Making Relatives of Them

NEW DIRECTIONS IN NATIVE AMERICAN STUDIES

Colin G. Calloway and K. Tsianina Lomawaima, General Editors

Making Relatives of Them

Native Kinship, Politics, and Gender in
the Great Lakes Country, 1790–1850

REBECCA KUGEL

UNIVERSITY OF OKLAHOMA PRESS : NORMAN

Publication of this book is made possible through the generosity of Edith Kinney Gaylord.

Library of Congress Cataloging-in-Publication Data

Names: Kugel, Rebecca, author.
Title: Making relatives of them : Native kinship, politics, and gender in the Great Lakes country, 1790–1850 / Rebecca Kugel.
Other titles: New directions in Native American studies ; v. 21.
Description: Norman : University of Oklahoma Press [2023] | Series: New directions in Native American studies ; volume 21 | Includes bibliographical references and index. | Summary: "Explores how Native ideas of kinship went beyond creating families and tracing descent, defining the boundaries of tribal inclusion and exclusion and informed Native constructions of political power and authority, and how this affected relationships with the recently founded US"—Provided by publisher.
Identifiers: LCCN 2023002393 | ISBN 978-0-8061-9282-6 (hardcover)
Subjects: LCSH: Indians of North America—Kinship—Great Lakes Region (North America)—History—19th century. | Kinship—Political aspects—Great Lakes Region (North America)—History—19th century. | Ojibwa Indians—Kinship—Great Lakes Region (North America)—History—19th century. | Dakota Indians—Kinship—Great Lakes Region (North America)—History—19th century.
Classification: LCC E98.K48 K84 2023 | DDC 305.897/333—dc23/eng/20230223
LC record available at https://lccn.loc.gov/2023002393

Making Relatives of Them: Native Kinship, Politics, and Gender in the Great Lakes Country, 1790–1850 is Volume 21 in the New Directions in Native American Studies series.

The paper in this book meets the guidelines for permanence and durability of the Committee on Production Guidelines for Book Longevity of the Council on Library Resources, Inc. ∞

Contents

Acknowledgments

It seems to be a "truth universally acknowledged," in the words of Jane Austen, that scholarly works take much longer to produce than anticipated. This book, which began over a decade ago, has taken even longer than most. Indeed, it is with something like wonder that I contemplate the actual completion of a book that has endured not only the usual academic and personal distractions but also the chaos and disruption of the global Covid-19 pandemic. The last few years in particular have slowed the work of scholarship, but the community of scholars has endured. Colleagues in history, anthropology, ethnic studies, and other disciplines have listened to my conference papers and read my publications. They have offered camaraderie and friendship along with critiques and suggestions. I have picked their brains and drawn inspiration from their work. Some, sadly, did not live to see this work in press, but their contributions to my thinking about how one writes Native history loom among the largest. My deepest thanks to the late Raymond D. Fogelson, the late Michael D. Green, the late Melissa L. Meyer, and the late Helen Hornbeck Tanner. It was my privilege to know and learn from you all. Gratitude and thanks also extend to Karen Wilson Ama-Echefu, Ben Barnes, Heidi Bohaker, Jennifer S. H. Brown, James Joseph Buss, Brenda J. Child, Alan Corbiere, Alejandra Dubcovsky, Regna Darnell, Jill Doerfler, Gregory Evans Dowd, R. David Edmunds, Michael W. Fitzgerald, Keith Goulet, Rayna Green, Mattie M. Harper, Brian Hosmer, Frederick Hoxie, Judy Kutulas, Wesley Leonard, Malinda Maynor Lowery, Harvey Markewitz, James McClurken, Michael D. McNally, Cary Miller, Lucy Eldersveld Murphy, Larry Nesper, Margaret Noodin, Chantal Norrgard, Jean O'Brien, Katherine Osburn, Laura Peers, Theda Perdue, Katrina Phillips, Carolyn Podruchny, Dylan Rodriguez, Nancy Shoemaker, Susan Sleeper-Smith, Nicole St.-Onge, Christina Snyder, Heidi Kiiwetinepinesiik Stark, Rose Stremlau, Clifford E. Trafzer, Stephen Warren, Jill Watts, Devra Weber, Bruce M. White, and Fariba Zarinebaf.

The University of California Riverside's Center for Ideas and Society has offered an intellectual home and gathering place over the years I've worked on this project. I benefitted from a series of summer workshops for second book authors that both helped me to theorize the book and gave me the proverbial room of my own in which to write early drafts of chapters. A second CIS project, the "Reclamation and Native American Communities Faculty Commons," has provided something all too rare in academic circles, a gathering space for scholars in Indigenous Studies and related fields. In this congenial environment, we have created that much-desired community of scholars, but even more importantly, we have extended the circle to include members of local tribal communities. Such connections would be invaluable at any time; they have been even more so during the isolation of the pandemic years.

Throughout the research and writing of this book, I have been awarded a number of University of California, Riverside Academic Senate Research grants, which have enabled travel to archives and to conference venues where I've presented early iterations of the book's ideas. A generous grant from my estimable colleague, Clifford E. Trafzer, the Rupert and Jeanette Costo Endowed Chair in American Indian Affairs, allowed me to purchase a new laptop computer at a critical moment. Library staff at the University of California Riverside have been extraordinarily helpful, especially as we've transitioned to online formats. Krystal Boehlert, Digital Initiatives Specialist, walked me through the process of working with digitized collections and provided valuable information concerning copyright regulations. Janet Reyes, Geospatial Information Librarian, provided useful information for creating the book's map. Kimberly Noon of the Interlibrary Loan Department and Sabrina Simmons, Interlibrary Loan Coordinator, were of tremendous assistance in locating online copies of the illustrations.

Although it has been several years since I conducted research in person, the unsurpassed research staff at the Minnesota Historical Society deserve mention as well. Ruth Ellen Bauer Anderson, Steve Nielsen, and Research Director Debbie Wilson, now all retired, made researching at their facility an absolute joy. They guided me to manuscript collections, located obscure photographs, and fielded phone calls from California. Their expertise has facilitated my research from its earliest days to the present project. My enduring thanks to you all!

My research assistant, Russell M. Fehr, has proven an incomparable and peerless sleuth, capable of teasing the most obscure documents from their homes in distant archival depositories. Other former graduate students have assisted with research projects that ultimately found their way into this book, among them Ian D. Chambers, Michael L. Cox, Jon Ille, Elizabeth Von Essen, and Amanda K. Wixon. Special thanks to Kali M. Krishnan (BA UCR 22) for invaluable initial assistance on the map. My brilliant and patient editor, Alessandra Tamulevich Jacobi at the University of Oklahoma Press, has been the ideal person to shepherd this manuscript through the publication process. Project Editor Helen J. Robertson oversaw the work of production, while Susan Walters Schmid, Ph.D., of Teton Editorial Services, Gardnerville, NV, was the ideal copy editor, both exacting and good-humored. Erin Greb, of Erin Greb Cartography, Doylestown, PA, created the amazing final map.

Material from chapter 2 appeared in an article titled "Planning to Stay: Native Strategies to Remain in the Great Lakes, Post-War of 1812," *Middle West Review,* special issue titled "Indigenous Midwests," 2 (Spring 2016): 1–26. Grateful permission to the University of Oklahoma Press and Shannon Gering of the press's Rights and Permissions department for permission to adapt the book's map from Map 20 in Helen Hornbeck Tanner's *Atlas of Great Lakes Indian History.* The illustrations, which serendipitously include portraits of many of the people mentioned in this work, are taken from James Otto Lewis, *The Aboriginal Portfolio, or a collection of portraits of the most celebrated Chiefs of the North American Indians* (Philadelphia: Lehman and Duval; 1836). Adam Matthew Digital Publications. https://www.aihc.amdigital.co.uk. Originals from the Edward E. Ayer Digital Collection, the Newberry Library.

Friends and extended family outside of academia deserve special recognition. They have been my behind-the-scenes cheerleaders, always ready to listen to a story about amazing archival finds or remind me why it is that the work of writing Native history matters. Many thanks to all the cousins and special acknowledgment to Lesley and Charlie Spooner, Mark Newman, and Bill Whitacre for their support and enthusiasm for this project over the years. Sadly, both the Covid-19 pandemic and the inexorable passage of time have also taken their toll. I dedicate this book to those who have walked on: my cousins Paul Smith, Tim Kugel, and Nancy Kugel, friends Anita Andrew, Tim Bradley, Roxanne ("Rocket") Gilmore, and Dayra Jensen, and to my father, Robert B. Kugel. Final thanks and boundless love go to my partner, Larry, daughter Sky, son Dylan, and daughter-in-law Steph. Gizaagi'ininin!

Introduction

In the summer of 1795, twelve allied Native nations from across the eastern Great Lakes country gathered at the town of Greenville, in present-day western Ohio, to negotiate a treaty with the United States. Beginning on June 16 and continuing into early August, tribal delegates from the Wyandots, Delawares, Shawnees, Ottawas, Ojibwes, Potawatomis, Miamis, Weas, Piankashaws, and others met with American representatives. Their mutual objective was to end the Northwest Indian Wars, the series of armed conflicts that had wracked the trans-Appalachian border country since the end of the American Revolutionary War. After considerable deliberation, in which both Native and American negotiators spoke, employing the formal metaphoric language of Native diplomatic undertakings, they succeeded, and the terms of their agreement were recorded in written form in the Treaty of Greenville.[1]

At first glance, the treaty's ten articles appear unrelated to the subjects explored in this book. This is a study of Great Lakes Native peoples' constructions and practices of kinship, gender, and social belonging across an eventful span of decades from the late eighteenth through the first half of the nineteenth century. While recognizing kinship was a daily lived reality that allowed individuals to interact appropriately with other persons who were either kin or non-kin, the book devotes the bulk of its attention to exploring the ways that kinship formed the metaphoric foundation for a regionally shared Native political discourse. An expansive intellectual construct existing in complex but often unrecognized relationship to gender, kinship discourse allowed Great Lakes Native peoples to theorize the nature of the spiritual and material worlds in which they lived.[2] Furthermore, because all living beings dwelled in social groups organized by comparable constructions of kinship, human communications and actions in this world were made possible. In at least one English translation, Indigenous peoples referred to the kin-based discourse of politics as "the Customs of All the Nations." Clearly defined yet endlessly elastic, the Customs of All the Nations generated a shared vocabulary of kinship—concepts, symbols, analogies, and of course kin terms—that proved an able vehicle for navigating the encounters between the Great Lakes' many Indigenous political collectivities. Whether gathering to trade, negotiate political alliances, secure permission to travel across one another's territories, share hunting ranges and use rights to land and water-based resources, or arrange peace conferences after periods of warfare, Native political bodies engaged in frequent interactions at which they spoke the shared metaphoric language of kinship.[3]

The discourse of kinship, like the daily exchanges between relatives, should not be understood as based on equalities of status or condition among kinfolk, however. Indeed, the language of the Customs of All the Nations, with its pairings of elders and warriors, women and children, older and younger brothers, indicates the opposite. In daily life, Native peoples interacted with one another in full awareness of the varied kinship statuses existing among them as well as the ways that social power and prestige were accessible along lines of age and gender. Yet the inequalities inherent in the concept of kinship also signaled its considerable flexibility. In encounters and negotiations between Indigenous polities, these attributes of kinship became potent political symbols by which tribal nations depicted their relationships with one another. While friendly ties might be described as those between brothers, relative degrees of political power were frequently added. A dominant partner in an alliance was often identified as the elder brother and one or more others were referred to as younger brothers. Certain tribal nations that were accorded widespread respect were termed grandfathers. Perhaps most significantly, the symbol-laden language of kinship could be used to question, challenge, and even overturn and redefine the relationships among Indigenous polities. Carefully worded statements that realigned relationships between collectivities formed an important element in intertribal diplomacy. For example, Oneidas newly arrived in Wisconsin from New York state in 1827 attempted to assert their political dominance at a treaty to which they were not a party. They reminded the assembled Ojibwes, who lived in Wisconsin and *were* parties to the treaty, of their former alliance with the Six Nations Iroquois, an alliance in which the Iroquois had claimed preeminence. As the "offspring" of the Six Nations, the Oneidas sought to minimize the Ojibwes' claims to political power in Wisconsin by calling them "Grand Children," reducing the Ojibwes to the status of the least politically empowered social group in the language of the Customs of All the Nations, while also asserting their own claims to leadership. The Ojibwes politely but firmly rejected this effort, reminding the Oneidas that the Covenant Chain agreement to which the latter had referred had been negotiated in the distant past, so long ago that "few among us remember it." Given the passage of so many years, the Ojibwes suggested that a more seemly description of their renewed ties would be cordial but more distant, "as friends."[4]

Starting in the seventeenth century, when they began interacting with European colonial regimes, Great Lakes tribal nations incorporated the French and British into their existing diplomatic and political proceedings and employed the symbolic language of kinship to describe and manage their relationships with these newcomers. Despite multiple imperial claims to dominance, as Michael Witgen has observed, the real power in North America remained in Native hands from the early 1500s through the mid-1800s, especially with respect to their knowledge about and possession of the land itself. European and later European-descended regimes adopted the language and diplomatic protocols of the Customs of All the Nations because they were not in a position to do otherwise. They needed Native allies if they were to maintain their colonies and fend off imperial rivals. Certainly they attempted to manipulate the language of kinship to benefit their own interests, and enjoyed some success at it, but ultimately, they continued to participate in an alliance system that remained defined by Native realities and articulated through a Native discourse of kinship. Even the fledgling United States operated according to the Customs of All the Nations in its earliest decades of independence, leading Great Lakes Native peoples to regard the Americans initially as another nation much like the British and the French had been. Over the course of the seven decades covered by this study, that perception would be proven incorrect, as the United States remade itself as a settler-colonial nation, intent on implementing a very different relationship with the Great Lakes tribal nations than the prior colonial regimes had sought.[5]

During the same decades that the United States committed itself to a form of colonialism defined by eliminating Native peoples and replacing them with settlers like themselves, its European-descended citizens also began redefining their conceptions of "race." Older colonial constructions of racial identity, while recognizing the existence of the three phenotypically differing races of humankind identified in biblical writings, nonetheless had also included a range of cultural and personal attributes by which the "race" of individuals might be determined. By the late eighteenth century, Americans increasingly calling themselves "whites" began investing physical features, especially skin color, with the ultimate power of deciding a person's race. Not coincidentally, this American reconfiguration of race developed alongside the commitment to a new form of slavery that classified human beings as enslavable based on these newly rigidified, racialized identities. Anglo-Americans also embraced the idea that Native peoples constituted a "race," a project that fit within their larger settler-colonial objectives of eliminating Native peoples from lands Americans now considered theirs. But Great Lakes Native peoples, with long histories of intermarriage with Europeans as well as among themselves, challenged the new ideas of circumscribed and unalterable races. Despite American efforts to introduce racialized distinctions, differentiating persons whom they described as "mixed-bloods" or "half breeds" from those persons they considered "full-blooded Indians," Native peoples continued to view their communities in terms of kinship ties.

This is not to suggest that the introduction of the new terminology never created confusion or disagreement within or between tribal nations or that alternative views and practices did not emerge and contend for acceptance. As Americans insisted on employing racialized identities in such significant new contexts as treaty negotiations, Native peoples wrestled with the implications of identifying some of their relatives by this new term. Sometimes tribal spokespersons appeared to accept racialized labels as accurate descriptions of tribally recognized categories of difference between tribal individuals. At other times, they rejected translations of words that seemed so unlike tribal concepts, instead offering their own translations. Yet although racialized identities became potent ways of categorizing people and would come to generate significant controversy within Native communities, they never succeeded in supplanting the older tribal conceptualizations of kinship and gender as the bedrocks upon which human social belonging, and thus human societies, were created. Because Great Lakes Native polities articulated the principles of kinship discourse as part of the process of political decision-making, records such as the Treaty of Greenville that preserve their words and actions become important sources, albeit often incomplete ones, for understanding the continued Indigenous commitment to the constructs of kinship, gender, and belonging. With this realization in mind, the Treaty of Greenville, initially seeming so unhelpful, invites another look.

The written treaty itself represents only one of the documents that were generated by the process of negotiating the formal agreement at Greenville, Ohio. Several additional records were enclosed with the treaty when the Americans' head negotiator, General Anthony Wayne, forwarded it to the appropriate government official, Secretary of War Henry Knox. Of particular interest is one titled "Minutes of a Treaty with the tribes of Indians," a daily record of the major speeches given and agreements reached by the tribal and American representatives. The "Minutes" prove to be a multivocal record of the negotiations, amplifying the seemingly neutral descriptions of lands sold and sums paid for them contained in the treaty's articles. Comprising nineteen pages of transcribed Native speech, often with descriptions of the speakers' accompanying actions, the treaty minutes represent what the political theorist and anthropologist James C. Scott might call "hidden transcripts—concealed or disguised knowledge that contested official narratives.[6]

Once the "Minutes" are viewed as containing multiple layers and perspectives, they expose realities that would have been obvious to both the Native nations and the American delegation gathered at Greenville. The treaty-making process, and the diplomatic context in which it was negotiated, were products of Native creation. The speeches and actions of tribal representatives, as well as those of the American negotiators, unfolded in an Indigenous political environment, which also included the presence of many tribal community members who acted as witnesses to the proceedings. All speakers would have employed the Customs of All the Nations, delivering their words in the adaptable, symbolically rich political discourse of the Native peoples of the eastern Woodlands and Great Lakes regions. Indeed, as the host nation that had convened the Greenville treaty, the Americans conformed further to Native protocols. They sent messengers to tribal villages to invite influential leaders to attend. While awaiting the arrival of the delegates, they prepared the physical space of the treaty ground according to Native cultural specifications. They cleared the ground of "brush and rubbish" and kindled a new council fire, which would burn throughout the negotiations as a symbol of the participants' commitment to "the good work of peace," as New Corn, a respected Potawatomi elder, expressed it upon his arrival.[7]

Native cultural knowledge, in particular respecting the practices and conceptualizations of kinship, gender, and tribal belonging explored in this work, is clearly in evidence in the treaty's attached "Minutes." For instance, the "Minutes" uncover Great Lakes Native perspectives about how men and women cooperated in gendered but equally important forms of political work. Americans, like their European predecessors, had only an imperfect understanding of Indigenous gender roles and constructions and as a result they misinterpreted much about Native societies. Native women attended the treaty, but the Americans misunderstood and trivialized their presence. Convinced of the universality of male gender dominance, and certain that Native women were doubly oppressed because Native men supposedly forced women to perform what Europeans and their descendants viewed as the male work of farming, Americans took it as a given that Native women had no part to play in politics. When Native diplomats mentioned women specifically, Americans mistook their meaning.

When read with an awareness of the Native perspectives they contain, the Greenville treaty "Minutes" disclose a much different reality from the one the Americans thought they saw. Words spoken by New Corn, the Potawatomi leader, provide both an instance of American misunderstanding and suggest an alternative when placed in their culturally appropriate context. An elderly man, New Corn made the long trip to Greenville, in his words, "because I feel for my young men, women, and children, whose happiness I have deep at heart." Americans presumed that New Corn was making a paternalistic allusion to the categories of social dependents on whose behalf adult tribal men acted, much as a patriarchal American male head of household would act on behalf of the family's inferior members—especially wives and children whose interests were assumed to be represented by the paternal head. Interpreting New Corn's remarks through their own cultural constructions of women, children, and families, Americans did not realize New Corn was, in fact, naming the three tribal political constituencies who, along with the tribal elders, composed Great Lakes tribal communities. Other speakers at other treaties likewise invoked the tribal constituencies, making it clear they spoke on behalf of these community members. In 1826, the Potawatomi leader Aw ban aw bee offered an especially detailed articulation, describing "our war chiefs and our peace chiefs, our young men, our warriors, and our women and children." They were "the voice of our nation," he added. Such elders as New Corn, whose past diplomatic successes demonstrated their concern for the social groups that constituted Native societies, did not make policy for dependents. They acted instead on positions previously agreed to by all the named constituencies that composed their communities. Rather than occupying a passive status as observers, the women, young men, and children present at treaty negotiations signaled their involvement in Native political processes that began before tribal peoples arrived at council grounds and continued after they departed. Neither the French, British, nor Americans comprehended these levels of community involvement in political processes and decision-making. As a result, they had only imperfect understandings of what Native women's political involvement entailed and how Indigenous gender relations shaped tribal communities. Yet as the acts and words of Native persons recorded in the Greenville treaty "Minutes" reveal, the evidence was present before their eyes.[8]

If Native understandings of the gendered nature of political activity remained opaque to Americans, Native indifference to the racialized identities that assumed ever-greater significance to Americans was also much in evidence. Unlike Native constructions of kinship and gender, the final subject explored in this work, tribal belonging and the racialization of individuals and groups of persons, did not emerge from within Great Lakes Native cultures or societies. Racialized identities developed from Old World precedents; their great power in the context of North American colonial societies deriving from the ways human beings used them to justify the oppression or privileging of other human beings. Earlier, more protean racial identities (which could be mediated by such factors as religious belief, literacy, or wealth) were in flux by the 1790s, in the process of solidifying into the phenotypically based categories that would fundamentally shape the economic, political, and social development of the United States. The social constructions of race in the treaty "Minutes" capture one particularly well-known facet of the process by which Great Lakes Native social identities would become complexly racialized yet, for reasons having everything to do with Native constructions of kinship, gender, and tribal inclusion, were never wholly confined within American racial categories.

The Greenville treaty "Minutes" again provide an example of this process. In several places, the "Minutes" make note of the presence of ethnic Frenchmen, persons who in 1795, the Americans regarded as "whites" and linked conceptually with the British as their European colonial forebears. In article 4 of the treaty itself, the Americans stipulated that land holdings within the ceded territories "in possession of the French people, and other white settlers" would be recognized as privately held property. Yet a conversation between an Ojibwe spokesperson named Masass and Anthony Wayne revealed that if the Americans were constructing the French as whites, Native peoples were continuing to conceptualize the French as people with ongoing kin connections to tribal nations. Masass, who spoke for the Three Council Fires of Ottawas, Ojibwes, and Potawatomis, inquired "what will become of the French?" The Three Fires, as this alliance was also called, maintained a large village at Detroit, and doubtless had kinfolk among Detroit's French populace. These relatives, worried about their future under American domination, had asked their Indigenous kin to help them navigate the new colonial order. Despite American attempts to construct the French as white, and thus a people separate from the Indians, both Native peoples and the interior French continued to recognize one another as related by kinship ties. The subsequent blurring of racial categories and identities would both frustrate and fascinate Americans, but their own understandings of race, unstable and changing as they were, would seldom permit them to understand Indigenous constructions of kinship on Indigenous terms. For their part, Native peoples would find racialized categories of identity inadequate replacements for their own constructs of kinship as a literal foundational social organizing principle and metaphor of political and social relations of power.[9]

Several bodies of scholarly theory and methodology facilitate the analysis of Native historical perspectives found in written records such as treaty minutes. The field of history itself, particularly since the development of social history beginning in the 1960s, has expanded to acknowledge the historical experiences of multiple groups of people whose pasts were not formerly considered worthy of study. Histories of women, of communities of color, of laboring peoples, and of persons of varying gender identities both within the United States and the colonial empires that preceded it, have increased significantly.[10] Beginning in the 1970s and 1980s, a robust field of Native history emerged. Often termed the New Indian History to distinguish it from the earlier historical studies that focused on the policies of the federal government and offered generally uncritical analyses of the acts of American political leaders, New Indian History practitioners self-consciously sought to write Native history from the perspectives of Native peoples themselves. In their efforts to locate Native voices in the written records generated by non-Native military explorers, missionaries, fur traders, and colonists, historians joined with anthropologists in employing the blended methodology of ethnohistory. Combining the historian's focus on human agency in effecting change over time with the anthropologist's emphasis on human cultures and Indigenous ways of knowing, these scholars could place recorded instances of Native speech, thought, and action in culturally accurate interpretive contexts.

Native knowledge is preserved in other forms as well. Native communities safeguarded their own understandings of their histories in community-based oral narratives. Carefully conserved within tribal communities, many such oral narratives included accounts of a sacred nature. Others might involve tribal histories. By the late eighteenth century and increasingly in the early nineteenth century, literate Native individuals also produced historical studies of their own.

Great Lakes Native persons such as William Whipple Warren, Peter Jones or Kah-ke-wa-quo-na-by, George Copway or Kah-ge-ga-gah-bowh, and Andrew J. Blackbird undertook historical projects that sought to render Native history comprehensible to Americans and Canadians of European descent. For these men, the first three of Ojibwe ancestry and the fourth an Odawa, this meant describing historical events according to European-derived historical conventions, yet each referenced tribal oral narratives and traditions as the ultimate sources of their information. Warren especially took pains to describe his efforts to seek out and consult knowledgeable tribal community members about the remembered past. While Jones, Copway, and Blackbird, all Christian converts, emphasized Indigenous religious traditions that coincided with Christian thought, they viewed this as evidence of the essential correctness of their ancestors' spiritual teachings. Each also took the additional step of publicly identifying themselves with their tribal heritages by employing their Odawa- or Ojibwe-language names.[11]

An additional form of Indigenous knowledge is available in the transcribed speech of Native individuals found in written records generated by non-Natives, such as the Greenville treaty minutes. An astonishing amount of such preserved Native speech survives, though scholars have been slow to recognize its value. Such recorded words are especially important for revealing Native thoughts about events as they unfolded. Recorded shortly after they were uttered, the words of Native speakers in these documents provide an immediacy similar to sources such as newspaper accounts, letters, or journals in which a non-Native eyewitness recalled an event. Frequently, the Native speech thus preserved was that of leaders like New Corn, whose words were recorded in formal venues such as treaty negotiations.

Transcribed Native speech was not confined to treaty documents, however. Native people's words were recorded in court testimony and quoted in the writings of American officials, fur traders, and non-Native missionaries. While government officials were accompanied by interpreters, traders and missionaries who were longtime residents in tribal villages often developed a working knowledge of the tribal language. Although the words of tribal leaders and spokespersons were more likely to be recorded, informal and even colloquial Native speech was also preserved. A fur trader might make note of the historical accuracy of the reminiscences of an elderly Indigenous woman, for instance, or a missionary might record the irony-inflected retorts of Native men at work. In each of these settings, Native voices articulated their perspectives. Their translated words can be compared with Indigenous-language dictionaries, grammars, and vocabularies, as well as examined by present-day speakers, to gauge the accuracy of the translations. Read judiciously, these written versions of spoken words reclaim Native historical knowledge and reveal contemporaneous Native thoughts on a wide range of their historical experiences.

Making Relatives of Them enters into dialogue with several scholars whose work has also explored themes relating to kinship, gender, and social belonging. Historian James Joseph Buss' *Winning the West with Words: Language and Conquest in the Lower Great Lakes* (2011), with its keen appreciation of the symbolic meaning of words and discourse as forms of domination, has sharpened my own awareness of the ambiguities present in the written records of Native speech while suggesting that they can be analyzed as examples of the hidden transcripts as theorized by James C. Scott. The work of two historians of Great Lakes Native women, Susan Sleeper-Smith's *Indigenous Prosperity and American Conquest: Indian Women of the Ohio River Valley, 1690–1792* (2018) and Brenda J. Child's *Holding Our World Together: Ojibwe Women and the Survival of Community* (2012), explore the significance of gender complementarity in Great Lakes Native societies, emphasizing the overlooked importance of Native women's copious agricultural knowledge and considerable agricultural labor. *Making Relatives of Them* expands on their insights to consider how gender complementarity was articulated in kinship discourse and how recognition of these facts makes visible the importance of women's political participation. The writings of political scientist and Native Studies scholar Heidi Kiiwetinepinesiik Stark on conceptualizations of nationhood among the Potawatomis, Odawas, and Ojibwes, three frequently allied Great Lakes nations, offer a discerning analysis of how these collectivities understood their first political acts of alliance-building as originating in spiritual encounters. Subsequently, human collectivities would continue to comprehend their own political actions as participating in a continuum of alliance-building that had begun with those earliest spiritual encounters. Each of these scholars has contributed to my thinking about the significance of kinship, though none make the study of its symbolism in political discourse their central category of analysis. In the ensuing five chapters, kinship, gender, and social belonging reveal themselves to be complexly interconnected, both as forms of discourse and as lived social reality. As these categories each in their turn amplify one another, they present a more complicated portrait of Great Lakes tribal life and thought in the decades from the 1790s to the 1850s, a period more often framed as one of dispossession and removal.[12]

The five chapters are arranged in loosely chronological fashion. The first two offer broad overviews exploring how Great Lakes Native peoples employed the interconnected constructs and practices of kinship, gender, and tribal understandings of belonging in their political interactions and diplomatic negotiations with one another and later with Europeans and their Anglo-American descendants. These chapters pay particular attention to kinship as a highly adaptable vehicle for expressing and enacting the relations of power between political entities. The French, British, and Americans, no strangers to metaphors of inequality articulated through gendered and familial metaphors, would attempt to exploit the Indigenous language of kinship to force Native peoples to acknowledge a symbolic status as dependent "children" while the European-descended power asserted a patriarchal dominance as "fathers." Their efforts at forcing this admission met with little success, as did their attempts to co-opt Native gendered discourse. These circumstances gave the Americans an additional reason to attempt to introduce racialized constructions of social difference in place of tribal notions of kinship and gender. They hoped to be better able to deploy the logics they supposed were inherent in the language of racialized identities to force Native peoples to admit the subordination that the malleable symbolism of kinship and gender continued to evade.

If Native peoples found the Americans' racialized concepts of human social difference uncompelling, it was not because they needed to be educated in the truths of the racial hierarchy that Americans believed were represented in their emergent recategorizations of human beings. The remaining three chapters of this work redirect the book's focus away from widely shared Native understandings and practices of kinship, gender, and social belonging. They concentrate instead on the thoughts and historical experiences of two specific tribal collectivities, the Ojibwes and, to a lesser extent, the Dakotas of Minnesota and Wisconsin, to explore the complexity of Native thought and actions in a detail unavailable in the broad stroke analysis of the first two chapters. Chapters three, four, and five probe specific Ojibwe and Dakota understandings of the significance of kinship, gender, and social belonging in a world where their cultural understandings and practices prevailed. These explorations demonstrate how the several constructs worked in Indigenous cultures and suggest why they remained as firmly fixed as they did. This in turn indicates why American constructions of race and gender were not able to dominate Dakota, Ojibwe, and by extension other Indigenous peoples' understandings. Ojibwe and Dakota conceptualizations of the persons Anglo-Americans increasingly racialized as "half breeds" or "mixed bloods," the subject of the third chapter, reveal that the Native understandings of persons of multiple heritages were both more expansive and more nuanced than Anglo-Americans imagined. Of far more significance to Dakotas and Ojibwes than the anomalous racialized identities that fascinated Americans was the possibility that persons with kinship ties that spanned different tribal nations might become a unique sort of multitribal individual. Such persons, with enduring kinship ties to multiple tribal nations, could become envoys and mediators in intertribal political contexts. Especially when relations between tribes were fraught or volatile, persons of shared multiple heritages could act as stabilizing forces and facilitators of renewed peaceful ties. The fourth chapter focuses on Ojibwe constructions of gender but departs from analysis of male and female gender roles. Instead, the chapter uncovers Ojibwe men's conceptualizations of another group of men—French voyageurs. Ojibwe men had decidedly mixed feelings about the French, whose dependence on their fur trade superiors for wages, clothing, and supplies deeply disconcerted Ojibwes who prized autonomy and self-reliance. Though evidence is scanty, Dakotas seem to have developed a similar construct, raising the possibility that what initially appears as a single tribal nation's negative evaluation of the French might have been more widely spread among Great Lakes tribal nations. It is well worth considering the ways that Native peoples communicated among themselves about the growing dangers that the several colonial regimes represented, not only for the concepts by which they articulated their concerns, but for the fact that such conversations indicate the vibrant intellectual exchanges occurring among Native peoples, exchanges that the records of non-Native authors seldom acknowledged even as they recorded inadvertent evidence of their existence. The fifth chapter reconsiders the multiple impacts of American settler colonialism on the level of daily lived reality, examining constructions of race, gender, and class in the lives of a multiracial couple of Ojibwe descent. Their experiences navigating a changing racial and gendered landscape reveal how the disempowering new American constructions mutually reinforced one another even as they affected Indigenous women and men in very different ways. At the same time, the complexities of the lives of these two individuals remind us that Native historical experiences are never monolithic or uniform; they are as varied and creative as the individuals who sought to create meaningful lives in frequently turbulent times.

Chapter 1

Gray Hairs and Young Dogs

Formulations of Social Equality and Hierarchy in the
Kin-Based Discourse of Politics and Diplomacy

In 1791, the Mohawk clan mother Molly Brant questioned a group of travelers
that had recently arrived at the town of Grand River, among whom was the well-
known and widely traveled Mohican diplomat, Hendrick Aupaumut. Brant was
skeptical about Aupaumut's claims that his party was pursuing peaceful objectives, and she voiced her skepticism employing the classic political language and
symbolism of the Native nations of the Great Lakes and eastern Woodlands of
North America. "If these people were on good business," she observed, "they
would follow the customs of all the nations. They would have some women with
them, but now they have none." Brant's reference to "the Customs of All the
Nations" indicated that diplomacy and political action were gendered activities, in which women and men performed different kinds of political work. In
addition, her words identified the larger body of political rituals, practices, and
highly metaphorical speech that was universally recognized—and utilized—
by the many tribal nations of eastern North America. Since time out of mind,
Algonkian-, Iroquoian-, and Siouan-speaking peoples had engaged one another
in political and diplomatic contexts, creating a shared body of distinctive, highly
metaphorical speech and ritual through which intertribal communication and
subsequent action took place. The Customs of All the Nations did not reflect
the nuances of each tribal community's kinship system; they were a more universalized version of kinship categories, responsibilities, and obligations best
understood perhaps as a lingua franca that, through long experience, tribal
peoples had come to agree upon. As Brant's criticism of Aupaumut indicated,
gender relations and roles were an important category of social differentiation
in Native cultures, but kinship underwrote the social construction and material
organization of the tribal societies of the eastern Woodlands and Great Lakes

regions. This foundational role in turn elevated kinship terminology into the most potent and expansive source of analogies for describing relationships of power, including those characterized by equality and by hierarchy. Employing the Customs of All the Nations, tribes expanded the language of familial kinship to encompass alliances with other tribal nations, encoding the relations of power between tribal collectivities. That kin terminology could describe both egalitarian and hierarchic relationships further expanded its usefulness in crafting political metaphors. Relationships of power between tribal polities could be asserted, and contested, utilizing the differing shades of meaning that adhered, for instance, to tribal understandings of the relationship between an elder and a younger brother.[1]

The French, Dutch, and British—the major European powers who sought to colonize northeastern North America in the two hundred years prior to the American emergence as an independent power—also possessed culturally trenchant kin metaphors that were similarly able to describe either hierarchic or egalitarian relationships. They recognized Native diplomatic speech as a discourse of political power and were quick to try to manipulate the Native kin terms deployed in diplomatic contexts in support of their own political objectives. In particular, European colonizers attempted to establish their dominance in political relationships with tribal nations by seeking to alter the meaning of Native kin conceptions. The numerous European attempts to redefine the Native conception of a supportive, comradely relationship between fathers and children to one of authoritarian dominance and obedient subordination stand as the most famous example of this. European powers had only limited success in such efforts, in part because they never fully grasped the complexity of the meanings Native peoples assigned to their understandings of kinship. One European response to their inability to repurpose kin metaphors would be to try to introduce new, and to their minds more convincing, metaphors of inequality to unseat kinship as the primary vehicle through which dominance and subordination were expressed. To this end, they sought to present or reframe concepts of gender, believing that the Native societies they encountered were also predicated on a hierarchic and oppositional relationship between men and women. These efforts also foundered, though as with kin metaphors, there appeared to be enough commonality that Europeans would attempt to use gendered metaphors and analogies as representing more ironclad hierarchies than kinship afforded.

Upon achieving independence, the United States also employed the language of kinship and sought, like its European forebears, to redefine the meanings of words for its own political and imperial purposes. As members of a settler-colonial nation, Americans were intent on creating a far different relationship with North America's Indigenous peoples than European nations had developed. Where colonizers based in Europe had focused on commodities that could be profitably exported to home countries and sought alliances with Native peoples as part of larger imperial objectives, Americans planned to settle the land and reap its benefits themselves. Their expectations of Native polities were that they would disappear, either through absorption into the United States or by removal from American soil. By the 1780s and 1790s, as part of a lengthy intellectual transformation in their ideas about "race" and human variability, Americans also began introducing new conceptions of human difference and hierarchy into the diplomatic language they employed in interactions with Native peoples. In these new configurations, "race" came to be seen as both a fixed characteristic of persons and the ultimate deciding factor by which individuals could be accorded social privilege and inclusion or condemned to dispossession and subordination. In an unappreciated irony, Americans sought to introduce these constructs in a region of North America where, in the context of the fur trade, European and Native peoples had intermarried for centuries. The new American ideas about "race" would be profoundly challenged by the composite societies of the Great Lakes and the multiple, overlapping identities of its peoples.

For their part, Native peoples of the North American interior recognized American efforts to alter the meanings of words for what they were, attempts to alter the terms of the political debate. Keenly attuned to nuances and shifts in political speech, tribal spokespersons deftly probed the meanings of the new racialized discourse that American officials employed. While they were ultimately unpersuaded that American efforts to fine-tune concepts of personhood by invoking racialized identities reflected any greater accuracy or higher truth about relations of power within human communities, their own words in councils and meetings reveal the combination of rigor and elasticity that characterized the Customs of All the Nations. Recognition of the intellectual agility and strength of the Customs goes a long way toward explaining why its central construct of kinship remained the primary metaphor through which eastern Woodlands and Great Lakes Native peoples understood the exercise of political and

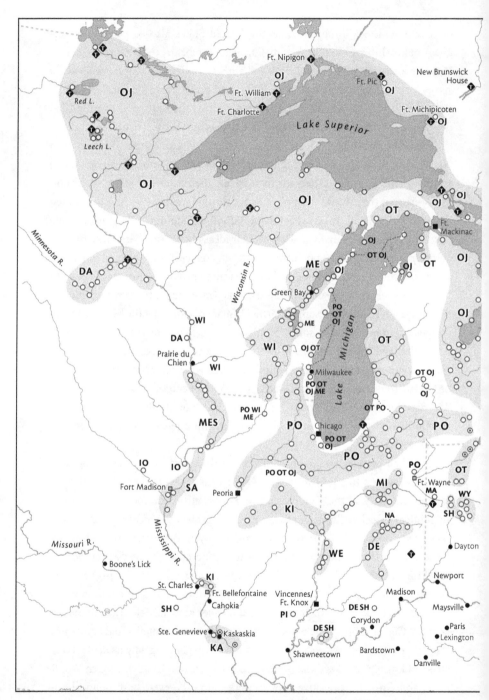

Great Lakes Native Communities, c. 1810. Map by Erin Greb.

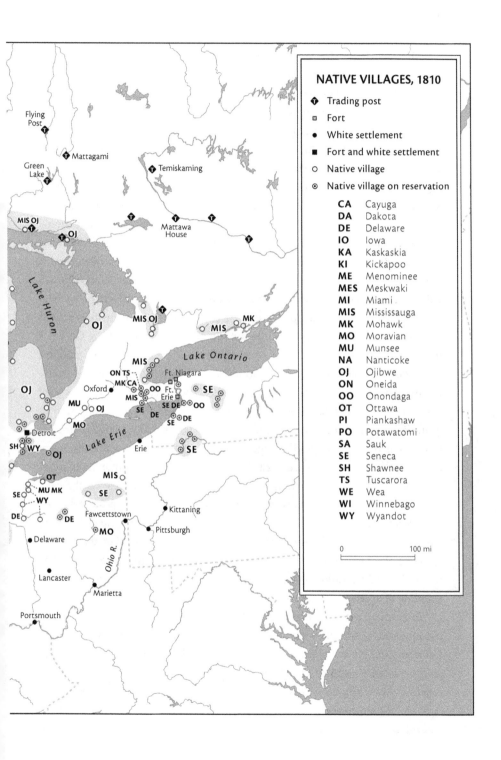

NATIVE VILLAGES, 1810

- 🛆 Trading post
- ▫ Fort
- ● White settlement
- ■ Fort and white settlement
- ○ Native village
- ◉ Native village on reservation

CA	Cayuga
DA	Dakota
DE	Delaware
IO	Iowa
KA	Kaskaskia
KI	Kickapoo
ME	Menominee
MES	Meskwaki
MI	Miami
MIS	Mississauga
MK	Mohawk
MO	Moravian
MU	Munsee
NA	Nanticoke
OJ	Ojibwe
ON	Oneida
OO	Onondaga
OT	Ottawa
PI	Piankashaw
PO	Potawatomi
SA	Sauk
SE	Seneca
SH	Shawnee
TS	Tuscarora
WE	Wea
WI	Winnebago
WY	Wyandot

0   100 mi

Flying Post

Mattagami

Green Lake

Temiskaming

MIS OJ

OJ

Mattawa House

Lake Huron

OJ

MIS OJ

MIS

MK

Lake Ontario

MIS

ON TS

Oxford

MK CA

OO

Ft. Niagara

Ft. Erie

SE

MU

OJ

MIS

SE

SE DE

OO

MO

SE

DE

DE

Detroit

Lake Erie

SH

WY

OJ

Erie

SE

OT

MIS

SE

MU MK

WY

SE

MO

DE

DE

Fawcettstown

Kittaning

MO

Pittsburgh

Delaware

Lancaster

Ohio R.

Marietta

Portsmouth

17

social power despite the considerable challenges Americans mounted through their newly constructed categories of race.

Great Lakes and eastern Woodlands Native conceptualizations of kinship were grounded in the recognition that kinship was the most important social organizing principle, but it does not follow that kinship was thus either simple or a fixed set of relationships. As the Customs of All the Nations revealed, kinship and the behaviors expected between categories of kinfolk were complex and highly flexible. Native people distinguished relationships between broadly construed family groups, as in the exhortation of Shinguabe Wossin [Zhingwaabe Aasin] at the 1826 Treaty of Fond du Lac that Ojibwes and Americans should "live as one family." They also invoked a comradely and egalitarian relationship between "Brothers and friends," as the Wyandot leader Tarhe expressed it at the 1815 treaty at Detroit establishing peace after the end of the War of 1812. Tarhe's colleague, a Potawatomi leader identified simply as LaBay, injected a martial quality into the relationship at the same treaty, addressing the assembly as his "Brothers and Warriors." While the kin-based language of the Customs described friendly and familial relationships within and between nations, it was also capable of expressing relationships in which one nation was clearly the more dominant. Two of the most common such metaphoric pairings were between nations that described themselves as older and younger brothers or as grandfathers and grandchildren. Ojibwes and Odawas characterized their relationship as one of older and younger brothers on numerous occasions; more famously the Delawares were described as the grandfathers of a number of tribal nations, among them the Shawnees, Potawatomis, and Ojibwes. To the east, where the Six Nations Iroquois dominated the political landscape, a metaphor of uncles and nephews similarly encoded a relationship of political dominance and subordination. Fully aware of the ability of words to shape thoughts, Native speakers also utilized the subtlety the Customs could convey to contest other nations' characterization of their political status or to assert a differing understanding of an allied nation's relationship to their own.[2]

Beginning with the French, the European powers also recognized the manipulative possibilities inherent in the Customs and sought to co-opt Native kin terms and kin relationships for their own political purposes. In their struggles for colonial ascendancy, the French, Dutch, and British all attempted to redefine Native kin metaphors to reflect what they believed was the proper relationship of dominance and subordination between themselves and the Native nations that they wished to believe were their dependents. Since Europeans recognized Native metaphors as the power-encoding analogies they were, and since they sought to shift the meanings of those analogies to force Native admission of European dominance, it might be assumed that they would deploy the metaphors that underwrote the most profound inequality in their own societies, namely those that constructed gender hierarchies that justified male dominance and female subordination. Certainly, the language of the Customs of All the Nations often employed male kin terms such as brother, nephew, and uncle, and many of the Native political figures Europeans negotiated with were men, facts that could lead Europeans to assume more similarity between their own societies and those of Native peoples than truly existed. Yet such gendered metaphors, with their assumption of male control of all temporal and spiritual power and consequent female powerlessness, failed to convey to Native audiences the appropriate political messages of hierarchy and command, dependence and obedience.[3]

Despite some outward similarities and Europeans' efforts to create further similarities where they did not exist, both Native political organization and the processes by which political actions were accomplished in tribal societies differed fundamentally from those of Europeans. This is strikingly evident in the operation of Native political decision-making processes and in the access to political power of various tribal social groups. In European societies, the subordination of women meant that women lacked any legitimate political role. As dependents, their political interests were subsumed under (and in legal theory, anyway, represented by) those of the men to whom they were subordinated, their husbands or fathers. A far different understanding of politics existed among the Native peoples of the eastern Woodlands. Across the old French *pays d'en haut* and the western Great Lakes, Native societies conceptualized men and women as each representing germinal political constituencies, neither of which could make decisions for the other, or significantly, without each other. The importance of women as symbols of peaceful intent, conveyed in Molly Brant's remark at the opening of this chapter, further helps define Native women's political participation. Two important Native conceptualizations of men and women regarded men as warriors (or life-takers) and women as peacemakers (or life-givers). These two different relationships to earthly life and its animating symbolic substance of blood were by no means the only ways that men and women were conceptualized, but they were seen as emblematic of the overall gender complementarity that undergirded eastern Woodlands and Great Lakes Native societies. As foundational constituencies, men and women also performed two very different kinds of political work. There were reasons for warfare and reasons to restore peace. In Native thinking, powerfully grounded in spiritual understandings of reciprocal relations between categories of ensouled persons, those with blood on their hands could not also be the ones to restore peace. Similarly, those who literally embodied life-sustaining activities should not, as a collective, participate in warfare. While there were always individual exceptions (usually initiated through a person's dreamed encounter with a spiritual being), as social categories, men and women had very different political responsibilities.[4]

While men and women acted in different political arenas, and were constructed as having differing political responsibilities, they both remained essential political constituencies. In contrast to Europeans, who viewed difference as a reason for excluding social groups from the political process, eastern Woodlands and Great Lakes tribal nations recognized different social groups as requiring inclusion, to make the political process represent the several types of persons who composed human societies. Thus, across eastern North America, Europeans encountered Native women as a political constituency whose views were important. Their support had to be gained for political actions and agreements to proceed. When the core political constituencies could not agree, political decision making was stalemated. In 1821, the Potawatomi leader, Me-te-a, acknowledged both the several constituencies and the difficulty of building unanimity. Speaking at the council held at Chicago to negotiate yet another land cession, Me-te-a observed that Potawatomis were gravely concerned over this most recent American request to purchase tribal land and were anxious that their several views be conveyed accurately. "[W]e have therefore brought along, the chiefs and warriors, the young men, women and children of our tribe," he explained, "that one part may not do what the others object to." Additionally, despite European and later American efforts to redefine politics as the domain of men, Native women remained a core political constituency within tribal nations. In the late 1830s, the Ojibwe leader Flat Mouth described his work as a political leader as involving his responsibility to the core constituencies of his nation. He attended councils and negotiated with the Americans, he stated, so "that our young men, women, and children may go home with their hearts at ease."[5]

One example of an attempt to alter the language of diplomacy reveals how difficult and uncertain a prospect it was. As the work of Gunlög Fur details, an effort by the Six Nations Iroquois and their British colonial allies to transform the accepted political and social roles of women exploded in their faces and, rather than containing an increasingly chaotic political situation as was its intent, only accelerated its collapse. In the mid-eighteenth century both the British and the Iroquois attempted to redefine the long-standing and intertribally recognized political role of the Delawares as the former two sought to maintain their own increasingly tenuous hold on political power in the decades leading up to the Seven Years' War. The Delawares had long been recognized as "a nation of women," a metaphoric status that empowered them to mediate and negotiate between warring tribal nations. The Iroquois (and the British, following their lead) redefined the Delawares' status as "women" to mean they had been politically conquered and humiliatingly subordinated. Implicit in this definition of women was an understanding that female behavior could be controlled by men employing sexualized violence. The status of women in this context signaled that the Delawares were not free to make their own political decisions, and instead must do as the Six Nations told them. The language of these diplomatic exchanges described women in terms that reflected European conceptions of women as a politically dependent group; they also reframed Native women's sexuality in ways that reflected European views that some female sexual activity deserved sexualized violence in response.[6]

This startling redefinition of the political symbolism of Native women brought neither the desired immediate effects nor did it introduce a long-term change in Native thinking about gender. In the short term, the Iroquois-British attempt to redefine the political symbolism of women only further alienated the Delawares. Many Delaware leaders stoutly resisted this new interpretation of what it meant to be "a nation of women." In place of this Europeanized view of women as politically dependent on, and sexually controlled by, men, they reasserted instead the symbolism of women as intertribal mediators. Over the longer term, the attempt to introduce this new definition of women as political symbol also failed; Native peoples did not accept the gendered hierarchy of Europeans as foundational to their societies or as a compelling metaphor within their diplomatic speech. This example, drawn from the mid-eighteenth century when British and French colonial empires were well established, ended disastrously for the British. Earlier attempts, when neither of these European powers (or any of their earlier competitors such as the Dutch and Swedish) had a strong presence in North America, had fared equally badly. Given such experiences, Europeans sought other kin-based metaphors that would serve to convey the desired political message of subordination.[7]

While Europeans discovered that metaphors of male dominance and female subordination were confusing and problematic in the Indigenous political contexts of the eastern Woodlands and Great Lakes regions, another kin relationship, and, interestingly, one strongly linked conceptually to women, did exist in these tribal societies. This was the analogy of a father and his children, and it appeared to approximate the forms of dominance and subordination that Europeans sought. In early modern European societies, the father-child relationship exposed another form of profound male dominance, one that extended patriarchal power over both women and women's children. Male power was embedded in fatherhood itself, as the Latin origin of the word "patriarchy" reveals. The father-child duality found its strongest iteration as a statement of the relationship between a God depicted as an all-powerful father and his dependent and often-errant human children, but it was also replicated in western Europe's germinal social institution, the conjugal family. Notwithstanding the love European fathers felt for their children and the multiple forms of economic and social support they sought to provide to their children, the households formed by married couples routinely displayed and enacted the dominance of the male head over all his dependents. The patriarch's dominance extended to all members of the family, including children. Indeed, a man's control of his children was as important as his control of his wife in maintaining his patriarchal honor. Authoritarian fathers dominated family life through their control of the family's resources and youth were reminded, often forcibly, of their duties to be obedient and submissive.[8]

Since metaphors of patriarchal authority and power over women found little traction in Native societies where social inequality was not grounded in male/female gender hierarchies and female political inclusion was normative, Europeans sought to construct patriarchal metaphors based on their views of an authoritarian and decidedly nonegalitarian father-child relationship. Styling themselves fathers and calling Native people their children, Europeans attempted to behave as if these relationships reflected the dominance and subordination they desired. The several upheavals—political, economic, demographic—unleashed by European colonization in eastern North America gave many Native nations reason to make selective alliances with European powers and to seek a common diplomatic vocabulary by which to negotiate agreements. Native peoples conceptualized the father-child relationship far differently than did Europeans, stressing not authority and power but kindliness and support. Yet there was some overlap of diplomatic language; Native metaphoric speech did make prominent mention of children, and in the volatile and shifting world of the seventeenth and eighteenth centuries, Native people engaged with the metaphors, manipulating them in the classic manner of the Customs of All the Nations. The fact that neither the French nor British managed to subordinate all neighboring Native nations and always needed Native allies in their frequent colonial wars also mitigated the subordination inherent in their symbolic language of fathers and children. European fathers could not be too domineering or demanding of their Native children or they risked losing the very real military and economic support these "children" provided.[9]

Through long trial and error, European colonizing regimes had learned that the Customs of All the Nations represented an important diplomatic and conceptual tool that they ignored at their peril. In the 1790s, the newly independent Americans would relearn the lesson when they fought the Northwest Indian Wars, as they would come to be called, and were handed humiliating defeats by tribal warriors in the first two of three conflicts. The United States managed to claim a technical victory in August 1794 at Fallen Timbers when they forced the Northwest tribal alliance to abandon its defensive position and evacuate the surrounding villages and cornfields, which the Americans subsequently torched. The allied tribes spent a winter miserable enough to make them willing to meet the Americans for peace talks in the summer of 1795, but they were by no means prepared to abandon their position as independent peoples who allied with other nations as they chose. They employed the Customs of All the Nations, much as it had heretofore been done, as an assertion of their enduring power. Despite its rhetoric to the contrary, the United States recognized it was in no position to contest the continued strength of the tribes; it too would continue to employ the Customs of All the Nations, including its language of fathers and children.[10]

Some twenty years later, the Customs of All the Nations still retained their political relevance as the War of 1812 concluded and Americans faced the daunting task of once more negotiating peace with the dozens of tribal nations of the Great Lakes country. In an echo of the Revolutionary War, many of these nations had supported the British war effort and were anything but reconciled to an American victory. The 1812–1814 conflict had also served as a grim reminder to Americans that Native peoples still represented a formidable fighting force that they could not afford to discount. Despite having bested Great Britain a second time, the United States remained a weak and impoverished nation in 1814, its resources depleted by the war. Americans recognized they needed to continue employing diplomacy with the Native nations of the lands they now called the Northwest Territory. They would continue to use the language and rituals of the Customs of All the Nations, with every intention of manipulating its symbolic conventions to forward their own ends.

While Americans continued to make the father-child metaphor the centerpiece of their diplomatic efforts in the decades following the War of 1812, they were simultaneously investing the metaphor with new meanings that reflected broad socioeconomic changes occurring in their society. A dreadful new profitability had been injected into the American system of chattel slavery with the late-eighteenth-century invention of a new cotton gin, combined with American appropriation of extensive tracts of Indigenous land in the southeast. It was in the context of seeking to justify the continued enslavement of Africans and persons of African descent that Anglo-Americans began formulating new ideas about human difference. As they grappled with their new understandings of the meanings of human variation, Americans seized upon the older term, "race," which, until the middle of the eighteenth century had been rather fluid, capable of describing a variety of types of human cultural, ethnic, and national differences in addition to skin color. Increasingly in the decades after the Seven Years' War (1756–1763), British colonists and their Anglo-American descendants began to emphasize skin color as the key defining characteristic of human "races." In the early nineteenth century these new understandings were powerfully bolstered by supposedly scientific studies of human body parts, particularly skulls and other bones, which concluded that racial differences were measurable and real. Based on these measurable differences, certain scientists argued that races were not flexible ethno-national categories as previously thought. Instead, they were bounded and bordered categories that reflected unchanging identities grounded in visible physical differences such as skin color, eye color and shape, and hair color and texture. Not only did these physical differences mark human "races," Americans came to believe a host of cultural attributes, including intellectual ability and even moral characteristics, were innate in the different races as well. These traits too were believed to be inherited through the generations much as physical features were.[11]

In the years following the War of 1812, Anglo-Americans deployed their emergent understandings of race in their diplomatic meetings with Native nations confident that Native peoples either already recognized the significance of race-based differences among human beings or would be easily persuaded of their new significance. As they considered the language of the Customs of All the Nations, Americans had good reason for this belief. Several key words already existed in the diplomatic speech of the Customs that differentiated

Native peoples and Europeans in ways that could be read as racially based. Such words as "red men," "white men," "Indians," and "whites," had been present in the Customs from at least the early eighteenth century. As their own understandings of race were transformed, Americans pointed to Native peoples' use of such words to underscore the supposedly universal human recognition of their own newly emerging constructions. In the early nineteenth century, the words of Native speakers in councils were seen to validate American beliefs, as tribal speakers at a wide variety of political meetings used what appeared to be, in translation at least, language that acknowledged racial difference. At the 1825 Treaty of Prairie du Chien, for instance, a political leader identified only as the "Fox Chief" cordially declared, "I am glad to see all my relations these red skins assembled together." On the same occasion the Ojibwe leader Zhingwaabe Aasin offered his greetings to "my red brethren." One year later, at the follow-up meeting held to acquaint tribal leaders who had not attended the Prairie du Chien treaty with its provisions, another Ojibwe leader, Big Marten, opened his remarks by observing to the American commissioners that they had previously "met the Red Men in Council at the Pra[i]rie."[12]

Tribal leaders not only appeared to understand themselves as "red," they also seemingly recognized Anglo-Americans as a different race from themselves, as "white." "Nobody shall trouble your white men where you shall put them," Spotted Arm, a Ho-chunk leader, assured Anglo-Americans during a discussion of permitting a ferry to operate across Wisconsin's Rock River in 1828. Present at the same negotiations, the Sac elder, Quash-quam-may, invoking what he understood to be universal political constituencies, reminded Americans that the Sacs had abided by the president's request "[n]ot to frighten your white brothers, their women and children." Native leaders even seemed to articulate understandings of the divine creation of the races that were like those of Americans. The Miami leader LeGros remarked that "[t]he Great Spirit made us with red skins," while the Ho-chunk leader White Crow described a similar divine origin for the white race. "[T]he Great Spirit," he observed, "has made your skin white."[13]

Such language encouraged American officials to think they and Native peoples would soon reach a mutually intelligible understanding of human "races" and with it, an acknowledgement of the hierarchic relations between them. Those Anglo-Americans who had political dealings with Native peoples—territorial governors, treaty commissioners, Indian agents, and military officers—downplayed the importance of distinct tribal or national identities and worked instead to convince Native peoples that this one universalized racial identity as "red men" represented the more meaningful social and political construct. "The Great Spirit made you all of one colour & placed you all upon this land," Superintendent of Indian Affairs William Clark explained to the nine nations assembled at the 1825 Treaty of Prairie du Chien. Treaty commissioner Thomas McKenney echoed the idea of a single racial identity for all Native peoples at the 1827 Treaty of Butte des Mortes near Green Bay. "[Y]ou are of the same blood, all red men," he informed the gathered Menominis, Ho-chunks, and Ojibwes.[14]

Beginning in these same decades, Americans attempted an additional shift of emphasis in the diplomatic metaphors. Returning once again to the older language of red men and white men, Americans attempted to link their new understanding of race to masculinity in a way that departed dramatically from the language found in the older Customs. In their new metaphor of social difference and inequality, Americans asserted that male dominance was no longer based on patriarchal masculine power alone; it was now also explicitly contingent upon race. An instance of this newly inflected language of race and gender is found in the words of Michigan territorial governor George B. Porter, speaking at a treaty council held at Chicago in 1833. "Your Great father loves you and knows more about everything that concerns his red children than any war chief in the great nation of the white people," Porter assured tribal representatives of the composite community of Ojibwes, Odawas, and Potawatomis known as the United Band. As Porter's words reveal, in American thinking, Native peoples were not simply the children of a benevolently patriarchal American father; they were the *red* children of that father. Porter also contrasted "red" Native children to the "white" people of the United States, reinforcing a race-based hierarchy between the great father's children and redefining the older constructs of maleness to privilege white male power over all others. In American thought, Native subordination was thus reconfigured to be based on the two mutually reinforcing categories of race and masculinity. Native men might yet be men and fathers, but they were not racially white and thus lacked the more important of the two categories that were now necessary for claiming dominance.[15]

Although Americans believed that Native peoples were also accepting the new primacy of race with its implicit linkage to gender over other forms of dominance, they overlooked considerable evidence this was not the case. Indeed, not only were Native peoples not admitting the connections between race and patriarchy, but they had also never accepted constructs of race to the extent

Americans had assumed they had. The evidence of translated Native speeches, seemingly so persuasive, was in fact far more ambiguous than it first appeared. In a number of documents, both those written by Anglo-Americans and those written by Native individuals, Native speakers used other words than the racialized terms red men and white men that Anglo-Americans employed. These other word choices suggested that Native peoples continued to view a host of ethnic and cultural markers as more significant indicators of personal identity than an individual's "race," especially as Americans were redefining the word to focus on immutable physical traits instead of malleable cultural attributes. Ojibwes and Odawas, for instance, referred to the French, the first Europeans they encountered, as "the people who wear hats." By the 1830s, the expression had been expanded to include the British and the Americans. Que-we-shan-shez [Gwiiwizhenzhish], the Ojibwe leader from Sandy Lake village quoted above, used it when speaking to American negotiators at the 1837 Treaty of Fort Snelling. Yet the original meaning endured. The year prior to Gwiiwizhenzhish's use of the phrase to describe the Americans, the Leech Lake *ogimaa* (premier civil leader) Flat Mouth spoke fondly "of the French, of those who wear a hat."[16]

Nor were the French the only European nationality that Native peoples distinguished by a specific name. The Ojibwes gave distinct names to each European people or those of European decent that they knew, in the same manner as they named other tribal nations. In both instances, the names reflected notable characteristics of the named communities, but not the "race" or skin color of the people. Ojibwes called the Odawas "the Trading People," in recognition of their longstanding role as facilitators of Indigenous trade and exchange. Acknowledging the Potawatomis' political significance in a regional alliance network, Ojibwes called them the "Keepers of the Fire," a reference to fire-tending, a political role as well as a key metaphor describing the nurturing of an alliance. Similarly, the British, according to William Whipple Warren, the nineteenth-century multiracial historian of Ojibwe descent, were called "Shaug-un-aush," written as "Zhaaganaash" in the widely accepted double vowel orthography of the present-day. The ethnonym meant "to appear from the clouds," a reference to the "sudden and almost unaccountable appearance" of British troops at the pivotal Battle of Quebec in 1759 during the Seven Years' War. The Americans, famously, were the "Gichimookomaanag," or the Big Knives, seemingly a reference to the hunting rifles the earliest Americans had carried. In the first half of the nineteenth century, during the years when Anglo-Americans were investing the term "race" with new meaning based mainly on skin color, there was not one all-encompassing word or concept in *Anishinaabemowin,* the Ojibwe language, to describe all white people as a race.[17]

Culturally descriptive ethnonyms and such phrases as "the people who wear hats" represented two ways Native peoples ascribed identity to people by using ethnic and behavioral criteria that did not foreground physical features or skin color. A third representation focused less on ethnic attributes and more on political associations between tribal nations. In keeping with the Customs of All the Nations, these political relationships were conceptualized and articulated in terms of kinship. At the council at Detroit in 1815, for example, a speaker identified only as "the Potawatomi Prophet" utilized an enigmatic phrase to describe those Potawatomis, Odawas, and Ojibwes who had fought for the British and at war's end remained in Canada. These people, he asserted, were "the same species of inhabitants with us." As the War of 1812 concluded, the Potawatomi Prophet evidently felt it important to reemphasize the ties of kinship and alliance among peoples who had been separated by the war. While no dictionary of mid-nineteenth-century Potawatomi exists, in its closely related cognate languages of Ojibwe and Odawa, two words translate as "inhabitant," *abiitan* and *bemiged.* Both refer to people whose connection to one another is through a kin-constructed entity, the household. The Potawatomi Prophet's phrase reasserted a form of alliance articulated as a kinship connection, as members of one extended family or one household of relatives. A kin-based metaphor of this sort, rooted in the metaphoric and physical spaces of households as Indigenous peoples created them, would have represented a more meaningful concept of identity for the Native nations assembled outside Detroit than the American appeals to their collective race. While the precise meaning of the Potawatomi Prophet's words remain elusive, it is clear Native peoples were not describing themselves according to American racial categories of red and white.[18]

Perhaps the most compelling evidence suggesting Native peoples continued to understand the meanings of supposedly racialized words quite differently than Anglo-Americans comes from a rare surviving bilingual petition prepared by Ojibwe leaders in 1864. Written in Ojibwe and English on opposite sides of the page, the petition reveals that the Ojibwe-language words are given English translations that do not accurately convey the words' meanings in the Ojibwe language. With respect to American attempts to introduce the racial construct "Indian" into Native thought, the word that the petition consistently translates using the racialized term Indian is in fact the tribal name, Anishinaabe, rendered "Anichinabe" in the text. Because the writer-interpreter of the petition translated this name to mean Indian, Americans might well conclude that Native peoples were articulating an idea akin to their own concept of an "Indian race," but the Native-language use of an ethnonym like Anishinaabe, or, more properly, in the plural, Anishinaabeg, suggests Native peoples continued to think in terms of their distinct tribal nations and were not according all Native peoples the new racialized identity as Indians.[19]

Despite American attempts to introduce new and supposedly more accurate racial meanings into treaty discourse, Native leaders and spokespeople continued to invest such words as red men and white men with the older, more fluid meanings. These constructs, with their ability to encompass multiple types of cultural and ethnic difference, remained the staples of Native diplomatic speech. Me-te-a, a Potawatomi leader, emphasized the cultural characteristics of Anglo-Americans more than their race when he observed in 1821, "You white men eat at certain fixed times, we Indians do what we have to do, and eat when it is convenient." Similarly, at the July 15, 1830, treaty negotiated at Prairie du Chien, Waw-row-csaw, a Dakota speaker, compared American and Indigenous practices for asserting truth. Anglo-Americans "have writings and books . . . to tell the truth by," he observed, but when he or other Native speakers "want to speak the truth," they would "look up—first to the heavens, next to the earth," while consecrating a pipe of tobacco. Still other speakers emphasized the concept of national identity that Native peoples understood to be present in the older racial words. Ah be te ke zhick, the speaker at the 1833 treaty at Chicago, understood that he was enumerating the nationalities when he described "the Potawattamies, Ottowas & Chippeways and whitemen," who had assembled to negotiate.[20]

Even more importantly, the newly racialized metaphors did not begin to supplant the older and far more subtle language of kin relations that had always been at the heart of the Customs of All the Nations. Native speakers at councils continued to characterize nations as relatives, encoding multiple political messages of dominance and subordination in the finely tuned distinctions. From the earliest treaties that multiple Great Lakes tribes negotiated with Americans, such as the pivotal 1795 Treaty at Greenville, Ohio, speaker after speaker described his nation's kin relationships with the other assembled nations. At Greenville, Potawatomis, Ojibwes, Shawnees, and Miamis each acknowledged the Delawares as their grandfathers and the Delawares reciprocated, naming each of these nations as their grandchildren. The Shawnee leader Blue Jacket changed his seat at the council to reflect the proper kin relations among the nations, noting that: "the Shawanese are the older brothers of the other nations present; it is therefore proper that I should sit next my grandfathers and uncles." The Wyandot speaker Tarhe, who performed the opening condolence ritual essential to reestablishing peace between the tribes and the Americans, also named the Wyandots' kin relationship to each of the several nations present, mentioning nephews, younger brothers, and elder brothers. Signaling once again the primacy of kinship over race, Tarhe addressed the Americans in their turn as "Brothers of the Fifteen Fires."[21]

Native diplomatic language did not noticeably change over the next thirty years, the time at which Americans began negotiating treaties in the Great Lakes region. Tribal speakers continued to acknowledge one another by kin terms and offered explanations of the power differentials between Native nations to American negotiators. For instance, the speaker for the allied Potawatomis, Odawas, and Ojibwes assembled to negotiate in 1833 at Chicago, Ah be te ke zhick (also spelled Ap-te-ke-zhick), was an Ojibwe even though the Ojibwes were not the numerical majority of the United Band that had gathered to negotiate with the United States. At the start of the talks Ah be te ke zhick explained why the Ojibwes took the lead role in the negotiations. "The Ottowas & Potawattamies are our younger brothers and have chosen me to speak their words . . . that there may be no confusion." Tribal speakers also continued to use councils as opportunities to contest those relationships or offer criticism of one another, a far subtler form of contestation. The Miami leader LeGros, speaking at the Treaty of 16 October 1826, acknowledged the power relations between his nation and the Indiana Potawatomis, whom he referred to as "our older brothers." Once these words of respectful recognition were spoken, however, he continued with a critique of the Potawatomis' past willingness to trust the Americans too readily. After signing an earlier treaty, LeGros explained, the Potawatomis "were the first to open their hands to" the Americans, despite Miami warnings to them that they "did not know what kind of men you were." The result was repeated land losses, as the Potawatomis "sold then and have continued to do so since, until experience taught them better." The implication was clear: had the Potawatomis listened to their Miami younger brothers in the first place, they might not have found themselves in such dire straits.[22]

As LeGros' words reveal, kin-based language did not only express amicable political relationships; deeply contested relationships could also be conveyed and even renegotiated utilizing the language of diplomatic kinship. At a council meeting in 1827 where the Menominis considered a request by several eastern tribes to share some of their land, the Oneidas also spoke to a delegation of Ojibwes, who were wary of these eastern tribes settling near their country. Trying to place the new political relationship in Wisconsin within an older tradition of Covenant Chain alliances between the Six Nations Iroquois and their western allies, a relationship which the Six Nations had dominated, the Oneidas reminded the Ojibwes of "the covenant of friendship made between our forefathers." They greeted the Ojibwes as "Grand children," and asserted that the political relationship established so long ago remained in effect. "I address you by the name which the covenant of friendship . . . established," said the Oneida speaker, "and which is used by us their offspring to this day." After claiming political preeminence in kinship terms, they concluded by giving the Ojibwes some political advice, their prerogative as Grandfathers, the elder and dominant members of the (newly rekindled) political relationship. "Do not listen to any bad birds that may be flying about," they cautioned, a reference apparently to the number of residents of French descent from the nearby town of Green Bay who attended the talks.[23]

The Ojibwes present at the council likewise used the opportunity to put forth their view of their long-term relationship with the Iroquois. Addressing the latter as "Brothers," the Ojibwe speaker placed the relationship on a very different footing than did the Oneidas, He cordially agreed that the Ojibwes wished for peaceful relations between the two nations, stating "We have no wish but to live as friends, since you desire it." At the same time, he subtly shifted the terms upon which that relationship would be based. Expressing himself "glad that you bear in mind the covenant made by our forefathers," he then dismissed the significance of that long-ago agreement by noting "the time has been so long that few among us remember it." Such a nearly forgotten relationship would not do for the present, he concluded. He rearticulated the current Ojibwe-Oneida relationship on a very different, and firmly egalitarian, footing: "Whenever we meet any of you hereafter we shall know that we are friends."[24]

As both friendly and adversarial uses of kin terms suggest, the metaphors of the Customs of All the Nations were finely calibrated to express a distinctive Indigenous construction of social inequality and hierarchic relations of power. Although Native societies acknowledged gender differences, they did not construct unequal power relations and forms of social hierarchy based on differences between men and women, whether biological or socially constructed. Instead, and particularly in the Great Lakes country, Native societies analogized relations of unequal power and categories of social difference using the constructs of age and youth. At its most basic, age represented wisdom while youth represented foolishness. Not surprisingly, the foundational power relationship was frequently articulated in sacred origin stories and accounts that explained why the world was constituted as it was. Oral narratives of the various tribal nations contained numerous references to the wisdom of elders and the foolishness of youth. Mythic stories of Nanabo'zho, the culture hero of a number of the Algonkian-speaking nations, among them the Odawas, Potawatomis, Ojibwes, and Menominis, relate how he embarked upon a series of adventures where his youthful impatience and impetuousness had disastrous results. Since Nanabo'zho began his adventures by ignoring his grandmother's advice, the relationship between the wisdom of age and foolishness of youth was present in the narratives from the beginning. In a more subtle expression of the power and authority of elders and its deep connection to the sacred, an Ojibwe man named Agabe-gijik related how, when he was old enough to undertake his vision quest, it was his grandfather, not his father, who oversaw the event. When asked why, Agabe-gijik explained, "My father was still young. My grandfather was old. For all such affairs old men have the most experience and knowledge."[25]

The linked subordination of youth and the dominance of elderly adults was not confined to expressions of spirituality; it pervaded almost every aspect of ordinary daily life. Elders occupied the more desirable seating places in lodges and wigwams and at public gatherings sat nearest the speakers and the council fire. Periodically at a critical moment an elder would step forward and graphically demonstrate the respect and esteem in which she or he was held to the community at large. John Tanner, an Anglo-American adopted into an Odawa-Ojibwe family in the early nineteenth century, described in his autobiography how an elderly man "whose head was white as snow, and who was so bent with age that he walked on two sticks" was able to calm a "bloody brawl" between Cree, Ojibwe, and Assiniboine youth and did so after the combined tribal leaders had failed to break up the fighting. The actions of this anonymous elder deeply impressed Tanner and the other young men of the community and he noted that "extravagant reports circulated among us respecting" the old man. Elders were also quick to remind younger people of their subordinate status when youth attempted to invert the relationship of age and knowledge. In the late 1870s, when a youthful Ojibwe deacon attempted to conduct classes to teach elderly Ojibwes the tenets of Christianity, the younger man was soundly rebuked with the words "You are only a child; you do not know anything; I ought to teach you, instead of your setting yourself up to teach me." The affronted elder concluded his remarks with an observation that both articulated and explicated the Ojibwes' understanding of the connection between a long life and the acquisition of knowledge. "I have lived a long time and learned a great deal." The privileged status of the elder remains acknowledged to the present day. In Ontario, Ojibwes reply when they've been outwitted or proven wrong by saying "Ay! You're older than me!"[26]

As such wide-ranging cultural practices reveal, the status of age was clearly esteemed. Achieving old age was a cultural goal of the greatest importance, the culmination of a life well lived and an affirmation of aged persons' strong spiritual power, since Great Lakes tribal nations understood a long life to be made possible largely because individuals had forged enduring ties to powerful spiritual beings. Community members routinely observed the elderly, searching out those who embodied personal characteristics such as humility, patience, and forbearance, for it was believed that such attributes signified that an elderly person had acquired not just old age, but also wisdom. These individuals were doubly distinguished as community elders, called *Kijanishinaabeg* in the cognate languages of Ojibwe, Odawa, and Potawatomi. By their longevity these elders had become repositories of accumulated cultural knowledge. They conserved sacred rituals and practice, as well as a vast array of practical skills such as how to procure food when the snow melted early or the best herbal cure for an earache. Their long memories further preserved knowledge about past events and about community responses to notable historic occurrences. When the Ojibwe community of Sandy Lake witnessed an astonishing number of shooting stars shortly before dawn one morning in early November 1833, some villagers were concerned and wondered if the display was a warning of bad times to come. An elderly woman reassured the community that she remembered a similar meteorological event in her youth, and it had not portended disaster.[27]

As a stage in the life cycle as well as a social construct, youth was viewed with more ambivalence and anxiousness. Children were cherished and attentively raised, and the vitality and strength of youth were admired and applauded, but the young were also understood as being unfinished and in process, an idea expressed in the multiple translations of the Ojibwe, Odawa, and Potawatomi cognate *oshki,* which in addition to "young" also could mean "new, recent, fresh, [and] . . . first." Youth was an experimental period of life, a time when people learned the skills and life lessons (and established the connections to spiritual beings) that would allow them one day to achieve their own respected old age.

Until that time, however, youth were seen as unfinished, as not yet wise, and thus as vulnerable. Babies and young children who had not yet created relationships with spiritual beings were especially viewed in this light. The vulnerability of the very young clearly necessitated adult protection and even restraint, but as the young reached their teens and twenties they exhibited behaviors of deep concern to mature adults. They were rash and impetuous and acted without giving due thought to the consequences of their actions, a situation that often led to danger or trouble.[28]

In no place was the subordination of youth and the dominance of age more evident than in the political institutions and decision-making processes of Great Lakes tribal societies. As noted earlier, the language of political discourse held abundant age-related statuses that astute speakers carefully and strategically deployed in diplomatic contexts. Tribal political leaders also frequently invoked their age to validate their right to speak in public councils and to make political decisions: "I am not a new man," Bizhiki of LaPointe told treaty commissioners Lewis Cass and Thomas L. McKenney in 1826—the unknown interpreter of his words emphasizing the Ojibwe equation of youth with inexperience by translating the word *oshki* as "new" in place of the more usual "young." And the redoubtable Flat Mouth coolly stated the obvious reason for his presence in Washington, DC, at the negotiation of the Treaty of 1855: "My old head and gray hairs tell for themselves."[29]

This cultural conceptualization that the elders were the proper persons to exercise political leadership was so strong that younger men who found themselves in positions of leadership often felt obliged to begin their words in council with acknowledgements of their inexperience and pledges to act responsibly despite their youth. "[Y]ou see I appear young in years," Bayezhig, an Ojibwe leader from the St. Croix River region, commenced his remarks at the 1825 Treaty of Prairie du Chien. Having drawn attention to his evident youthfulness, Bayezhig continued by reassuring the gathered tribal and American representatives that, despite his youth he acted with wisdom and "listen[ed] to the words of the collected chiefs." His sentiments were echoed in 1832 by a diffident young speaker named Whitefisher, who began his speech with the observation that "[t]hough I am only a little dog (. . . a pup) without hair, yet I will say a word." In 1837 a youthful Fond du Lac leader named Spruce also acknowledged, "Altho' I am but a child, I speak to the middle of the subject, and you shall hear straight about my lands."[30]

The hierarchy of age and youth was also strikingly visible in the well-known bifurcation of political leadership, with mature civil leaders and youthful war leaders assuming leadership under two quite different political conditions and in ways that highlighted the qualities associated with each. Quasi-hereditary civil leaders occupied the preeminent roles within villages and in negotiations between nations. As negotiators they were closely associated with creating political agreement and the reestablishment of peaceful relations in the aftermath of wars. Despite the semihereditary nature of the civil leaders' positions, their claims to represent the entire community meant they had to demonstrate the behaviors and abilities Great Lakes peoples expected of their leaders. They had to be generous, giving gifts to their people in reciprocal cycles that bound the members of tribal communities together in bonds of mutual obligation. In addition, they had to demonstrate skill at building political consensus, bringing the people together to be of "one heart" and to "speak with one voice." In short, they had to be publicly validated and accepted as village leaders by their communities. Their culturally exemplary behavior was continually on display.[31]

War leaders were considerably younger than civil leaders and were differentiated from them in ways that underscored the oppositional nature of their actions while reminding people how much the state of war contrasted unfavorably to the state of peace. Where civil leaders sought consensus and unanimity and employed persuasion and negotiation to achieve it, war leaders behaved aggressively, even antisocially. War leaders issued commands and employed coercive force rather than negotiating consensual agreements, the very behaviors that tribal societies ordinarily disavowed. Furthermore, war leaders did not need the acceptance of entire communities for their ventures; they only needed the acceptance of the men they led. Such actions might be necessary in defense of villages or on war expeditions, but tribal nations were troubled by the implications of such leadership in village politics and governance. They sought to confine such violent acts and coercive behavior to spaces outside their villages, requiring extensive rituals of preparation before warriors left villages and rites of purification and reintegration upon their return. At particularly important peace councils, war leaders sometimes publicly renounced their leadership roles and returned political authority to the civil leaders. At the 1795 Treaty of Greenville, the influential Shawnee war leader, Blue Jacket, performed such an act, calling attention to the change in authority at the propitious moment in the treaty's transaction when peace terms had just been agreed to. "[Y]ou see me now present myself as a war chief," he stated to the assembled tribal and American delegates. Laying aside unnamed personal items (perhaps a war pipe and wampum belt) that were emblematic of warfare, Blue Jacket described his next action as "plac[ing] myself in the rear of my village chiefs, who, for the future, will command me." Blue Jacket's actions occurred in a shared political space, the council ground, and marked the transfer of governing power with the reestablishment of peace. Within the space of communities, where the core cultural values of unanimity and consensus prevailed, war leaders were firmly subordinated to the civil leaders and the councils of the respected elders.[32]

Relations between civil leaders and war leaders were rarely so neatly contained, and it is no coincidence that political disagreements and dissention crystalized along this deepest marker of unequal social power in the Native societies of the Great Lakes and the eastern Woodlands more broadly. Successful war leaders often challenged civil leaders for political power and advocated political policies in opposition to those advanced by the civil leaders. As protectors and defenders of their nations, war leaders were often very popular with their fellow villagers and their policies of more aggressive responses to tribal adversaries often garnered significant support within villages and nations. The civil leaders acknowledged this reality. In council meetings with Americans, the British in Canada, as well as their European predecessors, civil leaders referred continually to their inability to control the actions of their young men. Yet as an organized political opposition, the warriors were deeply disadvantaged. In opposing the elders, the war leaders were understood once again to be exhibiting the rash and impulsive behaviors that justified their symbolic construction as youth. The act of opposition was not simply a challenge to the political policies or objectives of the civil leaders, it was also construed as a threat to the ideal of political unanimity that the civil leaders embodied. Warriors and war leaders by their mere presence once more reminded tribal communities of the ideal relationship between age and youth and, by their divisive actions showed why reckless young men were meant to be subordinate to wise elders.[33]

The political subordination of youth, while quite evident in Great Lakes and eastern Woodlands Native societies generally, should not be viewed as a form of disenfranchisement or dispossession. Youth's claim to leadership might be denied, except in the drastically altered circumstances of wartime, but youth were prominently acknowledged among the constituencies that made up tribal political bodies. They were also divided into two socially constructed categories, the young adults or "young men" and the children, the youngest and weakest members of

Great Lakes and Woodlands Native societies. In 1826 the Potawatomi leader Aw ba naw bee clearly stated this understanding of tribal political constituencies when he enumerated "our war chiefs and our peace chiefs, our young men, our warriors, and our women and children." These groups, he declared, comprised "the voice of the nation." Within tribal society so constructed, youth were included as members of valued constituencies whose views were solicited and whose assent was necessary for nations to reach the desired unanimous decisions that were the diplomatic ideal. What youth were not allowed to do was assume roles as political decision-makers. Their subordination was, in fact, encoded in the ritualized recitation of the tribal constituencies. In political speech, both young men and children, the representations of the two symbolic categories of youth, were paired with and subordinated to older, wiser constituencies. As in Aw ba naw bee's speech, young men were linked with warriors or war leaders while children were always linked with women. Elders, of course, included both women and men.[34]

As political metaphor the category of youth was given greater elaboration than any other named constituency. Youth could refer to the inexperienced and foolhardy junior adults of Great Lakes and Woodlands societies. It could also describe a second, more particularized kind of youth, children. As a symbolic category, children represented a different yet still distinctive set of attributes. Children were described as petty, quarrelsome, and divisive. If the rash behavior of the younger adults led them to make bad decisions, the behavior of children made it impossible for them to reach any decision at all. The critical tribal political objective—arriving at consensual agreement—was thus rendered impossible. The Sac leader Keokuk, protesting a questionable land sale in 1824, employed a classic version of the metaphor of the behavior of children to underscore the seriousness of his tribe's complaint: "I mention this that you may not have the Impression that we are children, and that we doe not know our owne minds." Similarly, Ojibwes from LaPointe, Wisconsin, pondering whether to grant missionaries permission to settle in their village, emphasized that a decision of such importance could not be rushed or hurried; it would take time. As one of missionaries impatiently awaiting their decision recorded their words, villagers stated that "[t]hey did not wish to act like children, but have everything done by the whole in council."[35]

In the metaphoric language of diplomacy, children, as the second and least powerful category of youth, had yet another symbolic meaning; they represented the extremes of powerlessness and weakness. Reliant on adults for food and shelter, and lacking connections to spiritual beings, children were vulnerable and unprotected. Such persons, in Native thought, were potentially subject to coercion and control by others, and children, who were in fact controlled and disciplined by parents and other adults, exemplified this potential. As the only group of persons in Native societies who could be coerced without concern about their ability to retaliate, children occupied a sharply ambivalent position as political symbols. On the one hand, the symbol of "children" became a potent vehicle for condemning egregious political acts or behavior that smacked of coercion or force. Indeed, the strongest metaphors of political inequality and political disapprobation in the Native diplomatic vocabulary described adults who presumed to treat other adults as if they were children. "I am not like those [Indians] in the East whom [the Americans] call their children and whom they treat like three- or six-year olds, a rod in their hand," declared Flat Mouth in the 1830s. Another Ojibwe leader, Hole-in-the-Day the younger of Gull Lake, echoed the construct thirty years later. Detailing the actions of a high-handed Indian agent who refused to release treaty-mandated funds to him, Hole-in-the-Day described himself as "mortified to think that he should be treated so much 'like a child.'"[36]

On the other hand, however, like most things in these societies that were culturally attuned to the possibilities of ambiguity, the weakness and powerlessness of children had another dimension, one that referenced the deeply esteemed and spiritually charged action of taking pity on another being. Because youth were dependent, relying on elders for food, shelter, spiritual guidance, and other training for adult life, adults took pity upon children and assumed the responsibility of supporting them. In political discourse, this acceptance of responsibility was articulated as nurturance, symbolized as the kind father who offered advice and support, often by literally distributing food and supplies, to allies who described themselves as like children, pitiable and in need of aid. This second view of children as a political symbol was also much in evidence in Native diplomatic negotiations with the French, British, and Americans, though considerably distorted by the attempts of each of these latter groups to turn the metaphor into an admission of tribal subordination.[37]

Despite the fixed relationship of dominance and subordination between seniors and juniors as social constructs and as symbolic figures in political speech, it is important to distinguish the language of social metaphor from the lived reality of Native youth. While youth as a category remained in constant subordination to age similarly constructed as a category, individual young people matured, gained experience and wisdom, cultivated relationships with spiritual beings, and with the passing of years took their places among the community's aged, acquiring the respect and social power that old age conferred. This was as tribal peoples expected it to be, such maturation reflected the journey of a human being over the course of a lifetime. Apart from some war captives, Great Lakes peoples did not envision individual persons or groups of persons living within their societies as members of a permanently subordinate group. Individual youth grew out of their subordinate status and joined the dominant group. It was as symbols that youth and age existed as permanent categories.[38]

With metaphors of age and youth so deeply woven into the cultural fabric of Great Lakes tribal societies, it is not surprising that American attempts to substitute their newly sharpened definition of race as the primary indicator of social inequality were unsuccessful. An emphasis on a physical characteristic as variable as skin color simply could not supplant the complex cultural constructions and equally complex social manifestations of youth and age as symbols of social inequality in tribal societies. Thus it was that Native people, whether diplomats, political leaders, or ordinary tribal members, paid so little attention to the Americans' emphasis on white skin or red skin; such descriptions struck them as politically conventional and thus unremarkable. They concentrated their attention where they always had, on the political relationships encoded as kin relations. The speech events that most deeply concerned them were those where they recognized that Americans were manipulating the kin language of fathers and children to try to force their acquiescence to an unequal political relationship. When a territorial governor attempted to silence the Menomini leader Grizzly Bear by informing him that "Your Great Father knows better than you do what will be for your good," or a treaty commissioner chided Ojibwes to "behave as dutiful children should," Native peoples recognized alarming assertions of political subordination framed in kinship terms. Native speakers repeatedly rejected the inequality thus insinuated. The redoubtable Flat Mouth of Leech Lake delivered the masterful counterstroke in a speech to the newly appointed Indian agent J. W. Lynde in 1858. In a curt rejoinder to Lynde's condescending talk of red children and white fathers, Flat Mouth ignored race altogether to focus on the core political message of Lynde's words. "I am too old to have a father," Flat Mouth informed the Indian agent, "but accept you as a brother." In one short sentence, Flat Mouth summarily denied the American attempt to assert political dominance and deftly returned the Ojibwe-American relationship to its proper foundation in an alliance of equals.[39]

While it might seem that the continued Native insistence on the kin language of the Customs of All the Nations would have relegated racialized characterizations to the margins of discourse, the social realities of the Great Lakes country were both too complex and too unstable for such an easy resolution. In the same decades that Americans sought to introduce constructs of red and white races as the defining metaphor of inequality into their relations with Native nations, they confronted in the western Great Lakes a multiracial and multiethnic social reality that they did not expect, and which threatened to overturn their notion of bounded racial categories altogether. To a much greater extent than in areas east of the Appalachians or even in the Ohio and Virginia backcountry, the western Great Lakes was home to a substantial number of people of mixed Native and European and, less frequently, Native and African, ancestry. Present-day scholars have used the French word *métis*, which describes a mixed racial heritage, to describe this population, but this word was rarely used in the early nineteenth-century Great Lakes country. Its current-day usage to describe all multiracial persons also perpetuates an existing confusion with the Métis Nation of the Red River region of the present-day Canadian Plains, who were engaged in a different process of self-creation in the same early decades of the nineteenth century. The multiracial people of the Great Lakes region employed other self-identifiers, the most prominent English-language one being "half breed." Not initially a pejorative word, half breed would become so over the course of the nineteenth century, especially in the United States, where the word mixed-blood emerged as a less insulting alternative. Estimated by Jacqueline Peterson at some 10,000 to 15,000 persons in the late 1820s, multiracial or mixed heritage people worked overwhelmingly in the fur trade and often clustered in the fur trade towns, among them Sault Ste. Marie, Michilimackinac, Green Bay, and Prairie du Chien. They also lived in symbiotic but variable relationships with tribal nations.[40]

The sociopolitical situation was made even more complicated for all parties because individuals claimed identities that contradicted the "racial" identity Americans thought was self-evident either in phenotype or phenotype in combination with cultural characteristics. Physical features such as skin, hair, and eye color, or secondarily, selected cultural attributes such as occupation, language spoken, and styles of dress and bodily adornment, ought to have been accurate predictors of "race," at least by American thinking, but disconcertingly, they were not. Zhaagobe, an Ojibwe war leader from the Snake River region on the Wisconsin-Minnesota border, whom Americans considered an

Indian, proudly proclaimed himself a half breed. Gesturing to the American delegation at the 1837 Treaty at Fort Snelling, Zhaagobe told the baffled negotiators "I sprung from the same stock with . . . you . . . white men." The complexity of Zhaagobe's self-identification did not stop with this observation. He took pains to clarify that his position of leadership (and thus his presence at the treaty negotiations) did not derive from his connections to the local multiracial populace. His claims to leadership descended from his Ojibwe forbearers. Gesturing to another Ojibwe political leader, Zhaagobe said, "His and my ancestors were the chief men of the country that you want to buy from us." In another baffling instance, Jean Baptiste Chandonnet, a bilingual fur trader who interpreted at the Chicago Treaty of 26 September 1833, possessed numerous cultural features such as a European name, literacy in a European language, and a distinctively European occupation that should have identified him as a Frenchman, or at least have acknowledged his multiracial heritage by referring to himself as a half breed. Yet Chandonnet said of himself, "I am, it is true, an Indian." Clearly neither a phenotype Americans identified as displaying racially mixed features, nor a series of cultural characteristics Americans felt were indicative of a specific nationality, reflected the realities of the western Great Lakes. [41]

Americans remarked upon the large number of mixed-race people from their earliest exploratory ventures into the old *pays d'en haute,* but it was in the context of negotiating land-cession treaties that they came to view multiracial persons' definitions of themselves as problematic. While they claimed a separate social identity from tribal nations, multiracial persons also claimed that their tribal affiliations entitled them to inclusion in treaty negotiations and they pressed hard to receive treaty benefits. American officials, especially treaty commissioners, tended to view these assertions skeptically, believing multiracial persons were trying to manipulate an accident of birth into a claim on treaty funds. They expected tribal leaders would subscribe to a similar view when they sought clarification of the relationship of multiracial individuals to tribal nations. The answers they received were unexpected and flew in the face of the logic of American perceptions of race. Much to American consternation, Native people did not emphasize what Americans viewed as the obvious connection between Native and multiracial peoples, their common racial heritage, or "Indian blood," as it was frequently phrased in the nineteenth century. Instead, Native leaders repeatedly described multiracial people as kinfolk and relatives. A Menomini council speaker employed the standard descriptive phrase in 1831, when he referred to "our children the half breeds." In 1842, the

Ojibwe leader Marten of Lac Courte Oreilles utilized another variant, calling multiracial persons "our half breed relations," while Zhingwaabe Aasin of Sault Ste. Marie referred simply to "my half breeds." When Anglo-Americans did not grasp the larger meanings implicit in these kin terms, especially the heavily freighted pronouns "our" and "my," Native leaders tried to explain the organic ties of kinship more fully. Pizhiki of LaPointe emphasized this physical connection when he remarked in 1843 "[m]y half breeds . . . [t]hey grow from my side." And in 1826 Maangozid of Fond du Lac employed a metaphor drawn from the Customs of All the Nations to describe a good and enduring relationship. "Our half breeds," he stated, "live in our hearts."[42]

Significantly, Native spokespersons also spoke of multiracial individuals and families as having connections to specific places on the land. They meant by this that multiracial persons came from specific villages and their connections to those villages were formed in the usual way, by intermarriage, with its creation of enduring and multiplying kin ties. At the Treaty of 27 October 1832, the Menomini leader Grizzly Bear described this social reality by which certain multiracial persons were connected to certain communities: "[M]y village was at Buttes des Morts—," he told the treaty commissioners, "and . . . these half breeds were with us there." Speaking at the 1837 Treaty at Fort Snelling, the Ojibwe speaker "Ma-ghe-ga-bo," [Mayaajigaabaw] of Leech Lake described the origins of multiracial persons, locating them in kinship ties and emphasizing the pivotal role of women in creating the marriages that made kinfolk out of strangers. "Our women brought the half breeds among us," he explained. Having thus established the basis by which multiracial individuals claimed relationship with specific communities, he underscored the place-specific nature of such kin ties. "What you propose to give us, we wish to share only with our half breeds."[43]

Americans were quick to grasp the idea that the multiracial persons were linked to tribes by ties of kinship, but, as the words of Grizzly Bear and especially Mayaajigaabaw suggest, they did not understand the relationship in its full complexity. Intent as they were on forcing tribal nations to act as unified political bodies, both to facilitate political negotiations and to conform to American views of how a tribe was socially organized, Americans preferred to view multiracial persons as connected to tribal wholes rather than to individual villages and kin groups, the types of political entities Americans sought to consolidate into the larger units they defined as tribes. Just as race was a homogenizing construct that lumped together as undifferentiated "Indians" such independent Great Lakes nations as Ojibwes, Odawas, Potawatomis, Wyandots, Menominis, Ho-chunks, Oneidas, Dakotas, Miamis, Sauks, and Meskwakis, the concept of half breeds or mixed-bloods likewise collapsed and distorted a complex social reality.

Despite the explanations of Native leaders and spokespersons, American views of the multiracial persons would continue to focus on their perceived race. This is unsurprising, given the growing American conception that race and racially based difference were the unassailable criteria by which human individuals and their societies could be explained and judged. The corresponding American belief that races represented bordered and circumscribed categories that should not be breached also insured that they would continue to view the existence of multiracial persons as a profound challenge, both conceptually and in daily social practice. Multiracial persons would prove a source of great fascination to Anglo-Americans. Individual American writers emphasized cultural characteristics and behaviors they deemed undesirable as evidence of the degeneracy of mixed-race individuals, providing a justification for the separation of the races. Others, in confirmation of another race-based theory, argued that the mixing of white and Indian blood would improve Native people, endowing them with greater aptitude for adopting Anglo-American civilization. Yet, as both these views show, whether Americans viewed multiracial persons positively or negatively, they never contemplated viewing them outside of racially constructed categories. Although Native spokespersons articulated conceptualizations of multiracial persons that had little to do with race and instead emphasized kinship and belonging to places on the land, Americans did not recognize such constructs as the culturally distinctive understanding that Great Lakes Native peoples employed to negotiate categories of social sameness and difference.

Native peoples, for their part, continued to define belonging and inclusion within tribal groups using the Indigenous constructions of kin group and village. These differing perceptions would be present throughout the nineteenth century and would surface again and again when Native peoples and Americans met and spoke together, whether in a formal diplomatic session like a treaty council or in a more casual conversational exchange. While Native peoples remained convinced that their categorizations more accurately described the relationship of multiracial individuals and families to the tribal villages and communities, American efforts to substitute racially based criteria required Native peoples to articulate their own differently constructed understandings. As the next chapter reveals, those understandings were fluid and variable, combining Native understandings of kinship, social power, gender roles, and ethnicity in complex and shifting and oftentimes contested ways.

Chapter 2

"Our Children, the Half Breeds"

The Political Construction(s) of the Multiracial French

The intellectual reconceptualization of race in American thought and practice that began in the mid-eighteenth century continued its uneven trajectory into the nineteenth century. Older conceptions of race continued in widespread use and enjoyed considerable explanatory power. In the decades following the War of 1812, most Anglo-Americans continued to understand multiracial people and the construction of race itself according to the welter of ideas that had their roots in medieval European understandings of the meaning of human bodily difference. European ideas about embodied difference had changed in response to the historical circumstances of a centuries-long process of European colonization of the Western Hemisphere, but race remained a protean and changeable construct in these centuries, less irreducibly linked to phenotype and supposedly innate race-based characteristics than it would become. Racial identity could be mediated by numerous factors, including wealth and class status, occupation, literacy, fluency in a European language, or adherence to the Christian religion. Significantly for the interior of North America, race could also be powerfully influenced by gender. Given the malleability of these systems, multiracial persons often could be understood to be white. By the 1830s such conceptualizations of race were being supplanted in American thought and practice by the view that races were fixed and unchangeable and that somatic features such as skin color, hair texture, and eye shape were unfailingly reliable identifiers of an individual's race. Moreover, these racialized identities involved much more than physically embodied difference. A wide range of culturally constructed behaviors, practices, and personality traits were conflated with race and understood to be perpetually inherited through the generations, by children from their parents. In such an environment, multiracial persons were subjects of much concern and lively arguments developed over whether white blood, so-called, elevated a multiracial child or whether the degraded blood of its Indian (or African) parent corrupted the child to a level beneath its "pure-blooded" counterparts. These changing intellectual environments would frame the first several decades of Native–Anglo-American interaction in the Great Lakes country following the War of 1812. Anglo-American efforts to make sense of racial and ethnic identities in the region would take place in an environment marked by shifting and uncertain definitions of the very categories they sought first to stabilize and then to manipulate on behalf of their own economic, political, and social objectives.[1]

Great Lakes Native peoples would also seek to manipulate the postwar political and intellectual landscape, but their concerns differed substantially from those of the Americans. Despite a round of treaties reestablishing peace and friendship at the close of the War of 1812, Native peoples quickly realized that Americans had no interest in restoring the back country's previous political and economic relations. Instead, the Americans embarked on a policy of aggressive, high-pressure land purchases from Native nations of the very sort that had fueled controversy and turmoil within Native communities before the war. Central components of these sales included not merely purchases of Native lands, but also the blunt expectation that Native peoples were to move away from the alienated tracts, never to return. The land would then be thrown open to Anglo-American settler-colonists, whose patterns of private land ownership and agricultural land use, which included the use of enslaved labor forces, would radically transform the previous Indigenous world of communal lands and multiple seasonal land-use patterns. In the post–War of 1812 period, Anglo-Americans first engaged in sustained treaty-making, with its accompanying contestations over land, with the Native peoples of the region of the Northwest that would come to be called the Lower Great Lakes—the present-day states of Ohio, Indiana, and Michigan.

The Native nations of the Lower Great Lakes envisioned a different postwar world. They wanted their peoples and Anglo-Americans to continue to share the land that Americans were now calling the Northwest Territory. They envisioned living in symbiosis with Americans while pursuing different economic activities and cultural practices, in a series of interlocking societies much like those that had characterized the prewar frontier exchange economy involving trade in furs or other commodities. "[W]e should live by each other, like brothers," the Miami leader LeGros told the US treaty commissioners in 1826, "That is what we wish to do—we want to live like neighbours, and barter and trade with each other, if we can agree, if not, to part peaceably and each keep his own." In their efforts to reestablish this system of interdependent societies, Native peoples drew on their extended kin networks, often involving family members who Anglo-Americans understood to be French and thus, initially, as white. As Lower Great Lakes Native peoples deployed the expertise of their French relatives, Americans confronted a first (and unexpected) challenge to their racial comprehension of the Great Lakes country. For their part, Native nations found themselves drawn into a series of debates with Americans, often in the context of treaty negotiations, about social difference, social inclusion, unexplored assumptions about gender, and the incorporative power of kinship.[2]

Although multiracial people would come to be a point of political and social contestation as the decades progressed, they did not initially figure in the postwar political calculations of any of the recent combatants. Of far more importance from the Americans' perspective was the opportunity to extend meaningful political and economic control over the region that stretched from the Appalachian Mountains to the Mississippi River. This long-sought prize, the "first American West," (which produced such enduring representatives of an imagined American frontier experience as Daniel Boone and Davy Crockett) had been nominally under American control since the end of the Revolutionary War. In reality, it had remained hotly contested. The British had refused to vacate their trading posts and forts despite treaty provisions to the contrary, and Native nations had never considered themselves defeated in a war fought between the Americans and the British. With hindsight, both contemporaneous Americans and later scholars would come to view the War of 1812 as a watershed event that decisively altered the several regional balances of power in the entire Great Lakes country. In the years immediately following the end of hostilities, however, it was anything but certain that power relations had shifted conclusively in the North American interior. Native peoples had been battered by the war, certainly, but both Great Britain and the United States also recognized their continued importance in the region and the absolute necessity of negotiating a return to peaceful relations with the tribes if the Treaty of Ghent was to hold. Article 9 of the treaty specifically charged the American government with reestablishing peaceful relations with the multiple tribal communities in the Great Lakes and Upper Mississippi Valleys, while His Britannic Majesty was tasked with ending hostilities with tribal nations within his Canadian territories. The United States thus found itself in the ironic position of having won the war and concluded a peace with Great Britain, yet still being obliged to negotiate an extensive number of treaties with Britain's ostensibly defeated Native allies in order to bring hostilities to a conclusive end. [3]

For their part, the numerous tribal nations that had been involved in the war were similarly eager to end hostilities and begin the business of rebuilding their communities. Many of them had been hard hit by the fighting and, in numerous instances, were still riven by prewar sociopolitical divisions involving support of or opposition to the intertribal resistance movement championed by the Shawnee brothers Tecumseh and Tenskwatawa. Regardless of their actions during the war, whether they had supported the British or the Americans, had sought neutrality or had seen their warriors aligned with both sides, tribal nations expected to end hostilities and reestablish peace, two complex and ritually interrelated states of political being, employing the long-standing treaty protocols of the eastern North American Woodlands. Besides structuring intertribal political relations since time out of mind, the old Customs of All the Nations had always been the vehicle for negotiations with Europeans and their New World descendants. As Great Lakes tribal peoples surveyed the immediate postwar world, observing the small American populations returning to provincial towns such as Detroit and Chicago and modestly sized British and American military forces ceremoniously returning forts captured from one another during the conflict, they saw few signs that the American victory represented a radical break with past practice.[4]

The Americans launched their first efforts at reestablishing peace with Native nations less than six months after the Senate's final ratification of the Treaty of Ghent, which occurred on February 17, 1815, and ended the war. In July of that same year American officials stationed at St. Louis, the town now at the westernmost edge of the United States, issued invitations to tribal nations to attend conferences at long-recognized regional council places, such as Portage des Sioux on the Missouri River less than twenty miles north of the city. These postwar treaties, of which there were ultimately sixteen, made no demands for land cessions or other reparations. They focused on reestablishing peace and reaffirming ties of alliance, the very goals that had characterized prior treaty-making in the eighteenth century. As with the Treaty of Ghent, none of these immediate postwar treaties made references to multiracial persons. Americans did not view such persons as in some manner related to tribal communities, nor did they understand the multiracial populations to have any collective legal or social standing within tribes that would entitle them to participate in the tribal political decision-making process. The French-descended population, along with those former British subjects from the thirteen seaboard colonies residing in the lands between the Appalachian Mountains and the Mississippi River, seemed to have been an afterthought. The treaty's real business, at least in the minds of Anglo-Americans, was compelling the British to acknowledge in practice, not just theoretically, that the boundaries of the United States were those that had been agreed upon some thirty years before at the Treaty of Paris ending the American Revolution.[5]

The fact that the multiracial heritage of the French was not explicitly mentioned in the Treaty of Ghent that ended the War of 1812 should not be understood to mean Americans were unaware of the French population's multiracial ancestry. To the contrary, Anglo-Americans had been remarking upon the distinctive culture and racial heritage of the region's French inhabitants since their first excursions into the Great Lakes region in the decades before the War of 1812. In either 1805 or 1806, while heading the expedition that bore his name, Zebulon Pike commented on the large number of multiracial persons living at the long-established fur trade town of Prairie du Chien. Although Pike did not explicitly identify as French the many persons whom he described as having "the blood of the aborigines in their veins," his contemporary General William Hull did. The American commander at Detroit prior to and during the War of 1812, Hull noted that the French had "been in the habit of friendship with the Indians" since childhood, with the result being an "ongoing connection" between their peoples. Although there were multiracial persons whose European ancestry was English, Scots, or other nationalities, it was the French whose multiracial ancestry was most remarked upon and pointed out as a defining group characteristic by the Americans. After the war, when President James Monroe followed the earlier example of his predecessor Thomas Jefferson and sent several expeditionary forces to reconnoiter the newly secured territories, members of these forces also made note of the multiracial heritage of the French population. In 1817, on the first of these expeditions, Major Stephen A. Long described the people of Prairie du Chien as "principally of French and Indian extraction." A young Henry Schoolcraft, on his own initial western exploration as a member of the 1820 Cass expedition, described with his trademark linguistic flair the "Gallico-savage population" of the old French empire. Three years later, William H. Keating, geographer and official chronicler of the second of Long's expeditions, less ebulliently described the people of the trading town of Fort Wayne, Indiana, as "chiefly of Canadian origin, all more or less imbued with Indian blood."[6]

Schoolcraft wrote approvingly of French-Native intermarriage, but his optimistic views were not universal. Other Americans expressed considerably less confidence in the elevating power of "white" blood and pointed to the multiracial French as proof of their contention. Among the other early postwar explorers, Long, for instance, described the people of Prairie du Chien as "degenerating," while Keating characterized the people of Fort Wayne as "apparently very worthless." Keating was particularly taken aback by what he viewed as the cultural degeneration of the French. Besides noting that the Fort Wayne French population had Native heritage, he described his "disgust" at seeing "the degraded condition in which the white man, the descendant of the European, appears," when, like the French, he lived, worked, and married among Native peoples. Keating was deeply disturbed to see Frenchmen who, far from claiming the racial advantage they were entitled to, were "throwing off [their] civilized habits to assume the garb of a savage."[7]

The unease of people like Keating notwithstanding, in the immediate postwar years most Anglo-Americans considered those of French descent as racially white. The issue had been addressed, and seemingly resolved, decades earlier at the 1795 Treaty of Greenville. Besides encoding into national law a pivotal political relationship between Anglo-Americans and Native nations of the Old Northwest, the Treaty of Greenville had extended American legal and social institutions over the region's non-Native inhabitants. These included Anglo-Americans, many of whom were squatters who had been moving into the trans-Appalachian region in the decades since the Proclamation of 1763, first in defiance of British law and later in attempts to goad the American government into making more land available for its own citizens to occupy. The French-descended population was also included under the Treaty of Greenville's provisions and described in language that left no doubt of their essential European cultural orientation, regardless of their actual ancestry. In the treaty's fourth article the United States recognized the land claims "of the French people and other white settlers." This telling phrase expanded the category of "white settlers" to encompass the multiracial French and linked them to the larger community of the Anglo-Americans who comprised those "other white settlers." It was not an entirely disinterested gesture, of course; it was meant to ensure the political allegiance of the French inhabitants to a not-yet-twenty-year-old United States that was uncertain of its ability to maintain its hold on the backcountry. Implicitly, such a construction of the French also distanced all white settlers from the Native societies that still lived on the same lands and had established other relationships with the United States under the same treaty. In all these ways, the construction of the French as white revealed that Anglo-American political considerations would regularly be a subtext in their views of French racial identity.[8]

Anglo-Americans were able to construct the multiracial French as white because they viewed the French as sharing their own commitment to the best parts of their common European cultural and religious heritage. While Anglo-Americans rejected elements of their European past (especially, in the post-Revolutionary decades, European political institutions and odious monarchical ideals), they regarded other aspects of European life as evidence of human social advancement that they were proud to claim. Foremost among these cultural attributes were the Christian religion and a solid commitment to a type of human society founded upon agricultural subsistence and private land ownership. Indeed, such societies represented the pinnacle of human social achievement in American minds, and they regarded themselves and their democratic revolution as dramatically advancing humankind's efforts to create a more perfected world in which such societies were spread over more and more parts of the globe. While strongly reinforced by Enlightenment theories of the evolution of human societies from the so-called hunter state to civilization, these Anglo-American constructions of "civilization" had much older roots in European social theory that emphasized God's post-Edenic command to humanity to transform the wilderness into habitable agricultural lands. In this view, humankind was meant to "improve" the land by felling trees and draining wetlands, plowing and fencing fields and planting them with domesticated grains, maintaining domesticated livestock, and owning such "improved" plots privately, as individuals. The social evolutionist advance of humanity could thus be literally marked upon the land, as the land itself passed from "wild" to "civilized."[9]

A gendered division of labor, also sanctioned by God, which empowered men and reduced women to economic and social dependency, underwrote such agricultural societies. These gender roles appeared natural to Anglo-American eyes, reflecting the supposedly inborn natures of men and women. Precisely because gender roles were perceived as organic and unchanging, they could be mustered as a powerful condemnation of other human societies where gender roles and economic production were so different as to appear unnatural. Few things invoked American ire and invective as strongly as Native gender roles. Native women farmed and gathered and Native men hunted and trapped, a labor division so repellant to European and American constructions of gender roles—and the social power they reproduced—that when either Europeans or Americans theorized the different levels of human society, "the savage state" was almost unfailingly represented by Native gender roles. The gender roles of the trans-Appalachian French-descended population were far more like those of Anglo-Americans than those of Native peoples, a point that cannot be overlooked in the American ability to construct the French as white. French men not only worked for wages in the fur trade, reflecting their commitment to private property and commerce and sharply distinguishing them from economically communal Native peoples, they also performed the agricultural labor on their small farms while women remained out of the fields, instead focusing their work on the household and barnyard. Multiracial Frenchwomen were also highly visible and devoted practitioners of what Susan Sleeper-Smith and others have termed "frontier Catholicism," and they adhered to standards of sexual behavior similar to those of Anglo-Americans, additional serendipitous overlaps in gender expectations that substantially underwrote French "whiteness."[10]

These basic French commitments to a society based on sedentary agriculture, private land ownership, Christianity, and patriarchal gender relations were deeply familiar and deeply reassuring to Anglo-Americans. Despite the French population's nonchalance about adopting many Native cultural practices and marrying into Native societies, it was clear that they had not abandoned the basic social precepts that distinguished "civilized" humanity from "savage." Anglo-Americans might sneer at the small peasant subsistence farms of the French, with their antiquated tools, narrow "ribbon" fields, and rusticated houses, but they nevertheless could clearly differentiate French landowning and land use practices from those of Native peoples. An embodied construction of "race" seemed less compelling in the earliest years after the War of 1812, and Anglo-Americans were more likely to emphasize that the French retained their European cultural heritage of "civilization" and Christianity rather than define French whiteness as grounded in their racial descent from Keating's white "European." Still, Keating's anxiety over white racial degeneration reveals the degree to which race-based identifications of people were already present in American culture.[11]

Over the next thirty years, Anglo-Americans would become less certain of the French racial identity. As representatives of the United States met and negotiated dozens of treaties with Native tribal nations and French-descended persons at locations such as Chicago, Green Bay, and Prairie du Chien, initial American constructions of the "races" of the Great Lakes region would be called into question. In particular, Anglo-American understandings of the French-descended population as white would be frequently challenged, yet, significantly, never completely overturned, or rewritten. Reasons for this were complex. Native peoples' repeated refusals to accept a logic of race based on somatic features without regard to cultural context or self-identification were clearly pivotal. At the same time, Americans' own ambivalence over which criteria—European cultural orientation or bodily features such as skin color—more accurately described a person's race remained an important factor explaining why they continued to define French identity in multiple ways. The older definitions of race that relied on cultural characteristics, religious beliefs, personal comportment, hairstyles, food preferences, and the like still lingered in American society, especially at the level of popular thought and expression. But neither Native peoples' insistence on alternative constructions of social difference nor the ongoing uncertainty of Anglo-Americans completely account for the continued American tolerance of racial ambiguity. A third factor arose in the decades after the War of 1812 that provided powerful additional incentives for Anglo-Americans, especially those coming to settle in the trans-Appalachian west, to maintain the ambiguousness of race in the Great Lakes region. As the United States began negotiating postwar land cession treaties with Native peoples, select Anglo-American individuals and their political allies quickly grasped the lucrative potential of malleable and uncertain racial categories. These men, among them territorial officials, the influential local citizens who served on treaty commissions, ambitious Indian agents, fur traders, and merchants, realized there was money to be made from the negotiation of treaties. The manipulation of racial identity became one of several ways to do it.[12]

The fluidity of personal and racial identity in the backcountry, and the several uses to which such nebulous identities could be put, were illuminated within two years of the war's end at the negotiation of the first postwar treaty to involve a land cession. This treaty, signed "at the foot of the Rapids of the Miami of Lake Erie," on September 29, 1817, was referred to variously as the Treaty of Fort Meigs, the Treaty with the Wyandots, and the Treaty of the Maumee Rapids, the last being the name by which it is currently known.[13] A sweeping document that alienated millions of acres of Native land in northwest Ohio, the Maumee Rapids treaty was negotiated with several Indigenous communities including Wyandots, Senecas, Shawnees, Delawares, Ojibwes, Odawas, and Potawatomis. The American treaty commissioners, Michigan territorial governor Lewis Cass and General Duncan McArthur, an Ohio politician and military officer during the War of 1812, emphasized their success in alienating tribal lands, with lead negotiator Cass pointedly calling attention to the treaty's "obvious . . . financial and military" advantages to the United States. [14]

The commissioners were somewhat less forthcoming about several of the treaty's other provisions. Although it had supposedly extinguished all Indian land title in Ohio, the Treaty of the Maumee Rapids contained a number of provisions by which Native peoples could retain at least some of their lands. In addition to the land cession, the treaty stipulated that every Native "head of family who wishes to remain within the limits ceded should have a life estate in a reservation of a certain number of acres, which should descend to his children in fee, reserving to the widow (if any) her thirds."[15] While these terms contained strict requirements that Native people adopt Anglo-American private landownership and inheritance patterns, including their unequal gender dimensions, they also accorded these reserved lands the strongest American legal protections by granting these life estates in fee simple, that is, as owned outright without any form of indebtedness. Several of the larger tribal communities of western Ohio, including the Wyandots, Shawnees, Senecas, and Delawares, reserved a total of thirty-six land grants "by patent, in fee simple" under the Maumee Rapids treaty.[16]

The treaty's inconsistencies did not end with land reserves for Native peoples. As Cass and McArthur delicately noted, the treaty was "the result of mutual demands and of mutual compromises." Not only had "life estates" that allowed tribal persons to remain on permanent land bases in the ceded territory been granted to 493 Native people, additional fee simple grants had been awarded to a disparate group of approximately 23 persons. Among them were the widows and orphans of tribal men who had died fighting in the American service during the War of 1812, a Francophone adoptive son of the Odawa leader Tondaganie, the two multiracial sons of Potawatomi Indian agent Gabriel Godfroy, and the multiracial interpreter and trader Antoine Chêne, or Anthony Shane, a lifelong acquaintance of Tecumseh who had identified the Shawnee leader's body after the Battle of the Thames in 1813.[17] Also included were five adoptive Wyandots, Anglophones who had been "taken prisoner by the Indians" as children and had "ever since lived among them" and several Wyandots of multiracial ancestry who culturally and phenotypically presented as "whites." [18] The ambiguous racial identities of many of these persons were of deep concern to Cass and McArthur, since Congress had repeatedly passed legislation expressly designed to prevent white people from obtaining land as part of a treaty negotiation.

Several adoptive Anglophones, along with several of the multiracial Wyandots, were in the forefront of the postwar Native effort to adapt to Anglo-American cultural and economic norms as part of the tribal attempt to live harmoniously with the incoming Anglo-American population. They had advocated in favor of the treaty and expected in return that the commissioners would protect their economic interests and bolster their attempts to encourage other Native people to follow their adaptive example. Aware that they owed their success largely to these individuals, Cass and McArthur obliged, and took pains to craft expansive language that would describe these persons as "Indians by blood or adoption" to ensure they would be eligible for the lands granted them.[19]

The phrase "Indians by blood or adoption" was indeed fortuitous. It handily created what appeared to be an unambiguous binary describing two mutually exclusive sets of criteria by which a person could be determined to be an "Indian." Cass and McArthur certainly recognized the phrase's utility, but it was not wholly their creation. Negotiators for several of the tribes (among them the Wyandots, Odawas, Potawatomis, and Shawnees) had advocated strongly for inclusion in the treaty of adoptive and multiracial kin. They did so as part of a broader tribal strategy to retain lands in addition to those that had been granted the 493 Native individuals as life estates. It should be remembered, however, that while tribespeople valued their relations' skills in dealing with the growing American presence, they also viewed these adoptive and multiracial persons as legitimate members of tribal kin groups. This fact was obscured in the treaty's narrow definition of the concepts of blood and adoption. Adoption especially was described in limited terms that emphasized the youthful captivity and the eventual cultural incorporation of racialized white individuals. Native understandings of tribal belonging were more expansive, emphasizing not absorption and disappearance but connection to tribal families and the creation of networks of multiple kin ties.[20]

The descriptions of the final three persons included in the long list that comprised Article 8 of the Maumee Rapids treaty suggest the larger context in which Native peoples comprehended kinship and adoption. Those three persons, Richard and Alexander Godfroy and "Sawendebans, or the Yellow Hair, or Peter Minor," were depicted as adoptive tribal kin but there was no mention of their racialized ancestry, their youthful captivity, or long years spent living among the tribes. Instead, they were presented in ways that were more aligned with Native views of adoption; they were described in named relationships to tribal kinfolk. The Godfroy brothers were "adopted children of the Potawatomy tribe."

Sawendebans, whose first introduction in the document was by his Odawa-language name, further locating him within the tribal world, was "an adopted son of Tondaganie," an influential Odawa leader present at the negotiations. It is also notable that the three adoptees were described by words connoting a status as tribal children, a political category that signified they were part of a tribal collective whole but lacked the ability to act alone in political matters. Their Native kin would not, for instance, have understood them as empowered to dispose of the lands they were being granted.[21]

Ultimately, Cass and McArthur's concern that land grants to adoptive and multiracial tribal persons would raise the suspicions of the Senate proved unfounded. The treaty's greatest sticking point was not racially ambiguous recipients of land grants; it was the fee simple land grants to nearly five hundred Native individuals. Senators pronounced such titles "unprecedented" and "at variance with the general principles on which intercourse with the Indian tribes has been conducted." Native peoples, in the Senatorial view, possessed only collective rights to occupy the soil and could not reserve land individually in fee simple. The negotiating tribes, too, had objections; many of them felt the lands reserved as fee simple holdings were too small to sustain their communities. A delegation of Wyandots, Senecas, and Delawares traveled to Washington, arriving fortuitously as the Senate was debating the Maumee Rapids treaty. Further talks were held that resulted in an amended Treaty of St. Mary's. Under its terms, the tribes gained considerable additional acreage, expanding the size of several tribal reserves in exchange for agreeing to the Senate's demand that they retain these lands "as Indian reservations have heretofore been held." In an ironic concluding note, given the commissioners' expectation that adoptive and multiracial individuals would be ruled ineligible for land grants, the revised St. Mary's treaty placed their land titles under restriction, too. Though the grantees were recognized as individual landowners and their lands did not revert to communal occupancy status, they could not freely sell their land. Sales had to have presidential approval, the same as land sales by Native peoples on communally owned reservations. Altogether, the amended Treaty of St. Mary's proved satisfactory to the tribes. They retained more land in northwest Ohio, creating the conditions that would allow them to remain in the state for several decades to come. The advice and actions of multiracial and adoptive kinfolk were seen as part of the reason for this success. Tribes would continue to experiment with ways to include tribal kin with bicultural skills or multiple ethnic and national identities as they continued to craft strategies to allow them to remain on the land. [22]

Intent on concluding a treaty that ceded Native lands in the strategically important region of northwest Ohio, American officials and politicians paid little attention to the broader implications present in Native understandings of adoption. A further examination of the adoptions of the Godfroy brothers and Sawendebans suggest other ways in which Native peoples conceptualized adoption beyond the incorporation of persons who were initially taken captive. Certainly, tribal adoptions could originate from prior acts of capture, but ties of kinship could also be extended to valued outsiders who had formed voluntary connections with tribal individuals or communities. Sawendebans' adoptive father, Tondaganie, was an important Odawa leader and might well have considered it expedient to incorporate a Francophone trader into his community as a member of his family. The Potawatomis extended kinship recognition to Richard and Alexander Godfroy because the boys' father, Gabriel, was an Indian agent for the tribe. Creating a kinship tie to an important American official seemed a wise idea in the aftermath of the War of 1812 when tribes were exploring all options in their efforts to restabilize their war-torn communities.[23]

The tribally initiated adoptions of the Godfroy brothers and Sawendebans underscore the point that Native peoples and Anglo-Americans understood this form of deliberately created kinship in very different ways. Americans considered adoptions to be restorative acts, a means of reintegrating the orphaned or abandoned into their society's most crucial institution, the patriarchal conjugal family. Native peoples understood adoptions as expansive actions, rituals that enlarged tribal kin networks by incorporating new relatives into them. Following the logic of restorative adoption, Americans further presupposed that adopted persons lacked existing kin groups. Great Lakes Native peoples, in contrast, presumed that many adoptees would retain ties with their natal kindreds. This was regarded as an extremely important feature of adoption, since it allowed for the establishment of still more kin ties between members of the now-connected kin groups.[24]

As a Native social construct, adoption also had larger political implications. Through diplomatic rituals sometimes translated into English by the phrase "the making of relatives," adoption served as prototype of, and analogy to, the central political acts of negotiating intertribal peace and alliance. Just as individuals adopted into tribal kindreds became relatives–brothers, children, mothers, and fathers—nations at peace with one another signaled the new peace-based state of affairs by their use of kin terms. Speaking of the recently concluded 1825 Treaty of Prairie du Chien, which attempted to establish peace among ten tribal nations, the Ojibwe *ogimaa* Zhingwaabe Aasin articulated this concept. He praised the efforts of American representatives in bringing together so many tribal leaders and working to broker the peace that would allow their peoples "to live as one family." Similarly, in 1827, the Menominis recalled how the Oneidas and several other eastern Native communities had met with them some years earlier to discuss the possibility of a move to Menomini lands in Wisconsin where "they might live with us like brothers." Needless to say, the American view of adoption did not include the multidirectional kin-making components so central to Native practice. They had only an imperfect understanding of the institution's significance to the tribal nations, and this would affect their perceptions of French-identified persons who claimed and were granted tribal inclusion. [25]

If tribal forms of adoption contained implicit assumptions about the possibility that kin ties could be forged across important categories of social difference such as nation or ethnicity, tribal understandings of marriage, the other social institution deeply involved in the creation of kin ties, elaborated upon these beliefs. Tribal oral narratives that described how the world came to be in its present form recounted stories of marriages between human and Other Than Human persons that served as charters for human understandings and practices of marriage. These oral narratives featured Native women and articulated the importance of tribal women in creating and sustaining marriage-based ties in ways patriarchal Europeans and their New World descendants, who conceptualized marriage as predicated upon female subordination, never fully grasped. In such widespread stories as "The Woman Who Married the Beaver," analyzed in an Ojibwe telling by Bruce M. White, the foundational role of Native women was both described and enacted. Not only did the protagonist of the story marry a man of a foreign nation and have children with him, by these acts she initiated an alliance between their two nations that would endure long after she and her spouse were dead. Embodied first through their children, the alliance would endure in all their descendants, who would remember themselves and be similarly remembered within their nations as descended from their ancestors' two nations. While the woman who married the beaver recounted a marriage between a human woman and an Other Than Human man, boundary-crossing marriages occurred in the human world as well.[26] At the 1837 Treaty of Fort

Snelling, the Ojibwe political leader Zhaagobe disconcerted the American negotiators by proclaiming himself their relative based on his "white" ancestry. "I sprung from the same stock with the people who stand behind you– white men—" he explained to the treaty commissioners. The council minutes, as printed in the Dubuque *Iowa News*, sought to clarify this statement for its Anglo-American readership, who would presumably be confused by a Native man claiming relationship with white Americans. The writer added a parenthetical note explaining Zhaagobe's multiracial heritage. "(Sha-go-bai, half breed)" was inserted into the text.[27]

Oral narratives like "The Woman Who Married the Beaver" contained a second level of significance that spoke to the reasons why Great Lakes Native peoples valued the ability to transcend seemingly insurmountable social differences. Once again modeled on relationships between human beings and Other Than Human beings, oral narratives established the appropriate relationships of mutual aid and reciprocity that were to exist among kin. The spouse of the woman who married the beaver aided his wife's relatives in the proper reciprocal manner by presenting them with food. The narrative sent a powerful message about the importance of kinfolk. One's relatives, wherever they might be found, could be counted on for help in facing the vicissitudes of life, whether in the form of a crop failure, an enemy attack, or an uncertain political environment in which the intentions of multiple nations needed to be accurately understood and hostile intentions deflected or neutralized.[28]

Native conceptions of kinship as a social connection that bridged the boundaries of nation and ethnicity took on heightened significance after 1815 as the United States pressured the tribal communities living in the western Ohio Valley and the regions surrounding Lake Michigan to cede their lands and vacate the area. As the provisions in these treaties also reveal, several Lower Great Lakes tribes with long histories of intertribal cooperation, among them Miamis, Potawatomis, Odawas, Ojibwes, Wyandots, and Shawnees, strategically employed transnational and interethnic kin ties in a variety of ways to defend tribal land bases. Their efforts began, ironically, with the Treaty of Maumee Rapids itself. While that treaty highlights one of the earliest Anglo-American efforts to manipulate their own categories of racial identity for political and economic gain, it also reveals the first postwar efforts by Native people to employ Indigenous conceptualizations of kinship to their own advantage.

The new tribal initiative featured deliberate efforts to put forward select multiracial kinfolk as treaty negotiators. Individuals sought were those who demonstrated keen political instincts and had kin ties to influential tribal families as well as other Native or European nations or ethnicities. While the ethnic makeup of the largely Anglophone multiracial kin involved in negotiating the Treaty of Maumee Rapids would initially obscure the fact, in most of the Great Lakes area tribes, the preponderance of multiracial kin were of French descent. They often described themselves as possessing a French ethnicity, while simultaneously self-identifying as kin to Native families and thus as belonging to tribal nations. As additional treaty negotiations unfolded in the years after the Treaty of Maumee Rapids, Native peoples clarified the kin-based nature of the connections between themselves and the Interior French, refuting the initial American assumption that multiracial French-descended persons were unrelated to area tribes. The new initiative was evident only one year later at the several treaties negotiated at St. Mary's, Ohio, in 1818. Potawatomi, Wea, and Miami negotiators all asserted the tribal reality of composite extended families made up of indigenous and French-descended individuals.[29]

The Potawatomis and Weas further identified their multiracial kinfolk using Native constructions of relatedness that emphasized the incorporative importance of the marriages of tribal women to outsiders. Such marriages rarely resulted in Native wives leaving their own communities but instead involved foreign husbands' residence within tribal villages, or nearby. Tribal leadership families in particular employed such incorporative marriages as a strategy to attach outsiders they deemed important to their communities, as trading partners or military allies for instance. Americans unwittingly described the results of this strategy in their records of several of the 1818 treaties. They identified the mothers of the multiracial families whom tribes sought to have included within the terms of the treaty as women from leadership families. Among the Potawatomis, the multiracial Burnett family descended from Kakima, the "sister of Topinibe, principal chief of the nation," while Mechinquamesha of the Weas, in addition to being the mother of multiracial children and wife of a Frenchman, was a "sister of Jacco, a chief of the tribe." Although Native peoples believed that the presence of women such as Kakima and Mechinquamesha revealed the significance of women and indigenous kin networks in political actions, Americans interpreted the presence of such women according to their own gender conventions. Reflecting the patriarchal biases of their own society (and reinforced by their invidious "squaw drudge" image of Native women), Americans assumed Native women were firmly subordinated to Native men. They took pains to connect Kakima and Mechinquamesha to their influential male relatives to demonstrate that their anomalous positions of power were ultimately derived from men whose legitimacy as leaders Americans underscored by terming them "chiefs."[30]

In thus interpreting Native gender roles as analogous to their own, Anglo-Americans radically misunderstood Native objectives in negotiating the 1818 treaties. Land grants might conceivably be privately held tracts awarded to multiracial French kinfolk, as the Americans characterized them, but from the perspective of Native people, they were also lands entrusted to members of respected leadership families. While Americans recognized the claims of select multiracial people to land grants on the basis of their mothers' connections to male Native political leaders, they rarely considered the fact that these kin relationships entailed connections to, and responsibilities for, an extensive array of additional Native relatives. Every child of a chief's sister or daughter was also a niece, nephew, or grandchild of a tribal leader. They, too, were members of leadership families, and Native peoples considered that they also had responsibilities to their communities. The lands placed in their hands were not viewed as exclusively private land grants to individuals; they continued to be conserved for the common use of tribal communities that were understood to include both Native and multiracial French persons. Through the land grants awarded to Kakima's six adult children with William Burnett, for example, the Potawatomis preserved ten sections of land under the Treaty of October 2, 1818. The less populous Weas, under great pressure from the treaty commissioners to alienate all their land "within the limits of the states of Indiana, Ohio, and Illinois," nonetheless granted a section of land apiece to Mechinquamesha's two adult children, the land "not to be conveyed or transferred . . . but with the consent of the President."[31]

Of the several tribes, the Miamis launched the most ambitious effort at retaining land utilizing a partnership of French-descended and Indigenous landowners. The Miami treaty of October 6 also stated the case for French inclusion within tribes most strongly, defining them as either "Miami Indians by birth" or "their heirs." Miamis admitted no other categories of person to confuse the situation, avoiding the earlier muddle that had arisen from the dual notions of "Indians by blood or adoption." The treaty also enjoined Miamis and their heirs from selling their land without additional negotiation and presidential approval and granted such protected tracts to twenty-nine individuals. Strikingly, fully one-half of these twenty-nine persons had French surnames, beginning with the "principal chief," Peshewa, or Jean Baptiste Richardville,

whose father was a French fur trader named Joseph Drouet de Cherville (angli-
cized to Richardville) while his mother, Taucumwah, was a member of an influential Miami leadership family. By using both his names, Richardville signaled
to Native people his transnational heritage with its unspoken assurance that he
possessed the cross-cultural skills and knowledge that would allow him to work
effectively in both Native and American societies. His membership in a Miami
leadership family sent a different but similarly reassuring signal: here was a man
who could be counted upon to understand and fulfill his kin obligations to his
tribal relatives.[32]

The strategy of sheltering lands by placing them in the hands of French relatives spread quickly among the tribal communities whose homelands lay between
western Ohio and the regions surrounding Lake Michigan. From Odawas in
Ohio to Ho-chunks in Wisconsin, numerous peoples would employ the strategy, but it would be the Potawatomis (including a community of Ojibwes,
Odawas, and Potawatomis called the United Band) who would most frequently
entrust lands to the care of composite French-Potawatomi kindreds. With villages spread across the entire region and encircling the three sides of Lake Michigan located within what would become American soil, Potawatomis negotiated
dozens of treaties with the United States between 1816 and 1833. In each treaty,
tribal communities retained land by placing it in the custody of French kinfolk,
often the close relatives of tribal leaders. While the strategy did not protect every
parcel of land so consigned, it was successful often enough to remain a method
of first resort.[33]

Placing land in the care of French kinfolk had the unintended consequence
of elevating a number of multiracial persons to positions of prominence and
political leadership in tribal societies in the decades following the War of 1812.
This proved particularly the case among Native nations that found themselves
repeatedly negotiating treaties with the incoming Americans. In addition to Jean
Baptiste Richardville, multiracial Miami leaders included Francois Godfroy
and Francois Lafontaine; among the Odawas, Augustin Hamelin Jr. emerged
as a tribal spokesman and leader, and members of the French-descended Bertrand, Chandonnais, LeClaire, and LaFramboise families assumed leadership
roles among the Potawatomis.[34] These families publicly named their Native
mothers as their progenitrixes, while other prominent multiracial men proudly
acknowledged their dual ancestry, proclaiming in the words of the well-to-do
French and Odawa fur trader Alexis Bailly that they had no reason "to blush at
the relationship." The visibility of these men as tribal leaders and their embrace

of their multiracial ancestry challenged the American construction of the Interior French as a white-descended people with only remote ancestral ties to local Native populations.[35]

As Anglo-Americans gained firsthand experience with the formidable political skills of multiracial tribal leaders, they struggled to reconceptualize such men as "Indians." By the early nineteenth century, Americans took it as a given that Native peoples were "savages" who occupied the bottom rung of the social evolutionist ladder. They lacked every element of what Americans termed "civilization," from private landownership to literacy, sedentary agriculture to acceptance of the Christian religion. The multiracial kinfolk who dressed in European-style clothing and spoke French or English, proclaimed themselves Christians, and prospered (sometimes quite handsomely) from the fur and provisioning trades were clearly not unsophisticated "red children of the forest," as a cliché of the times described Native peoples.[36] Indeed, from the perspective of Anglo-Americans, the Interior French could hardly be less like the people they claimed as their tribal relatives. Anglo-Americans had always made note of the "Indian blood" of the Interior French, of course, and had constructed them as "white" on the strength of their many European-derived cultural attributes. When confronted by multiracial political leaders, traders, and others who claimed kin connections with Native people or asserted an Indian identity, Anglo-Americans did not immediately abandon their older framework for assigning racial identities based on the evidence of cultural orientation. Yet the very fluidity of the culturally derived definitions allowed Americans to shift with relative ease from an emphasis on the *cultural* whiteness of the multiracial French to a renewed awareness of the significance of their "mixed" *racial* heritage.

Americans were further able to shift the emphasis of the older definitions because, despite their attention to the cultural bases of identity, they had also acknowledged the significance of "blood." Another malleable term, this one with its origin in European practices of animal breeding, blood metaphorically described the transmission of physical and cultural characteristics assumed to be inherited. Particularly salient, of course, was "white" blood. Anglo-Americans differed over what meaning to assign to white blood, with some describing it as an elevating trait while others characterized multiracial persons as degenerate and depraved, physical evidence of the dangers of interracial mixture. Although Anglo-Americans did not agree on the consequences of possessing a multiracial heritage, almost to a person they agreed that a multiracial identity signaled an important form of social difference. To be of "mixed" race was to be anomalous in a society where races were being redefined as bordered, hierarchic categories. Furthermore, social evolutionist theory decreed that, if multiracial persons differed culturally from Indians, they could not *be* Indians. Anglo-Americans thus bestowed new significance on the fact that the French were of both French and Indian blood, and they did so in a manner that reinscribed a fundamental difference between French persons who were part Indian and those persons who were wholly Indians, and whose cultural (and increasingly racial) identities were assumed to be both readily identifiable and completely unchanging. Americans described multiracial persons using terms such as half breed and mixed-blood, constructing their racially "mixed" ancestry both as their defining feature and as an inseparable barrier between them and "full-blooded Indians."[37]

This construction of multiracial persons as related to but profoundly different from Indians, both in their cultural orientation and in their "blood" descent, had far-reaching consequences. One of the most important would be the continued American belief that half breeds lacked any meaningful inclusion within Native societies. Particularly when it came to the activities that defined a Native community as a political entity, such as governance and decision-making, Anglo-Americans dismissed the idea that multiracial people had any legitimate role to play. They also rejected the possibility, if they understood it to exist, that Native peoples might define categories of relatives according to kinship principles different from their own. The Native practice of deliberately employing people whose kin networks crossed ethnic and tribal boundaries to act as diplomats and negotiators in inter-ethnic and international settings was so unlike the American conceptions of negotiation and diplomacy that Americans were unable to recognize it as a culturally distinctive Indigenous political act. As multiracial leaders emerged in the decades following the War of 1812, Anglo-Americans were far more likely to view them as self-serving opportunists than as connected by kin ties and kin obligations to the tribal communities on whose behalf they sought to negotiate. When tribal leaders such as Jean-Baptiste Richardville of the Miamis or members of the French and Potawatomi Bertrand family participated in the making of treaties from which they and their immediate families derived substantial land grants and cash payments, Americans saw their claims to tribal inclusion as spurious and completely self-interested. Such persons, Americans charged, maintained the pretense of tribal belonging only to be able to cajole their Native kinfolk into including them in treaty benefits. George Boyd, Indian agent for the Menominis in 1839, expressed this American perspective with special venom. It was a "notorious fact," Boyd claimed, that "*all Indians*" were under the "entire control" of their "Traders & half blood relatives." Although Boyd condemned both traders and Native peoples as "designing & unprincipled," he saved his harshest words for the Menominis' multiracial kin, decrying the "influence" exerted by "their miserable halfbreed French Relations."[38]

It would be in the context of treaty negotiations where Anglo-Americans continued to wrestle most profoundly and most frequently with the uncertain racial and cultural identity of multiracial French kinfolk. The presence of multiracial kin at treaty councils and their inclusion in treaty benefits would quickly become topics of controversy. Americans already distrusted the treaty-making process, and though they recognized the need for it, they saw treaties as a tainted enterprise foisted on them by their recently overthrown British overlords. In reality, despite their fondness for hurling this sort of invective, Anglo-Americans shared the views of their British forbearers respecting treaty-making with Native peoples. The most important intellectual feature of this shared perception was a long-standing inability to recognize the political significance of gift exchanges within the tribal cultures of the Great Lakes country. Americans referred to gifts as "presents," a euphemism (also borrowed from the British) that not only denied the political legitimacy of gifting but implied that the giving of undeserved presents was but thinly veiled bribery. This coded language only reinforced the American view that both treaties and the Native leaders who negotiated them were fraudulent and duplicitous. Native peoples understood the exchange of gifts as the central act that enabled negotiation to occur. Unaware of this cultural context, Anglo-Americans saw the exchange of gifts as a series of cynical under-the-table payoffs to dishonest tribal leaders. Anglo-Americans were already inclined to view tribal leaders as corrupt and dishonest; they would quickly come to extend this view to multiracial tribal leaders as well. [39]

For the multiracial individuals who assumed leadership positions in the 1820s and 1830s, these several American views constituted a particularly ironic double-edged sword. Native peoples entrusted their multiracial kin with leadership authority because they were seen to possess the skills in intercultural negotiation that tribal nations needed. At the same time, these men needed, as any tribal leader did, to legitimate themselves by displays of generosity and gift-giving within the tribal community. Their successes—the lands they conserved and the cash, goods, and services they were able to provide their peoples via land sales—redounded to their credit within tribal societies but had precisely the opposite effect from the American perspective. Americans viewed multitribal leaders' efforts at validating their leadership as just that much more proof that treaty-making was inherently corrupt, accomplished by bribery not principled negotiation. They regarded multiracial leaders with contempt and often emphasized what they saw as evidence of the personal moral turpitude of these individuals, calling attention to their hard drinking and extravagant living. The scathing remarks of Peter Dougherty, the subagent for the Potawatomis in 1839, are typical. He described the highly visible multiracial political leader Billy Caldwell of the United Band of Ojibwes, Odawas, and Potawatomis as "a cunning, designing, dangerous, speculating, unprincipled drunken spoilt character." [40]

Multiracial leaders earned yet more enmity when, beginning in the 1820s and continuing through the Jacksonian period, a number of them made the hard decision to support tribal removal to the western side of the Mississippi River. After fighting what the historian Bradley Birzer has termed a strategic "series of rear-guard actions" in their efforts to remain on tribal lands in Michigan, Ohio, Indiana, and Illinois, a number of these multiracial leaders concluded that the better course of action was to sell what lands remained and move to the west. These decisions were not unanimous within tribal nations, and multiracial leaders who advocated for them could become controversial, even polarizing, figures. Their reluctant support of removal—and their hard bargaining to get the best terms possible once removal appeared inevitable—only added to the American perception that they were unscrupulous and self-serving, maneuvering to profit personally while selling off the tribal estate.[41]

American efforts to create a racialized identity for the Interior French reflected the heightened importance of "race" in American society in the decades of the early republic. Compelling as the necessity was to create races as fixed categories that embodied either social power or social dispossession, attempts to create an unambiguous racial identity for the multiracial French were never simple. Centuries of intermarriage between Native and French persons had blurred the clear phenotypical differences between Indians and white people that newly arriving Anglo-American emigrants expected to encounter. In this region, where Zhaagobe the Ojibwe war leader identified himself as a "half breed" and Jean Baptiste Chandonnais the French-descended fur trader proclaimed himself "an Indian," physically embodied race alone was simply inadequate as a guide to social identity. Too many people on either side of the supposedly impermeable racial border were not what they appeared to be if one relied exclusively on physical features. Although Americans grasped this reality only partially, the most compelling reason why cultural characteristics as well as somatic differences continued to have social meaning in the Great Lakes region was because on some level they reflected a crucial social reality. Individuals did self-identify (and assign identities to others) as members of Native nations or as "Frenchmen," although somatic features could not predict who would claim which identity. In a place where Indians could be half breeds and half breeds could be Indians, multiple forms of identification remained socially necessary. In such a place, embodied racial differences also remained less significant than either cultural characteristics or self-designation.[42]

In addition to constructions of race and social identity and the social power or subjugation they represented, a series of hard-edged material issues also exerted tremendous influence on the continuing malleability of race and identity in the Great Lakes country. The region's European-descended economic and political elite remained strongly committed to the idea that race was a fluid construct that could be manipulated to advance their business and personal interests. In the years following the War of 1812, the local elite underwent significant changes in membership as a new wave of American emigrants arrived to compete with the earlier generations of settlers. As the American government shifted from a policy of attempting the military conquest of eastern Great Lakes Native peoples to the new strategy of purchasing tribal land and pressuring Native peoples to remove from the area, the region's economic base shifted from the trade in peltries to supplying the annual payments in goods and services owed to Native peoples under treaty mandates. Some of the older traders joined the newly arriving emigrants in retooling their businesses to capture the lion's share of the new economy of the eastern Great Lakes region. Since that economy still consisted of trade and exchange with Native peoples, they lobbied hard in Washington for trading policies that would favor their private companies over the federally subsidized "factories," or trading posts, that the American state had experimented with in the decades before the War of 1812. As individuals and as companies they were largely successful. Their efforts involved cultivating mutually beneficial ties to incoming politicians and government officials at both the local and national levels. As the Federal government responded to pressure from its citizens to throw open the newly secured Great Lakes area lands to "white" settlement and began sending commissions to negotiate land-cession treaties with the region's Native nations, the traders and merchants again took full advantage. They provided the food, gifts, and other merchandize at the treaty negotiations, recommended interpreters, served as political consultants to both Commissioners and the negotiating delegations of Native peoples, influenced the appointment of Indian agents, and presented themselves as the dealmakers whose consent was crucial to the successful negotiation of a land sale.[43]

The traders and merchants involved themselves so closely in treaty making and negotiating because they recognized opportunities to make large sums of money during a time of political change and economic uncertainty. In addition to facilitating treaty negotiations with supplies and political expertise, they also submitted highly inflated claims for debts that Native peoples supposedly owed their posts and stores and speculated heavily in Native lands about to be thrown onto the open market. They colluded on the locations of town sites, city lots, sawmills, and stagecoach lines, and schemed to move the lucrative annuity payments to places convenient to their business operations—though decidedly inconvenient for the Native peoples who could find themselves trekking hundreds of miles in inclement winter weather to receive a yearly installment payment for the lands they had sold. No strangers to the region's racial and ethnic diversity, many of the traders and merchants had established unions of long or short duration with Native or multiracial women and had fathered multiracial children. Some were themselves of multiracial descent, while all employed multiracial persons in their businesses as laborers, subcontracting petty traders, and interpreters. They saw in the racial ambiguousness of the Interior French another profitable means of tapping into the sizeable sums being made available by the treaty-making and treaty-fulfilling endeavors. Malleable racial identity also suggested ways to evade the forms of Congressional oversight repeatedly enacted to prevent the very sorts of graft, fraud, and corruption they were engaged in.[44]

No one better grasped how the ambiguities of race and kinship could be manipulated to make money, reward political allies, and advance one's political career than Lewis Cass. As Michigan territorial governor eager to promote western emigration, Cass pioneered the process of racial manipulation at the 1817 Treaty of Maumee Rapids when he reconstructed Anglophone adoptees as "Indians." Two years later he helped to place nine apparently fictitious Native-descended children onto the list of persons who were to be awarded land under the September 24, 1819, Treaty of Saginaw, negotiated with the Ojibwe and Odawa peoples of Michigan. As at Maumee Rapids, this too was a scheme to get around the Congressional restrictions on awarding such land grants to racialized whites, though rather than declaring adoptive Anglophones to be

"Indians," this time Cass provided a number of Saginaw-area traders, prominent citizens, and Indian Office officials with multiracial children in whose names, and allegedly on whose behalf, they claimed their lands. The scandal-ridden negotiations (Cass also purchased 187 gallons of alcohol for the ten-day council and kept an influential Ojibwe opponent of the treaty too drunk to attend the daily meetings) generated a public outcry and some of the names of Cass's cronies were stricken from the treaty before it was ratified by Congress. The governor himself, however, was undaunted. [45] In 1826, he and his political protégé, the newly appointed Indian agent to the Ojibwes Henry R. Schoolcraft, again manipulated racial identity and kinship ties, this time on behalf of the largest fur trade company in the region, the aggressive and politically well-connected American Fur Company. At a treaty negotiation held at the Ojibwe village of Fond du Lac in present-day Minnesota, Cass and Schoolcraft inserted into the treaty exceedingly large land grants of one full section, or six hundred forty acres, for "half breeds, and Chippewas by descent." A schedule was drawn up and attached to the treaty identifying the multiracial individuals who were to receive the munificent grants. Unsurprisingly, nearly all were the wives and children (and in a few instances the grandchildren) of high-ranking American Fur Company personnel. These land grants were even more remarkable because they were the *only* land cessions in the treaty; the assembled Ojibwes ceded no land to the United States under the 1826 Treaty of Fond du Lac. [46]

Not unexpectedly, it was the potential duality inherent in a multiracial identity that made it so attractive to the commercial trading elite and their allies. Also not unexpectedly, they constructed racial identity around the familiar binary of either physically embodied traits such as skin color or cultural characteristics such as occupation, housing styles, or languages spoken. Maintaining the idea of blood descent yet insisting on social and cultural separateness allowed the traders and merchants to lobby for two mutually exclusive types of payments under treaties. The first repaid Native indebtedness owed to individual traders, merchants, and their several companies; the second involved separate payments for tribal "half-breeds." The traders, merchants, and their friends could thus press lucrative debt claims against Native peoples and speculate heavily in the landed assets and cash payments awarded to "the half-breeds of said Tribes." As additional treaties were negotiated, the trading elite submitted more debt claims and speculated anew in "half-breed" payments. It was an extremely profitable enterprise, making fortunes for a lucky few and creating the illusion of easy money for many more. As a political and economic strategy, it also meant that members of the commercial elite were deeply invested in maintaining the fluidity of "racial" categories.[47]

The trading elite's self-serving manipulation of multiracial identity would not go unchallenged, however. Anglo-American emigration increased rapidly in the 1820s, setting the stage for political rivalry between the newcomers, many of them from New England, and the fur trade-based society they encountered. As early as 1824, incoming "Yankee" emigrants to Michigan Territory challenged the "whiteness" of the multiracial French as part of an effort to undercut the political dominance of the commercial elite, who successfully courted the votes of the territory's multiracial French population. Allegations that ineligible men of color had voted in the close, hotly contested 1824 Congressional election rehearsed the language and cultural construction of "whiteness" as the newly arrived Americans understood it. The emigrants sought to define white persons as "those whose descent could be traced to a pure European origin," and the traders and their allies rebutted them with evidence of the European cultural characteristics of the multiracial French. "[T]he half breeds (so Called) . . . are not in their habits like wandering Indians," they asserted, "but on the contrary many of them are owners of comfortable houses, speak English or French, and dress like white men." Despite two government investigations into the alleged voter fraud, one at the territorial and the other at the Congressional level, neither investigative body attempted to define "whiteness" only in racially embodied terms. The Great Lakes territories, of which Michigan was the earliest to be organized, needed the votes of the multiracial French especially in the early decades of colonization when Native peoples were still in the numerical majority and the numbers of white Americans "descended from a pure European" were few. The eligibility of the multiracial French as voters and citizens was upheld by quiet legislative inaction. [48]

As a growing American population continued its efforts to understand racial and ethnic identities in the Great Lakes country, it also struggled to understand how "Indians" and "half breeds" were, in fact, related to each other. Americans readily accepted that there was a kin connection between the two groups, as the many treaty references to "half-breed relations" attest. Ironically, this American understanding of "half breeds" as kinfolk further reinforced their perception that the connections of multiracial persons to Native peoples were of an inherently nonpolitical nature. Long-standing, deeply held American beliefs located kinship within the private and feminized world of the family and home rather than the public and masculine world of politics and commerce. The fact that so many multiracial persons had Native mothers and European or American fathers only reinforced the characterization of multiracial persons as dependents, by linking them conceptually to those other dependents who lacked political personhood, women. American racial and gender hierarchies were thus employed as tools for defining relations between Native and multiracial persons while at the same time the definitions they crafted comfortingly replicated the crucial gender and race hierarchies that underwrote American society.[49]

As Americans sought to define and manipulate what they perceived as the kin connection between Native and multiracial persons, Native peoples advanced their own understandings of the relationships between themselves and multiracial French-descended persons. They too used the language of kinship, but close reading of their words reveals their definitions of "half breed children" carried far different connotations than the Americans' understandings of half breeds as subordinated dependents. Tribal spokespersons and political leaders located multiracial persons unambiguously within tribal kin networks, describing them as "our children, the half breeds," or "our half breed children." To Americans, such references suggested a Native understanding of children as the most powerless members of society, which certainly accorded with their own understanding of children. At times, however, tribal leaders elaborated on community affection for their multiracial kin, as when "Maw-Zaw-Zid" [Maangozid] an Ojibwe leader from the village of Fond du Lac declared in 1826 that "[o]ur half breeds live in our hearts." More frequently, tribal speakers asserted that because of their kin ties to tribal communities, "half breed children" deserved to share in treaty settlements. "Our children the half breeds also, we want to have provided for," said Bizhiki, or Buffalo, in a representative statement at the 1842 Treaty of LaPointe. Broken Nose, another speaker at the same treaty, echoed Buffalo's words, while elaborating on the familial nature of the relationship between Ojibwes and multiracial persons. "I have raised the half breeds," Broken Nose stated, "and I want you to provide for them." While the complex meanings Native peoples speaking multiple Algonkian, Siouan, and Iroquoian languages attributed to the words that were glossed into English as meaning "half breed" await further analysis, it is worth noting that words describing multiracial peoples did exist in Great Lakes Native languages by the early nineteenth century. Although none of these words, if accurately translated, carried racialized meanings comparable to those Americans were assigning to the term "half breed," their presence suggests tribal people did distinguish multiracial persons as unique social groups. The challenge for Native peoples, of course, was to make clear to Americans the deeper social realities that lay behind the words that were being uniformly translated by the gloss "half breeds."[50]

Native political leaders and spokespersons, especially those with long experience in international diplomacy with Europeans and their descendants, recognized that Americans had not grasped the full significance of the phrase "our half breed children" and sought to clarify it. At the 1837 Treaty of Fort Snelling, "Ma-ghe-ga-bo" [Mayaajigaabaw] of the Leech Lake Ojibwes attempted to place multiracial kinfolk in their political context by explaining their connections to the several villages of Ojibwes present at the negotiations. "Our women have brought the half breeds among us," he stated, referring to the acts of intermarriage that created kin-based alliances. When tribal women married foreign men, the children of those unions shared in the political and social identities of both parents' communities. By definition, they were brought into the tribal community of their mothers *by* their mothers. At the same treaty Zhaagobe, the Snake River Ojibwe war leader, tried to articulate the corresponding Native expectation that persons such as he formed the parallel links to their fathers' peoples when he identified himself as sharing ancestry with "white men." Such individuals, embodying multitribal alliances in their physical persons, further linked families across tribal and national (and eventually across what Americans would view as "racial") lines.[51]

When metaphors of embodied difference proved difficult for Anglo-Americans to comprehend, tribal leaders and speakers offered expanded definitions of multiracial persons in efforts to clarify tribal conceptualizations of such persons. Three mutually reinforcing ways of understanding multiracial persons as connected to, and included within, tribal communities found repeated expression. These conceptions clearly reveal Great Lakes Native constructions of kinship as a social practice that could cross ethnic and national boundaries. Additionally, Native peoples understood such boundary-crossing persons as capable of performing a crucial role in creating political alliances. Each of the three constructions was articulated in speech, usually at treaty councils, where the inclusion of multiracial persons within tribal nations was an issue of intense concern both to Native peoples and to Anglo-Americans. The first of these characterizations of "our half breed children" usually appeared as a qualifier, an assertion by tribal speakers that selected multiracial persons were not simply tribal children but had enduring connections with known tribal places. Recalling in 1832 a particular treaty he had negotiated some years earlier, the respected Menomini leader

Grizzly Bear remarked, "[M]y village was at Butte des Morts—and . . . these half breeds were with us there." Grizzly Bear did more than locate certain multiracial kin at his village; he acknowledged the wider meaning of their historic connection to his village. Multiracial kin were linked not only to spaces, but they were also connected to *places,* to those lands that human beings had inhabited and invested with meaning. Multiracial kin shared in the history of village places on the land, and in the collective memory of village inhabitants. Another Menomini speaker, "Sku-a-ne-ne," or Little Brave, attempted to describe these connections over time and space by characterizing the Menominis' multiracial kin as "half breeds who have been brought up among us and live among us." Other tribal spokespersons echoed the description of mutual residence together at selected village places. Referring to Ojibwe "half breeds," for example, "Pay-a-jig" [Bayezhig] an *ogimaa* who spoke at the 1837 Treaty of Fort Snelling observed that "many of them have been brought up among us."[52]

The second way that tribal leaders identified specific multiracial persons as kinfolk was closely associated with their long-standing residence in Native villages. Not only did multiracial kin "live among" Native peoples, but tribal leaders also considered their responsibilities as leaders to extend to the multiracial kin affiliated with their villages. Addressing an assembly of Ojibwes from multiple villages at the 1826 Treaty of Fond du Lac, Zhingwaabe Aasin demonstrated this understanding. "My relations," the Sault Sainte Marie area *ogimaa* said, "The land to be provided for my half breeds, I will select[;] I leave it to you, to provide your reserves for your own." Not only did Zhingwaabe Aasin assume responsibility to act for the benefit of the multiracial kin of his community, he anticipated that other village leaders would do likewise. Such expectations are of particular interest because Anglo-Americans such as Boyd and Dougherty routinely characterized "half breeds" as shamelessly manipulating their tribal kin. Tribal leaders clearly understood their actions very differently. "I will shew [*sic*] to my traders, the ground on which I wish my half breeds to live," said an Ojibwe *ogimaa* from Snake River at the same treaty where Zhingwaabe Aasin spoke. Far from being manipulated by "designing traders and half breeds," village leaders saw themselves as exercising the responsibilities incumbent upon them as leaders. These included instructing traders and "half breeds" to do their part in distributing treaty-derived resources for the benefit of the village's component parts.[53]

The third characterization of "half breeds" was the most symbolically significant to Indigenous peoples and the least comprehensible to Anglo-Americans.

While Anglo-Americans assumed "half breeds" occupied, at best, a tenuous status in relation to Native communities, Native peoples in fact located "half breed children" firmly within their foundational political constituencies. As discussed in the previous chapter, Great Lakes Native peoples conceptualized themselves as composed of several pairs of elder and junior political constituencies. Anglo-Americans, as well as the several predecessor European colonial powers, easily recognized the ranked pair of hierarchic male leaders, whom they called the "chiefs," or old men, and the "headmen," or warriors, as the obvious community leadership, analogous to civil and military authorities in their own societies. They would have much more difficulty understanding a second ranked pairing of women and children. Since Americans assumed male dominance and the corresponding dependence of women and children were human cultural universals, they assumed women and children occupied the same dependent status in Native societies. That Native women might inhabit an elder status parallel to those of men and possess forms of power in their own right was so removed from their thinking that they seem to have been unable to recognize it when they saw it, or, more frequently, when they heard it described. This cultural blind spot would hamper Americans in their efforts to understand who "half breeds" were and how they fit into tribal families and communities. As the phrase itself suggests, "half breed children" were collectively conceptualized within the political category of children. Herein lay the deeper import of Mayaajigaabaw's statement describing half breeds as brought into tribes by Native women. Half breeds were not simply biologically descended from Native women; they were paired with Native women in a set of political categories that acknowledged women's distinctive abilities to incorporate people into families and communities as spouses and affinal relatives, as well as children. Straightforward as this incorporation of half breed children might appear, their location as tribal children contained additional implicit levels of meaning. Children in Native political discourse also existed in a symbiotic relationship with tribal elders of all genders, whose long lives, judiciousness, and reliability personified ideal leadership qualities. As a political symbol, impulsive and unreflective children represented the antithesis of these qualities. They were constantly held up in political discourse as an example of how not to behave.

The fact that half breed children were incorporated as a group into this least empowered constituency suggests that Native peoples envisioned only the most limited kind of group political activity for half breed children. Children, *as a constituency*, were limited to voicing assent, as is evident in the statements of tribes speaking with one voice. Although collective political activity was denied them, individuals of multiracial heritage, such as the Ojibwe war leader Zhaagobe, might become political leaders in tribal communities. Under the right circumstances, their multiracial heritage might be a valuable political asset, linking them to other kin groups in other nations, as Zhaagobe himself suggested. In the uncertain new environment of American treaty making after the War of 1812, individual multiracial leaders might find themselves possessed of cultural, linguistic, and political skills that could prove useful to the tribe, but this did not, as Americans thought, transform half breeds linked to specific families by ties of kin into a united group that coalesced into a powerful lobbying force in tribal politics. Regardless of the achievements of individual multiracial leaders, as a group half breeds lacked a political status that would enable, let alone legitimize, any collective political actions they might undertake to advance themselves apart from the larger tribal whole. As tribes constructed them, they were already apart of political constituencies and their tribal kin lobbied on their behalf as a result; there was no reason for them to act independently from the tribal whole.

As these descriptions reveal, Great Lakes Native peoples' conceptualizations of their multiracial kin shared little in common with Anglo-American understandings of who these individuals were. At a general level Native peoples and Anglo-Americans agreed that there were persons who, however problematically, were termed "half breeds" who were connected to Native nations through kinship ties. Beyond this point their views diverged, as each employed their own culturally constructed categories of knowledge to describe how, and why, "half breeds" remained a part of tribal societies. Efforts to find analogous explanatory categories that would enable Native and American representatives to speak together across cultural and linguistic categories met with only limited success. Constructs of kinship and gender proved too culturally specific to work as sites of accurate cross-cultural dialogues. Certain similarities existed that made it appear kinship ought to be comprehensible cross-culturally. After all, both Native and Anglo-American kin systems organized family life and insured the physical and social reproduction of their societies. Each operated to provide economic security for kinfolk. But Anglo-Americans did not deploy kinship as the central vehicle for conceptualizing and enacting politics. Great Lakes Native peoples did. They invested kin terms and kin categories with intensely symbolic political meaning, as the phrase "our half breed children" exemplifies. This Native cultural practice was simply too unlike American ways of understanding how politics could be organized and enacted for them to recognize it for what it was. This was not a cultural blind spot unique to Anglo-Americans; neither the British nor the French had fully comprehended the kin-based diplomatic language they had attempted to utilize and manipulate for the two centuries preceding the nineteenth.

Despite their decades long familiarity with Native kin-based political language, in the first twenty years following the War of 1812 social, economic, and political developments all having to do with "race" rendered white Americans particularly unable to contemplate kinship across recently racialized lines. Race-based chattel slavery had become newly profitable, igniting disputes over the expansion of slavery, revealing its fearsome potential to fragment the American republic, and spawning a series of increasingly unsatisfying political compromises. Simultaneously, economic inequality among racialized whites, which had not disappeared with the widening of the franchise, was masked by the expanded political participation by "white" men while an associated discourse asserted that "whiteness" and maleness defined American citizenship. This was the context in which Anglo-Americans reconfigured their prior understandings of race. The significance of somatic features, never inconsiderable, would now become the defining and obviously visible markers of identity, the literal embodiment of one's social superiority or subordination. The substantial numbers of multiracial individuals in the Great Lakes country presented a profound challenge to the rigidifying American understanding of races as discrete and unchanging categories. Here in the northwestern hinterland Americans had fought so long and hard to control, were thousands of people who defied easy categorization in the new race-based system. Not only did multiracial Frenchmen and multiracial Indians resist the emerging system of race-based identification, their continued insistence on their kin relationships with each other undermined one of the new racial hierarchy's central organizing tenets, the impermeability of racial categories and the consequent inability of kinship to cross racial lines. Great Lakes peoples probably could not have come up with a more difficult set of constructs with which to confront Anglo-Americans than their refusal to accept racial difference as the most important indicator of an individual's social power or social dispossession.[54]

This is not to suggest that tribal peoples did not come to realize that Anglo-Americans were defining multiracial persons quite differently from themselves. Quite the contrary, the fact that Great Lakes Native peoples created categories of social personhood to identify and distinguish half breeds from other sorts of tribal individuals shows that they did. But their continued insistence on the inclusion of half breeds within tribal communities and political constituencies reveals the more important fact that Native peoples did not come to accept Anglo-American race-based definitions of half-breeds as more meaningful or more accurate or more scientifically evidence-based than to their own. Anglo-Americans, ever more certain of the primacy of race, might think that Native peoples also recognized the logic of blood descent, but they would be repeatedly confronted with the evidence that Native peoples had not. Despite Anglo-American assumptions that race and racial identity were self-evident, Native peoples would continue to view half breeds as tribal kinfolk based on their inclusion in a foundational tribal political constituency. This recognition would endure until at least the last two decades of the nineteenth century. The irony of this construction is considerable: Anglo-Americans struggled to reconcile what they saw as the contradiction at the heart of multiracial French identity, the facts of Indian blood on the one hand and European cultural attributes on the other. Native peoples, in contrast, saw no reason to explain who half breeds were beyond their construction as tribal children. Outside of treaty negotiations with Anglo-Americans, tribal people rarely spoke about these persons whose political inclusion within tribal nations was assured while their potential for group political action was limited by their status as children.

As Americans grappled with the fluid and shifting nature of race in the Great Lakes country, they sometimes recorded evidence of Native peoples' own well-developed ideas about categories of social identity. Careful examination reveals that these constructions were not the same as Americans' own views, especially their ongoing vacillation over a culturally based or physically embodied definition of race. Native peoples remained uninterested in identifying or defining multiracial persons in terms of the categories that so preoccupied Americans. Native constructions of several categories of persons, including the Frenchmen, the half breeds, and the mixed-bloods form the subject of the following chapter. Through an examination of the historical experiences of Ojibwes, and to a somewhat lesser extent, Dakotas, dwelling in the western Great Lakes region of Wisconsin and Minnesota, the next chapter considers Indigenous understandings of social identity and belonging that were predicated on terms fundamentally different from those of the Americans.

Chapter 3

"One of Those Near-Mixed-Bloods . . . Not a Real Half-Breed"

Ojibwe Constructions of Multitribal and Multiethnic Persons

In the spring and summer of 1914, several elderly Ojibwes testified as part of an ongoing federal investigation into whether certain persons of mixed racial ancestry were fraudulently enrolled upon Minnesota's White Earth Reservation. Federal investigators from the Interior Department and attorneys for the individuals whose enrollment was in dispute traveled to northern Minnesota to take testimony. The racial construction of Ojibwes, particularly their division into persons of "full" and "mixed" blood, was a pivotal component of the investigation. The Anglo-American investigators, attorneys, notaries, and other court personnel understood the division of human beings into distinct "races" to be an established fact, proven by scientific research and visible in the bodily characteristics of individuals. As the testimony unfolded, it became clear that the Ojibwe witnesses, though they used what seemed to be the same language of "mixed bloods" and "full bloods," had very different understandings of what constituted these categories of persons. Somatic features that Anglo-Americans felt signaled racial intermixture, such as multiracial men's heavier facial hair, Ojibwes attributed to using salt in one's food, a dietary change emblematic of the social transformations the witnesses had observed over the courses of their lives. When a skeptical attorney asked, "Where did you hear that story about salt making whiskers?" the elderly woman who was testifying replied this was common knowledge: "Everybody knows that." Ojibwe men, she added, "never had any whiskers when they didn't use any salt."[1] In place of determining "race" based on physically embodied characteristics such as light skin or heavy beard growth, Ojibwes emphasized cultural attributes. Pursuing a hunting and trapping subsistence, wearing Indigenous clothing instead of "pants and hats . . . like a white man," disdaining acquisitive economic behavior, and participating in Indigenous religious ceremonies identified a man or woman as a full blood instead of a mixed blood.[2]

This proved an exasperating situation for the attorneys as they realized that Ojibwes were not viewing the embodied "facts" of light skin, eyes, and hair as the incontrovertible proof of racial mixture that the court officials believed them to be. They ignored Ojibwe attempts to explain the nonracialized social realities that had existed in the early nineteenth century. When witnesses made clarifying statements as Ain-dus-o-ge-shig did when he explained that his great-grandfather "was one of those near-mixed-bloods; he was not a real half-breed," the legal teams did not explore the different meanings the terms half breed and mixed blood might have had to earlier generations, nor did they consider Ain-dus-o-ge-shig's own further modifications of the two terms.[3] While well aware of the multiracial ancestry of many of the Interior French, Americans had attempted to develop clear and unambiguous definitions of half breed and mixed blood beginning in the two decades following the War of 1812 as they began negotiating treaties with Native nations that often included provisions for multiracial persons. They defined half breed and mixed blood as race-based categories whose main purpose was to differentiate the several types of multiracial persons who were eligible for benefits under the terms of given treaties. Half breeds, in this understanding, were people who had one Indian and one European-descended parent while mixed bloods, the more expansive category, included all others. As American racial ideology grew even more rigidly hierarchic and exclusionary during the second half of the nineteenth century, Anglo-Americans would continue to assert that the most significant fact about multiracial Native people was their race, anomalous though Americans thought interracial mixture was. They would continue to emphasize an identity based in select physical characteristics to the exclusion of other possible forms of social identity, such as cultural orientation, kin ties, or self-claimed ethnicity or nationality.[4]

Yet the constructions of identity articulated by the elderly Ojibwe witnesses were far more important than any of the perplexed legal officials realized. Inadvertently, the investigation had asked these elderly persons to recall the social world of their youth in the first half of the nineteenth century, a time when Ojibwe constructions of identity still shaped their understanding of themselves and others and guided most interactions within and between human communities. In recollecting those years from the vantage point of the early twentieth century, the witnesses described several of the groups of persons who had inhabited that world of seventy-five years previous. In English, two of these groups were referred to by the names half breeds and "mixed bloods," with the two words often being used interchangeably in English-language records and spoken translations. Evidence present in the historical record makes clear that Ojibwes did not intend these words to be understood as synonyms. Half breeds and mixed bloods, in Ojibwe conceptualization did not refer to the same people, or the same categories of social being. They did not necessarily describe membership in the same national or ethnic groups. The elders also described several social features about these persons, one of the most compelling being the revelation that in the past Ojibwes had viewed the "race" of these persons, particularly their much-discussed racially mixed ancestry, as largely irrelevant in assigning them an identity. These several facts in turn allow a rare glimpse into Indigenous constructions of human social identities, and the features other than presumed racial identity upon which social, ethnic, and national forms of difference and sameness might be predicated.

The following discussion centers on the historical experiences of Ojibwes, or Anishinaabeg, as they called themselves, from communities in present-day Minnesota and Wisconsin. A sizeable body of historical information exists, drawn from these communities. Numerous surviving records reflect Indigenous knowledge, including tribal oral accounts, many of which discuss historical events. Another substantial body of material consists of recorded speech, words uttered by tribal leaders during treaty negotiations and other meetings with American officials. Much of this material was produced, or collected, or translated by bilingual Ojibwe or Ojibwe-descended persons. Careful reading of these various sources brings to light the unique social world of certain Ojibwe communities, a reminder that Native peoples' experiences with American constructions of "race" and racial identity were highly variable. At the same time that a distinctive regional portrait is revealed, major tenets of an Indigenous system of social and political interaction shared by the larger community of Great Lakes Native nations are also outlined. Not unexpectedly, the Indigenous ways of knowing and being in the world that are glimpsed in these sources disclose a social reality, and its underlying power relations, ordered along principles far different from those of Anglo-Americans, in either the nineteenth or twentieth century. The construct of race as a means of social identity upon which either inclusion or exclusion was subsequently grounded, was conspicuously missing, while Ojibwe speakers revealed the existence of several other types of persons whose existence Anglo-Americans were either unaware of or dramatically misunderstood.

As discussed in the previous chapter, when Americans reconnoitered the former French *pays d'en haute* in the 1790s they identified two populations as their predecessors in the region. The first was composed of Indigenous peoples and the second contained the relict settler-colonists of previous regimes. Eager for the support of the latter, Americans constructed them as French-speaking "white" people, affirming this status in the 1795 Treaty of Greenville, one of the earliest treaties negotiated between Native nations and the newly independent United States. The fact that multiracial French speakers would be singled out for special mention and provided with a unique social-political status in a treaty negotiated with Native nations—of whose sovereignty in 1795 the United States entertained no doubt—was not accidental. For all their whiteness, the multiracial Francophones would remain conceptually linked to Native peoples in both American thought and practice. Even as the Treaty of Greenville asserted their whiteness and extended American property protection to lands "in possession of the French people," it also captured the fundamental American ambivalence about the Interior French. The treaty constructed French speakers as residing in Native-controlled, and thus foreign, spaces. The "French people" lived "among" Native peoples at "other places" than where white Americans had settled. In the early decades of the nineteenth century, as American racial ideology shifted ever more decisively toward the construction of races as a finite number of enclosed and oppositional categories readily distinguishable on the basis of physical characteristics, individuals of Native and European ancestry remained a stubborn contradiction in terms. Their existence as persons who evaded the circumscribed races was problematic, yet as Americans would learn and relearn, multiracial individuals remained essential to American efforts to engage with the Native peoples of the Great Lakes country precisely because they were familiar with the multiple polities, languages, and cultures that characterized the region.[5]

In the years following the War of 1812, Americans were once again made uncomfortably aware of the multiracial Francophones and their ongoing connections to Great Lakes tribal nations. Emboldened by their victory over Great Britain, Americans quickly resumed their aggressive prewar treaty-making efforts. Within two years of the war's conclusion, they commenced a series of treaties involving land cessions, initially concentrating on the Lower Great Lakes area that would become the states of Ohio, Michigan, and Indiana. Implicit in these treaties was the expectation that Native peoples, once they had alienated the last of their lands, would move west of the Mississippi River, thus leaving American territory altogether. Multiracial Francophone intermediaries were involved in almost every aspect of the treaty-negotiating process. Francophone individuals were dispatched as messengers to tribal communities with invitations to assemble at longstanding council sites; often they were provided with further instructions to make sure the most influential leaders planned to attend. Francophones also guided the parties of commissioners to the council grounds and explained tribal political protocol and cultural practices to American commissioners. And, most importantly, the majority of interpreters were Francophones. Every word spoken in the formally convened daily deliberations, as well as much of the less formal, after-hours speech, was translated by one or more bilingual persons. American commissioners, government officials, politicians, and ordinary settler-colonists often downplayed the importance of multiracial Francophones to the successful negotiation of a treaty, but their presence and their unique cultural and linguistic skills were critical to that success.[6]

Although it would not be evident for a considerable period of time, the years following the War of 1812 would differ substantially from those preceding it. Gradually and unevenly across a significant portion of the North American interior, Americans were at last able to assert their control over lands they variously called the backcountry, the Northwest Territory, or the Old Northwest. As they began the process of settler colonization, expanding the legal, political, and social institutions of the American state into the region and regularizing settler access to its long-coveted lands, political relations with Native peoples assumed far greater importance than ever before. Even in the preceding tumultuous sixty years of recurring warfare in what Larry Nelson and David Skaggs have characterized as "the sixty years' war for the Great Lakes," Native nations and Americans had not engaged in as much diplomatic negotiation with each other as they would in the 1820s, 1830s, and 1840s, nor would the objectives be the same. The mediatory role of the Interior French also assumed greater importance as Americans continued to depend on them to facilitate the processes of treaty making and Indian removal. Beginning with the 1817 Treaty of Maumee Rapids—the first land cession treaty negotiated after the war—Americans relied on multiracial persons to perform all their usual duties as interpreters, guides, and intermediaries. Additionally, Americans sought their aid in marshaling support for land cessions among their reluctant tribal relatives. In exchange for this invaluable assistance, treaty commissioners entered into delicate arrangements with multiracial persons, agreeing to protect their property (especially any landholdings or individual land claims) under the terms of any treaties negotiated.[7]

Americans were often deeply ambivalent about such practices, which regularly became mired in controversy and certainly often smacked of chicanery and corruption. Congress repeatedly passed legislation designed to eliminate the conditions under which bribes, secret deals, or under-the-table arrangements might occur, but never with complete success. Treaty commissioners themselves approached this aspect of their duties with an array of expectations and justifications. These ranged from the matter-of-fact observation of Lewis Cass and Duncan McArthur that, in order to gain tribal assent to the 1817 Treaty of Maumee Rapids, they had "been compelled to admit the claims of a number of individuals," to Henry Schoolcraft's high-minded entreaty that the "half-breed relatives" of the Odawas and Ojibwes of Michigan should be granted lands under the 1836 Treaty of Washington because they had it "in their power to aid their Indian connexions" by demonstrating "their capacity to use and take care of property." But regardless of public distaste and acts of Congress, treaties continued to be negotiated that made generous provisions for multiracial kinfolk. Although Americans did not recognize it, they were observing the development of a new treaty-making approach by the tribal nations of the Lower Great Lakes. As tribal communities strategized ways to remain on the land and work out the means of living alongside a growing American population, they experimented with new ways of safeguarding their remaining lands. One promising method was to award substantial land grants to multiracial kin whose general familiarity with elements of American culture, especially its legal system and landholding practices, could be put to tribal benefit. As discussed in the previous chapter, Americans rarely recognized what tribal peoples sought to do by gifting land to "their half breed relations." Americans were more likely, especially as the 1820s gave way to the 1830s and 1840s, to view multiracial kinfolk as cynically manipulating their kin ties for individual gain not tribal survival.[8]

The postwar decades also saw growing numbers of American settler-colonists moving to the lower Great Lakes area, where they encountered a more complicated social landscape than they had anticipated. The region's Native peoples and French settlers remained deeply interconnected, linked by complex webs of economic exchange mediated through kinship ties and accommodative political institutions. The prominent role of multiracial French speakers in the treaty negotiations that made the American presence even possible was a further complication, while Americans also became uncomfortably aware that the old French settlers remained embedded within the kin-groups of Native nations. At a time when their own commitment to constructions of race as physically embodied categories was growing stronger, Americans struggled to find a place for such persons who resisted a single racial identity. They continued to rely on multiracial peoples as intermediaries, but they had difficulty reconciling how Francophones' claims to whiteness overrode the obvious phenotypic evidence of their "mixed" racial heritage. Words that specifically described multiracial ancestry became used more frequently to describe the Interior French as the decades passed. Americans spoke less of white French settlers and more often referred to half breeds, half-bloods, or mixed bloods.

Half breed was by far the most often used term, and its etymology is instructive for revealing the differences in the ways that Native peoples and Anglo-Americans understood the word's meaning and the people it described. Although the word half breed had existed in the English language since the mid-eighteenth century, it probably entered the vocabulary of English-speakers in the Great Lakes region as a translation of a French-language ethnonym already in use by multiracial persons themselves, especially though not exclusively by those whose European ancestry was French. This word was "Bois-brulé," which literally meant "Burnt-wood people." Most Anglo-American emigrants to the Great Lakes region adopted the English-language word half breed without recognizing its full Indigenous significance as an approximate translation of Bois-brulé, a word that implied a specific ethnic descent and culturally specific beliefs and practices rather than a blanket racialized identity. With their heightened sensitivity to race-based identities, Americans assumed the name referred to the skin color of multiracial individuals, who thus literally embodied their racial admixture, as "half-dark, half-white, like a half-burnt piece of wood." That Americans would make such an assumption speaks not just to their growing acceptance of race as a crucial marker of social difference, but to their additional belief that other peoples both shared their perception of race as a meaningful reality and accepted it as a principle of hierarchic social organization. In fact, it appears that multiracial persons did not consider either the word Bois-brulé or the word half breed to describe a race-based identity. In the early nineteenth century Great Lakes country, multiracial persons did use these two words as glosses of each other when translating Native languages to monolingual English or French speakers. They also employed them as a form of code-switching when speaking to other multiracial persons who spoke a different

European language from the speaker's own. They appeared to have considered half breed to be an ethnic identification indicating English ancestry, while its French-language counterpart Bois-brulé, signaled French heritage. Seemingly, multiracial persons whose tribal heritages derived from other language groups than Algonkian, adopted Bois-brulé as an ethnonym. Neither Anglophones nor Francophones considered these words to describe a race-based identity.[9]

It was also evident that Ojibwes had not assigned the racialized identity to multiracial persons that Americans assumed that they had. In the early nineteenth century the Ojibwe language spoken in Minnesota and Wisconsin contained two words that translated as half breed, which despite the single English-language gloss of their meanings, possessed significantly different Indigenous-language connotations. The most well-known was "Wiissaakodewinini" ("Wiissaako-dewikwe" in the feminine), which literally translated as "half burnt wood men" and was, in fact, the subject of the extended "half dark, half white" explanation given by the Jesuit priest and linguist Frederick Baraga in his authoritative *Dictionary of the Ojibway Language*. Wiissaakodewinini thus shared an almost identical meaning with the French ethnonym Bois-brulé. This suggests a possible origin for the Ojibwe-language word as a loan word from French rather than as an extended comment on Bois-brulé skin color. Such an origin would emphasize an Ojibwe understanding of the "half burnt wood men" as a distinct ethnonational collectivity with whom they interacted in multiple political, economic, and social ways. Although a few of the earliest Americans in the region shortly after the end of the War of 1812 recognized that Bois-brulé, and half breed were synonyms, Americans in general gravitated to the English language word half breed. They tended to ignore or overlook the clear ethnic dimension initially present in the definition of half breed, instead employing it as a race-based identifier for any and all multiracial people. The ethnic specificity of Wiissaakodewininiwak would be a long-standing source of confusion between Ojibwes and Americans. Additionally, since Americans considered the word half breed to be pejorative, when they heard the word translated in the speeches of Ojibwes, they assumed "full-blooded" tribal peoples also disdained multiracial heritage in much the same way Americans did, as a transgressive threat to a racial order predicated on supposedly impermeable and changeless racial categories.[10]

The second Ojibwe-language word that translated as half breed further suggested that Ojibwes understood the construct Wiisaakodewinini/ Wiisaakodewikwe as describing, not all multiracial persons, but a distinctive ethnic-national group. That word was "Ayaa'aabiitawisid" (in Baraga's orthography, "Aiâbitawisid") and it received only a short entry in Baraga's *Dictionary* as "a half-breed man or woman." The literal translation of the word was far more nuanced; it meant "to exist in a state of being half each." The elderly Ojibwes who testified at the White Earth disenrollment hearings in the early twentieth century distinctly recollected the word being used to describe a momentous event that had occurred in the distant but remembered past when the first "white man gave a child to an Indian woman." Such children were understood to embody the central concept of "living in a state of being half each," since they possessed "half one kind of blood and half of the other kind of blood." At that "long ago" time when the first half breed children were born, Ojibwes recognized them as an embodiment of the larger concept of "being half each" and "called [them] Ah-be-tah-wiz-ee [Ayaa'aabiitawisid]." Yet there is nothing in this more expansive definition of Ayaa'aabiitawisid that suggests the construct referred only to half breeds or involved only race-based identities. Existence in "a state of being half each" emphasized a duality in one's existence but could embrace multiple dualities beyond the one called to mind by a child who had "half one blood and half another." It has been suggested, for instance, that third- and fourth-gendered persons were comprehended as existing in a state of being half each. It is also possible that persons of two tribal backgrounds were understood to possess two distinct ancestries and live in a state of being half each. Since inter-tribal marriages and the birth of multitribal children predated any European presence in the Great Lakes country, these multitribal persons may have served as the analogy for comprehending children who were half Ojibwe and half European.[11]

Anglo-Americans remained largely unaware of the complexities of Ojibwe constructions of ontology and personhood, but they struggled with contradictory cultural constructions of their own. As their own ideas about race transformed, they reimagined the identity of those persons they had initially considered "white" Frenchmen. Their continued recognition of French ethnicity during decades when they increasingly conflated whiteness with "pure European" ancestry, sat uncomfortably with their larger expectations for the future of the Northwest Territory. In American thinking, these lands were their long-promised patrimony, a wilderness that they would settle and transform into agrarian, racially homogenous, patriarchal communities much like the ones they had left. Such replication held powerful political meaning as Americans believed that their democratic political experiment could only survive if anchored in widespread landed property ownership by independent white males. This vision of the future foresaw no place for Indigenous peoples. As long as Frenchmen were "white," they could participate in the emerging republic, but as Great Lakes tribes developed strategies to hold onto their land that involved placing it in the hands of their multiracial Francophone relatives, Americans reconsidered what kin ties to Native peoples meant for French whiteness. American certainty that the region was home to only a relatively small number of half breeds was shaken as they spent more time among the region's tribal villages and fur trade towns. It quickly became apparent that a large population of multiracial people lived in the Northwest whose identity was far more complicated than was envisioned by the conventional American definition of half breeds as "those [persons] one of whose parents was a pure-blooded Indian." This "strictly construed" definition did not reflect the region's long history with previous colonial regimes, nor did it reflect the "habits and customs" of either Native peoples or their multiracial relatives. Multiracial Francophones whose Native ancestry often involved generations of intermarriage, sometimes into more than one tribal nation, defied the narrow definition of half breeds that both settler colonists from the east and American officials such as John W. Edmonds, quoted above, expected to find. Even as Americans debated whether cultural attributes or racialized somatic features made a person "Indian" or "white," they found themselves adopting the more expansive but vaguer term "mixed blood" as they attempted to comprehend and contain the racially ambiguous peoples of the Northwest Territory.[12]

Preoccupied by their multiple colonial objectives and their own culturally constructed interpretations of what Native societies were like, Americans spent little time further familiarizing themselves with Native knowledge systems. This was especially the case regarding such intangible elements of culture as intellectual ways of knowing. Resolving the duality that they saw at the heart of a half breed identity consumed much American attention, and they rarely inquired beyond it to consider larger Native understandings of the nature of kinship and social belonging. That Great Lakes Native constructions of kinship routinely involved the expectation that entire groups of multitribal relatives could be created through rituals of alliance that included multiple intertribal marriages was beyond American comprehension of what constituted kinship. Certainly, Americans recognized that individual tribal persons might possess multitribal ancestry, sometimes noting in passing that a given Ojibwe tribal leader had "Sioux blood," or vice versa, but it remained only a point of passing interest. It simply did not cross their minds that Native peoples understood it to be possible to create new social collectivities that would possess permanent forms of inclusion in more than one of the polities of the *pays d'en haute*. There is considerable irony in this, for multitribal persons were in many ways far more significant in the Indigenous social landscape than the half breeds whose identity was so disconcerting to Americans.[13]

The strategy shared by Ojibwes and Dakotas of implanting new groups of relatives into both their own and another society, whether Indigenous or European-descended, is distinctive, but there are numerous historical instances of Native peoples similarly expanding their societies by creating new clans or kin-groups to incorporate new collectivities, often composed of adopted captives. A well-known instance of this is the Navajos, who from the 1500s to the end of the nineteenth century, incorporated sizeable numbers of outsiders by developing new Navajo clan identities for them. Navajos created clans for descendants of captured Apaches, Hopis and other Pueblo peoples, and Utes. Interestingly, they also created the Naakaii Dine'é, a clan originally for Spanish captives and their descendants. It is known presently as the Mexican Clan, a reflection of continuing geopolitical change in the Southwest border country and the continued vitality of Indigenous adoption practices into the twentieth and twenty-first centuries. Nor were they alone among the Native peoples of the Southwestern borderlands; the Tohono O'odham also created new clans in a similar incorporative manner.[14] In addition to incorporating captives, Native nations also absorbed refugees from tribal peoples with whom they were on good, or at least neutral, terms. In numerous instances in the American Southeast, smaller groups, battered by disease or weakened by enemy attacks, merged by mutual agreement into the societies of more populous allies. Probably in the early eighteenth century, Shawnees from the Ohio Valley sought refuge in Tuckabatchee, an important Creek, or Muskogi, town. The Shawnees were well-regarded by the Creeks, and upon their incorporation, several Creek clans formed a new grouping, or moiety, of clans called the "Sawanogalga," or Shawnee people. It is probable that incoming adoptive Shawnees joined these several clans. In this instance, the incorporation of outsiders worked well. In another case—the Creek incorporation of the Yuchis, there was considerably more friction. Yuchis held onto their own language and distinguishing cultural traits to a much greater degree than did most other incorporated groups, to the consternation of the Creeks.[15]

While the Indigenous creation of new kin-groups is widely documented, the specific form of making relatives employed by Ojibwes and Dakotas has received little attention from scholars. An extended discussion of Ojibwe constructions of multitribal persons appears in the writings of William Whipple Warren (1825–1853), the mid-nineteenth century Ojibwe-descended historian and ethnographer. Warren's posthumously published master work, *History of the Ojibway People*, represents one of the most comprehensive early efforts to compose a Native history based in Native sources of knowledge. Warren, who spoke Ojibwe fluently, interviewed well-informed Ojibwe individuals in the 1840s and 1850s, paying close attention to tribal oral traditions and narratives. While asserting the validity of his Ojibwe sources and emphasizing Ojibwe perspectives, he nonetheless regarded the written records left by successive French, British, and American explorers and colonists as the historical benchmark against which he compared his Ojibwe materials. He also accepted the western European-derived conceptualization of "history" as a chronological narrative of select events as the normative standard. He structured the *History* according to this convention. Like many educated men of his day, Warren was interested in synchronizing Indigenous knowledge with accepted western European interpretations of the past, particularly with respect to placing Indigenous people into the biblically based, linear narrative of human history that predominated in western intellectual circles. He pointed to Ojibwe narratives of a great flood, for instance, certain they represented a vestigial memory of the biblical story of Noah. Although he accepted much of the western epistemological tradition, Warren also wrote with a sense that his own lived experience mattered more than the "received opinions of more learned writers," who had erroneously described Ojibwe history and culture. His mother descended from a composite *pays d'en haute* family that included Ojibwe political leaders and Francophone fur traders, while his Anglo-American father was an early immigrant to the Northwest, moving in 1818 to the Lake Superior area to work in the fur trade. Born in 1825, Warren was familiar with the older interlinked world of tribal polities and fur trade communities and witnessed the changes that were transforming the Northwest. He described Ojibwe politics, history, and culture with considerable insight and sought to make Anglo-Americans appreciate the complexities of the world they were entering. His efforts at translating distinctively Indigenous cultural practices and political actions across linguistic and conceptual barriers for English-speaking Americans are thus of special interest.[16]

Most of Warren's discussion of multitribal persons involved individuals of Ojibwe and Dakota ancestry, not surprising since these persons were affiliated with the Native nations he knew best. Such dual-heritage persons exemplified the larger tribal practice of deliberately cultivating kin-groups possessed of multiple ancestries and identifying likely individuals within them to perform important diplomatic and political tasks. Because the existence of a multitribal kin-group with distinctive political duties was largely unknown to Anglo-Americans, and seemingly to their English and French predecessors as well, Warren struggled to find the English language words that would explain the concept to an American audience that possessed no analogous cultural practices. His understanding of history as a narrative chronicling mostly political and military deeds also guided his presentation of the Ojibwe past. Within these parameters, he focused his discussion of multitribal persons on their initial creation in the context of historic peace negotiations. In contrast to his treatment of the five Ojibwe origin clans, whose emergence he located during the time of mythic tribal creation, Warren took pains to determine the specific historical moment when the multitribal clans came into being. By his reckoning this occurred in the late 1690s, when Ojibwes and Dakotas living in the ecological transition zone between the northern hardwood forests and southern prairies of present-day Minnesota and Wisconsin, met and agreed to put a permanent end to their intermittent warfare. Cycles of intertribal war and peace were not uncommon across the Great Lakes region, and they were often most intensely contested in resource-rich ecosystems such as the present-day St. Croix River-Rice Lake-Mille Lacs region, where Warren placed the historic Ojibwe-Dakota peacemaking efforts. Ceremonies to reestablish peace after periods of hostility were correspondingly widespread, and involved formal speeches, gift exchanges, and ritual sharing of meals. Yet another part of the larger peacemaking ceremonies involved intermarriages between members of the participating tribal nations. The children of tribal leaders were among the first to initiate such intertribal marriages, again signifying the importance that the two Indigenous polities attached to the peace they were enacting. When children were born to these intertribal marriages, they became, in Warren's words, the first "mixed bloods of either tribe."[17]

Ojibwes incorporated these new "relative[s] by blood" into their existing kinship system of patrilineal clans but they did so in ways that signaled that these two groups would continue to exist as distinctive tribal entities. Although the children of Ojibwe men who married Dakota women could have been easily folded into the existing Ojibwe clan system, since they would inherit their clan affiliations from their fathers, absorption was not the ultimate objective of either tribal nation. Instead, the two tribes sought to create a new exogamous clan or kin-group as a lasting and visible reminder of the new relationship they had created. Multitribal Ojibwe and Dakota individuals would henceforth embody their dual ancestry in their physical persons; they were the literal instantiations of the alliance between their nations. Furthermore, they would also possess a form of dual nationality as Ojibwe-descended Dakotas or Dakota-descended Ojibwes. They would pass this heritage to their descendants, creating self-reproducing clans with a distinctive ethno-national identity that would forever remind their parent tribes that Dakotas and Ojibwes shared kinfolk in common. Indicating that he had had some personal interaction with Dakotas, Warren remarked that on several occasions he had met Ojibwe-descended Dakotas. He added that these distinctively multitribal Dakotas approached him and identified themselves as his relatives.[18]

Writing from an admitted Ojibwe perspective, Warren focused his attention on the actions of Ojibwes, specifically those living in the St. Croix River country as they created new kin-groups and tribal identities, and he paid much less attention to the Dakotas. He credited specific Ojibwe individuals as key figures in bringing the alliance to fruition. At the same time, he located the origins of the alliance in the actions of the clans to which these individuals belonged, since creating new kin-groups (rather than individual kin ties as through an adoption or intermarriage) was the focus of the intertribal peacemaking ceremonies. According to the oral narratives that Warren recorded, an unnamed leader, a member of the Awaasi or Fish Clan from Rice Lake, a village in the disputed St Croix country, was instrumental in brokering the initial peace. The leader's daughter, also unnamed but sharing her father's clan, participated in one of the first intertribal marriages. The daughter's children with her Dakota husband "inherited their father's totem of the wolf," and thus introduced the Wolf Clan among the Ojibwes. Paralleling her action, Ojibwe men from the Water Spirit or "Merman" lineage of the larger Awaasi cluster, married Dakota women and introduced the Water Spirit Clan among the Dakotas. Although Warren had had some interactions with Dakotas, he was not deeply familiar with Dakota culture or society. He assumed, incorrectly, that the Dakotas possessed a patrilineal clan system much like that of the Ojibwes, a circumstance that he described as allowing Dakotas to be easily "grafted among the Ojibway [sic] clans." Similarly, he appears not to have considered the extent to which Dakota beliefs informed the decision to designate the Water Spirit Clan for descendants of in-marrying Ojibwe men. Dakotas accorded great significance to spiritual beings that lived in water, and it seems probable that the Water Spirit clan affiliation drew from common Dakota and Ojibwe regard for water-dwelling spiritual beings, rather than representing only Ojibwe views. Such a melding of common cultural beliefs certainly echoed the purpose behind creating blended social identities in the first place, namely their ability to create and inhabit a new social space made possible by the state of peace existing between the two parent tribes. Regardless of his focus on Ojibwe perceptions of these events, Warren affirmed that the concept of a mixed blood kin-group came into existence among both tribal nations at this time. The central objective behind the creation of these new relatives was also achieved, for the members of these clans mutually recognized one another as kinfolk. "[A]t every peace meeting of the two tribes," Warren stated, "all persons of the Wolf and Merman Totem, in each tribe, recognize[d] one another as blood relations."[19]

Warren's discussion of the creation of multitribal kin-groups emphasized their origins in peace negotiations, but he was decidedly ambivalent about the lives led by individual multitribal persons. His consultants, who would have come of age in the tumult of the late eighteenth century, recalled that numerous incidents of violence were directed against multitribal persons. Their narratives underscored the uncertainty of kin protections for multitribal persons at times of escalating tensions between their parent tribes. In-married spouses, although they were the parents of multitribal children, made "sudden and secret flight to their former homes" and even kin ties as esteemed as the mentoring relationship between uncles and nephews were shattered under circumstances that suggested the dual loyalties of multitribal persons could be a source of great social tension. In an incident that Warren recounted in considerable detail, an Ojibwe-descended person living among his Dakota kinfolk was shot and wounded as he participated in a war dance with his Dakota relatives. Warren's consultants claimed that the multitribal man was shot by a "distinguished" Dakota warrior who justified his action by saying "he wished to let out the hated Ojibway blood which flowed in [the multitribal man's] veins." The wounded man recovered, however, sought support from his Ojibwe kinfolk, and in a ferocious retaliation, attacked the Dakota village, allegedly killing over 300 people. The number of casualties was probably exaggerated, but such narratives, and Warren's recording of them at length, clearly reflected the perceptions of at least some Ojibwes that the lives of multitribal people were precarious and uncertain. Since the combined material and spiritual conditions that fueled Ojibwe-Dakota warfare were not eliminated until the tribes were confined to Reservations, sporadic fighting continued throughout the eighteenth and the first half of the nineteenth centuries despite repeated peace negotiations. This situation reinforced the importance of multitribal persons though it also contributed to Ojibwe unease about the personal safety of their multitribal relations.[20]

Warren's realization that Ojibwes perceived the lives of their multitribal kinfolk as insecure and imperiled points to larger issues involved in Native practices of warfare, captivity, and adoption. Ties of kinship might not preclude dramatic forms of inequality and exploitation, while adoption might not bring full social inclusion and individual security in one's new tribal community. As James F. Brooks has observed in *Captives and Cousins, Slavery, Kinship, and Community in the Southwest Borderlands* (2002), the Spanish conceptualized the incorporation of Native individuals into Spanish families during the sixteenth, seventeenth, and eighteenth centuries as a form of adoption of orphaned relatives. Drawing on an Old World tradition with roots in the medieval conflicts between Christian and Muslim polities across the Mediterranean, the Spanish described their incorporation of captive Native persons as rescuing heathens and placing them into Christian families to be raised as kinfolk. The reality was frequently far less benign. Adopted Native captives were transformed into enslaved laborers in hierarchic, patriarchal Spanish familial units where they were often subjected to physical violence, abuse, and sexual assault. At the same time, however, through the mediation and bilingual skills of these adoptees and their children, the Spanish established kin-based ties to, and thus channels of communications with, regional tribal nations. Despite this important work of cross-cultural diplomacy and mediation, the social position of Native adoptees rarely changed materially. Most remained unfree laborers in the households of their Spanish "relatives." Simply being described as a member of the family did not guarantee equitable or kindly treatment. Writing about the Southeast, Christina Snyder in *Slavery in Indian Country: The Changing Face of Captivity in Early America* (2010) describes additional issues that could arise even when a war captive was adopted by an individual member of a tribal clan or other kin-group. Especially in times of war, and seemingly more frequently in the eighteenth century than earlier, other family members might oppose the adoption and take out their frustrations by tormenting and ridiculing the adoptive relative. Joseph Brown, a Virginia colonist who was adopted in 1788 as a nephew by a Cherokee leader named The Breath, described how relatives of his uncle mistreated him and threatened to kill him. The Ojibwe and Dakota strategy of creating new kin-groups differed significantly from the practices of captivity and adoption discussed by Brooks and Snyder, but it generated similar concerns about the violent origins of adoption in captive-taking during warfare. If creating multitribal kin-groups that would live in both societies seemed a solution to these problems, whenever a multitribal Ojibwe was injured or killed by Dakotas (and vice versa), people of both tribal nations were reminded of how tenuous and difficult the creation of mutual kinfolk was in daily practice.[21]

Despite an emphasis on warfare and the seeming implication that vulnerable multitribal persons were unable to prevent conflict, Warren also recorded other historical narratives in which multitribal persons successfully prevented hostilities. Such narratives tacitly reiterated the reasons why multitribal kin-groups had been created in the first place, while their successes subtly reinforced the wisdom of that decision. Although it might not be possible to prevent new conflicts from flaring up, multitribal Ojibwe and Dakota kin could, and often did, defuse them once they had begun. Not surprisingly, leadership families of both tribes recognized the importance of having "closely related" leaders who could mediate between their two nations. Warren recounted an instance of this practice in the story of an Ojibwe leader named "Ma-mong-e-se-da," [probably Mamaangiiside] who had Dakota half-brothers from his mother's first marriage. On one occasion, Mamaangiiside and his Ojibwe relatives were hunting near Dakota lands and their "camp was fired upon by a party of Dakota warriors." Mamaangiiside called out "in the Dakota tongue" to the attackers, identifying himself as their relative and asking if his brother Wabasha was with them. Warren reported that the "firing ceased immediately." Wabasha, by this time an important Dakota leader, stepped forward, and the two brothers shook hands in greeting. After the initial welcome, Mamaangiiside invited the Dakotas to his village and feasted them "in the style of a chief."[22]

In a passing observation that he did not explore in depth, Warren mentioned an important longer-term ramification that developed when substantial numbers of multitribal persons lived in local areas. In the St. Croix River-Rice Lake-Mille Lacs region where intertribal Ojibwe-Dakota contacts were frequent, multitribal kin-groups came to exert considerable political influence. By the 1840s when Warren conducted his research, several members of the Wolf Clan had become Ojibwe village leaders at the communities of Rice Lake, Pokegama, and Mille Lacs. Their influence was most apparent in their ability to resolve conflicts once they had broken out. A network of Wolf and Water Spirit relatives living in both tribes had created the institutional framework through which multitribal persons could work to resolve hostilities and restore peaceful relations. In Warren's words, when conflicts arose, "the ties of consanguinity which had existed between the Rice Lake or St. Croix Ojibways, and the Dakotas were such, that peace again was made between them." Reflecting the localized nature of both the intertribal clans and most tribal leadership, the Wolf and Water Spirit kinfolk enjoyed their greatest successes nearest their own communities. Their ability to broker peace at greater distances was far less certain. Warren put these local successes in the wider context. Although St. Croix Ojibwes and Dakotas "harmed not one another," they did so while "war raged between their tribes in other parts of their extensive country." This gave rise to a situation in which villagers could ensure some degree of protection for their relatives in nearby communities but were still subject to attacks from more distant enemies. Undoubtedly some of the ambivalence in Warren's many narratives about multitribal kin reflects this larger geopolitical insecurity. While the reach of interrelated leadership families was only local and could not guarantee a widespread or lasting peace, it continued to create the social and political conditions that made the institutionalization of multitribal kinship continue to be seen as a valuable tribal strategy.[23]

Multitribal Ojibwe-Dakota persons as a distinctive social category endured through the nineteenth century and into the twentieth. A generation of Ojibwes who were children when Warren was conducting his interviews reiterated the positive benefits of multitribal kin as late as 1914, the start of World War One. John (nicknamed "Jack") Porter of Fish Lake, Minnesota, by this time an elderly man, provided detailed information on the lives and actions of multitribal Dakota-Ojibwe persons whom he had learned of during his mid-nineteenth century youth. He remembered in particular a man whom Ojibwes called Ginoozhens, or Little Pike. "In times of war between the Chippewas and Sioux," Porter stated, using the common English-language names for the two tribes, Ojibwes "used to holler out his name; if they got on to the Sioux coming near the camp, would holler out his name, telling them [the Dakotas] that was Ke no zhaince's town." Ginoozhens "was part Sioux," Porter continued, "and was raised partly in his boyhood days as a Sioux . . . and therefore when they [the Dakotas] would hear that name hollered out they would leave the place, would not tackle it." Even though Ginoozhens lived in an Ojibwe village—not surprisingly, along the Snake River in the region of joint Dakota-Ojibwe occupation—and had an Ojibwe family, he was also a multitribal Dakota-Ojibwe person. Because Dakotas were loath to attack his town and possibly kill their relative, both his presence in the village at Fish Lake and his larger existence as a multitribal person protected his Ojibwe relations and their community from harm.[24]

Jack Porter revealed a final complicating fact about Ginoozhens and Ojibwe understandings of the term rendered into English as mixed blood. In an effort to clarify Ginoozhens' complex social identity, Porter described him as a mixed blood, because he was part Dakota. But Porter simultaneously understood Ginoozhens as a half breed, because he was also "descended from some Frenchman." In making these distinctions, Porter revealed how social and personal identities were differently constructed in the Ojibwe world of his youth. It was possible for a multitribal person to possess an additional identity as a multiethnic person. Porter's careful parsing of the words mixed blood and half breed also echoed Warren's use of the word mixed blood to refer to persons of dual tribal ancestry while the word half breed indicated a specific multiethnic heritage that involved French and Native ancestry. Furthermore, Porter's early twentieth century word usage suggests that Warren's use of the words half breed and mixed blood did not represent merely his own idiosyncratic efforts at translating complicated Indigenous concepts. Instead, Porter and his contemporaries continued to draw distinctions between two quite different kinds of persons in much the same way as Warren had some seventy years earlier. Though Porter's words appear only in English translation, the fact that he employed a word that was interpreted using the same English gloss of mixed blood that Warren had employed, suggests there may have been an Ojibwe consensus of some duration that a particular Ojibwe word describing certain types of persons was glossed as a particular English-language word. While it cannot be proven that the word being translated as mixed blood was Ayaa'aabiitawisid, it is certainly within the realm of possibility.[25]

Despite Warren's own recognition that mixed blood and half breed were not synonymous identities, the full significance of persons with multiple ethnic, tribal, and racial identities seems to have eluded him. He was conversant with the public debates of his own day and, while he accepted many of the conventional intellectual assumptions of antebellum Anglo-American society, he advocated strenuously for the older conceptualization that social identity was founded in cultural attributes rather than either phenotype or partial descent from Native persons. The logic of this position effectively prevented him from imagining the existence of people who viewed themselves as members of multiple societies, one of which was an Indigenous one. In Warren's understanding, French-descended multiracial individuals helped to civilize their Native kin; however, they were not in some capacity also Native themselves. As evidence that the multiracial Francophones had advanced beyond the "wild hunter state" in which Native peoples remained, Warren gave an example that resonated powerfully in the pious antebellum decades. He pointed to Francophones' adoption of Christianity, specifically Catholicism, and the cultural transformations that had followed. The Francophones' knowledge of the "the sacred book of God," not only offered them hope of salvation (Warren, a Protestant, was not prepared to say it guaranteed it), they also embraced a variety of European-derived cultural attributes ranging from standards of dress and cleanliness to notions of private property and appropriate gender norms. Since Warren, again accepting social evolutionist theory, considered women to be oppressed "drudges" in Native societies, the French adoption of more-European gender roles could hardly be emphasized enough. Changes in the gender roles of multiracial Francophones offered concrete proof that Native ancestry did not preclude individuals from adopting transformative components of western European, and by extension Anglo-American, religion and culture. Although Warren recognized and celebrated that individuals were capable of change, he did not question the assumption that types of human societies stayed the same. Native societies remained forever on the lowest rung of the social evolutionist ladder, where they typified the "savage and unenlightened state." Relying once more on evolutionist theory, Warren identified the social characteristics that epitomized primitive hunting societies. Foremost among them was the "bloody and exterminating warfare" waged between tribes, including, of course, Ojibwes and Dakotas. Despite some positive characteristics such as their hunting skill and oratorical ability, Native people remained "[t]he wild sons of the forest," destined as societies to disappear in the face of the superior agriculture-based civilization of the United States.[26]

This characterization of unremitting warfare may have faithfully recapitulated social evolutionist theory, but Warren's own evidence revealed a far different Ojibwe-Dakota social and political dynamic. Rather than endless bloodletting between "inveterate and hereditary enemies," their relationship was more accurately characterized as one of oscillations between states of peace and war. A strong sense of temporality further defined this dynamic relationship. Changing seasons marked changing social relations. The advent of colder weather signaled the shift from the activities of summer, the season when food supplies were abundant and war expeditions were launched. As the days grew shorter, Ojibwes and Dakotas negotiated new or reaffirmed previous peace agreements as part of their overall preparations for the harshest months of the year when food resources were at a minimum and people focused most of their energies on subsistence hunting and trapping. Multitribal individuals and kin-groups were once again pivotal figures in reestablishing the recurring seasonal peace negotiations between the two tribal nations.[27]

Their importance began with their language fluency. Multitribal persons who were raised among both their Dakota and Ojibwe families were often bilingual, an especially important skill since their Siouan and Algonkian parent languages were not mutually intelligible. In addition to the narrative of Mamaangiiside and Wabasha mentioned previously, in which Mamaangiiside's bilingual ability prevented a renewal of warfare, Warren included numerous other stories that underscored the crucial importance of dual language fluency. In one, an Ojibwe and a Dakota warrior "of some note" ritually adopted each another as brothers as part of larger peace negotiations. The Ojibwe first suggested the idea because he had gained a working knowledge of the Dakota language from his wife, who was an in-married Dakota herself. In another story, Ojibwes were struck with the behavior of a Dakota they had captured under extraordinary circumstances, but they could not learn the reason for the man's remarkable actions (which ultimately ended up benefitting the Ojibwes) until they could locate "an Ojibway who could speak his language." As such stories suggest, bilingual persons quite literally made the most basic communication between tribal nations possible.[28]

Equipped with knowledge of one another's language, multitribal persons were uniquely positioned to initiate the seasonal intertribal negotiations that would reanimate peaceful relations between their nations. Singly and collectively, they personified prior peacemaking efforts, their corporeal selves serving as a powerful reminder to their relatives in both tribal nations of the enduring importance of these transcendent kinship ties. Their symbolic roles converged with their diplomatic responsibilities when they undertook the actions necessary to allow for the ritual movement from states of warfare to states of peace. When Ojibwe peace delegations approached Dakota villages, multitribal persons literally took the leading role, bearing pipes and other emblems of peaceful intent. Warren made frequent mention of the "terms of peace" that were negotiated between Ojibwes and Dakotas, adding that they were usually "first brought about by the mixed bloods of either tribe." Such Ojibwe-Dakota persons were able to "approach one another with greater confidence than those entirely unconnected by blood." Once peace was established, multitribal kin-groups demonstrated one of the most important material-world considerations that motivated seasonal peace negotiations. Multitribal kin opened their hunting grounds to their relatives from other tribes, sometimes extending hunting privileges to entire villages in which their kinfolk lived. It is probable that the episode Warren related of Mamaangiiside and Wabasha originated in such an agreement. Mamaangiiside evidently knew his brother was camped nearby and, by announcing his presence within the Ojibwe hunting group, insured that the Dakotas would respond, not with hostility but as relatives. Acting in concert, the two brothers managed to reaffirm the ties of kinship and reestablish peaceful relations within and between their tribal nations. Even the feast that Mamaangiiside hosted offered a final comment on the importance of relatives caring for and sharing food with one another during the most difficult season of the year. [29]

Warren discussed the creation of the Wolf and Water Spirit Clans in some detail, but he did not supply an Ojibwe-language word that specifically identified (or was applied to) multitribal Ojibwe and Dakota persons. Instead, he relied on English-language phrases that described multitribal Ojibwes and Dakotas in terms borrowed from American conceptualizations of kinship. He portrayed multitribal persons as "the mixed bloods of either tribe" and as "blood relations" to one another and their parent tribes. Anglo-Americans and their British forbearers had long employed the construct of "blood" as a symbolic representation of consanguinity, or descent from common ancestors. In popular discourse, the word connoted ideas of kinship and lineage, as in such phrases as "one's own flesh and blood" or "blood is thicker than water." While its emphasis on descent and inherited traits lent it to co-optation by the new language of race, the older definition continued to enjoy a respected intellectual position, retaining the sanction of biblical authority which both asserted humanity's common creation from "one blood," while explaining by means of the Old Testament story of the Tower of Babel the dispersal of that blood among the world's many nations. Not only was Warren personally committed to the older understanding, but he also employed the older definition of blood with its associated symbolism because he thought its allusions to kinship and descent represented an analogy that his Anglo-American audience would readily comprehend. Yet the new race-inflected definitions were already in common use during the years when he collected his oral narratives and traditions. This new discourse that conflated cultural and physical attributes with an inheritable racial identity blurred the meaning of descriptions such as being "of mixed blood." As decades passed, Anglo-Americans were ever more likely to employ the word mixed blood as a racial identity for multiracial Native persons who were not literally half breeds, that is, descended from one Native and one non-Native parent. Ironically, Warren's reliance on the older symbolism of blood would obscure the identity of the distinctive multitribal persons that he sought to describe.[30]

Given the importance Warren attached to portraying multitribal persons in terms understandable to Anglo-Americans, it remains unclear why he did not provide an Indigenous-language name identifying multitribal Ojibwe and Dakota persons. Perhaps the most obvious explanation is that he was unfamiliar with such a word. While it is possible that "Ayaa'aabiitawisid" could have described multitribal persons, and Jack Porter's careful efforts to distinguish mixed bloods and half breeds in the early twentieth century suggest the two constructions of identity remained separate and distinct, there is no conclusive proof that Ayaa'aabiitawisid did, in fact, describe multitribal persons in the 1830s and 1840s. The word Porter used may have been coined later in the nineteenth century, after Warren's death in 1853. Constructs of multiracial (or mixed-blood) identity were coming to have heightened and quite negative significance for Ojibwes by the last two decades of the nineteenth century. They may have created a new word or invested an older word with new meaning to account for these changed circumstances. Alternatively, it is possible that early nineteenth-century Ojibwes saw no need to create a distinguishing name for multitribal kin-groups because they were viewed in the same manner as the other kin-groups before them who had been incorporated into the tribe as exogamous clans. The Water Spirit and Wolf clans had origin stories unique to their creation—as all clans did—and over time as they intermarried into other clans, they formed the same densely overlapping webs of kin connections that other Ojibwe families and individuals possessed. Their exceptional mediating abilities across tribal lines were much esteemed, but these abilities might not have placed them in a conceptual category so dissimilar that it could not be accounted for by reference to the origins of existing clans and their social responsibilities. Since Ojibwe clans were exogamous, all clans engaged in out-marriage and all clans contained within them the potential to connect to other kin-groups by the marriages of their members, especially women, who usually lived with their husbands' extended families while maintaining close ties to their own natal clan groups. It may be that Ojibwes thought intertribal clans were distinguishable by degree but not by kind. It is also important to remember that during Warren's lifetime, kinship, especially clan membership, remained for Ojibwes the crucial indicator of social belonging and inclusion. Individuals located themselves as social beings with reference to who their relatives were. Factors such as age, ability, and gender also powerfully shaped individual experience, but the responsibilities one undertook or the privileges one claimed were all mediated by one's numerous relationships to other kinfolk. The cultural logic and associated practices of creating kin ties would have been especially salient in the creation of multitribal kin-groups, since these actions took place wholly in Native political space and operated according to Native understandings of their needs. [31]

Despite Warren's keen appreciation of Ojibwe clans as creative social institutions that had guided and implemented Ojibwe innovations in the past, he was apparently unaware of the existence of a process of clan formation that was underway during his lifetime.[32] The new clans that would emerge from this process would come to be called "half breed clans" or "mixed blood clans." The fact that both terms remained in common use implies that there was widespread, though probably informal, agreement among both Native and non-Native peoples that the names half breed and mixed blood continued to refer to two different categories of social identity. The impetus for creating such clans, which strongly suggests that their origins dated to the eighteenth century, was the increasing number of British and American men who were only transitory members of Ojibwe or fur trade communities. When these men moved away, they not only abandoned their wives and children, but they also left their children with neither Ojibwe clan ties nor sponsorship into fur trade society. Ojibwes, along with Odawas and Potawatomis, their frequent allies and culturally similar tribal neighbors, met this challenge by creating new clans to provide the needed tribal social inclusion. Clan animals were determined after careful tribal observation of British and American material culture, particularly politically significant objects such as "British medals" or American "arms and seals." On the basis of this scrutiny, the three tribes concluded that the British *doodem*, or clan, was the lion and the American *doodem* was the eagle, an astute recognition of the ways that the two colonial powers deployed the symbols of the British Lion and the American Eagle as representations of their nations. While these innovations seem to have begun in the eastern portion of Ojibwe country, in Michigan and Ontario, they spread quickly, so that Ojibwes in Minnesota were adopting them, or experimenting with variations on them, by the early decades of the nineteenth century. [33] Even without Warren's detailed analysis, it is clear that Ojibwes and other tribal nations engaged in ongoing processes of expansive social inclusion by means of creating new clans. The earlier creation of the multitribal Water Spirit and Wolf Clans around the turn of the eighteenth century provided the conceptual and possibly the actual mechanisms for the later mid-eighteenth-century inclusions of multiracial persons. In each case, new clans developed in response to a felt tribal need. It is also worth considering whether multiracial persons were similarly constructed as another kind of boundary-crossing group, as the members of multitribal clans were.

While much remains unclear about Ojibwes' and Dakotas' social expectations for multitribal kin, historical evidence from two individuals in discrete periods in the nineteenth century offers additional glimpses into the ways that multitribal persons facilitated communication and interactions between tribal peoples, in both intertribal and international contexts. These incidents further reveal that intertribal persons might be called upon to act in a wide range of social situations and that Native women as well as Native men navigated social landscapes by enlisting the assistance of multitribal persons. The first of these individuals was discussed in a previous chapter. Zhaagobe was, in 1831, the "war-chief of Snake River," an Ojibwe village in the St. Croix River region. In that year, then-Indian agent Henry Schoolcraft conferred with Zhaagobe and the Snake River "principal chief," or village civil leader, Kaabemabi, to restore the peace between Ojibwes and Dakotas that American negotiators had helped to broker at the 1825 Treaty of Prairie du Chien. A war party of Dakotas had recently fired on a canoe traveling down the St. Croix River, killing four people of Ojibwe or multitribal heritage, and imperiling the peace agreement. In an intriguing instance of tribal leaders employing literacy for their own purposes, Kaabemabi and Zhaagobe had composed letters to two influential Dakota leaders, Wabasha and Little Crow (or Le Petite Corbeau), urging them to use their influence to keep the situation from escalating. Schoolcraft endorsed this plan and penned his own letters to the Dakota leaders. In addition, he supplied important material items to underscore the Ojibwe leaders' good intentions, contributing "a flag, tobacco, wampum and ribands [sic], to be used in the negotiation." Zhaagobe, as the village war-leader, was responsible for political relations with the world outside the village and he would be the person who performed the diplomatic acts of delivering the message and gifts to the Dakotas. After the meeting with Schoolcraft, however, Kaabemabi stated that "he would himself go with the chief Shakoba [sic] to the Petite Corbeau's village." Schoolcraft believed that Kaabemabi felt emboldened by the "protection" of the American flag he would be bringing as a gift, but it is just as likely that the prospect of renewed warfare was worrisome enough that these St. Croix Ojibwe leaders felt the presence of both the premier civil and war leadership of their village was warranted in this diplomatic negotiation. Regardless of what factors motivated Kaabemabi to join

Zhaagobe in his mission to Little Crow's village, it is clear that, as a war-leader, Zhaagobe was the individual responsible for initiating intertribal contacts with potentially hostile nations.[34]

In his capacity as a war leader, Zhaagobe also attended several treaty negotiations with the Americans over the first three decades of the nineteenth century. He accompanied Kaabemabi to the August 5, 1826, Treaty of Fond du Lac, placing his name, rendered "Chaucopee," directly beneath that of the civil leader, "Kaubemappa." Eleven years later, he attended the July 29, 1837, Treaty of St. Peters at Fort Snelling, the first treaty at which the United States sought a substantial land cession from Wisconsin and Minnesota Ojibwes. From the start, the Fort Snelling treaty was plagued with difficulties, ranging from the imperfect bilingual skills of the two US government interpreters initially selected to translate the treaty negotiations, to the delayed arrival of the Ojibwe representatives whose villages were located within the lands the Americans sought to buy. General William R. Smith, one of the two American treaty commissioners, was unable to be present at all. This left the remaining commissioner, Governor Henry Dodge of the Wisconsin Territory (which in 1837 encompassed present-day Minnesota), to wonder if he was authorized to treat by himself and complaining of the vagueness of his overall instructions from the Commissioner of Indian Affairs. Dodge compounded the problem when he sought to begin the talks with only those Ojibwe leaders who were present when he arrived at Fort Snelling. Several of these *ogimaag* explained to the commissioner the inappropriateness of his actions and quizzed him at length about his ultimate objectives.[35]

As a war leader, Zhaagobe remained uninvolved in the civil leaders' efforts to convince Dodge to follow the appropriate political protocol, but he intervened in a second controversy. He seems to have done so because he possessed a special expertise due to his multiple heritages. The dispute involved whether multiracial French relatives, some but not all of whom were also fur traders, should be granted a cash payment of their own in the Fort Snelling treaty. A number of important civil leaders, provoked that certain traders had been aggressively lobbying on behalf of their own economic interests, came out in opposition to any payment for "half breed relatives." Several war leaders in turn advocated for the traders. On July 24, the fourth day of the treaty talks, this debate grew heated and Zhaagobe attempted to mediate. Addressing the American delegation, he identified himself as uniquely capable of speaking to the issues involved because he was a multiethnic person. "[I] am related to all the half breeds in the country where I live," he informed Dodge, seeking to clarify his fitness as a representative of the regional multiracial French population. At the same time, Zhaagobe directed Dodge to "look at the man who is standing near me," a reference to an Ojibwe speaker who had preceded him. "His and my ancestors were the chief men of the country that you want to buy from us," he told Dodge. Having thus established his kin relationships to all parties involved in the negotiations, both Ojibwes and multiracial French, Zhaagobe offered to become involved in brokering an agreement between the disputing parties.[36]

At this point, the government interpreters' lack of facility with intercultural translation became painfully evident. They were unable to provide the cultural context that would have explained Zhaagobe's unique personhood and his consequent offer of assistance. Instead, Dodge and Commission secretary Van Antwerp were left to puzzle over what they considered the war leader's enigmatic words about his multiracial relatives and his simultaneous kin ties to the region's tribal leaders. They recognized that Zhaagobe was of both European and Native heritage ("Shagobai is a half breed," Van Antwerp noted in his journal), but they did not realize that Zhaagobe was also an Ojibwe. Nor did they grasp the larger implications of his multiple heritages. Zhaagobe was a particular kind of boundary-transcending person with particular skills and responsibilities. Not only that, as Zhaagobe himself pointed out, he was also fortuitously descended from Ojibwes in "the country you wish to buy from us." A multiethnic person with appropriate kin connections was offering his assistance in the discussion of a treaty payment by one of his kin-groups to another. This should have facilitated dialogue, but it did not.[37]

With the negotiations in danger of foundering, two of the most influential and respected civil leaders present, Flat Mouth of Leech Lake and Hole-in-the-Day the Elder of Gull Lake, intervened, firmly redirecting the talks back to the larger issue of the land sale. "[W]hen I came here this morning, I supposed you wanted to talk to us about the land you wished to get from us," Flat Mouth reproached Dodge, "[And] not about the traders." His words and a corroborating speech by Hole-in-the-Day returned the conversation to the most important business, a sale of Ojibwe lands negotiated by leaders representing the affected communities. The issue of a cash payment to multiracial relatives resurfaced five days later, after a deliberative and carefully qualified land sale had been concluded. Zhaagobe once more assumed a role as mediator in the lesser business of garnering support for payments for "our half breeds" and "our traders." By this time Van Antwerp seemed to have developed some understanding of the war leader's actions. He described Zhaagobe as taking on the role of "a peacemaker."

He further detailed the larger series of actions that Zhaagobe participated in, noting that Zhaagobe had "placed himself at the head of the Braves" as part of an effort "to conciliate both them and the Chiefs." With the more important issues involving the land sale resolved, Zhaagobe's mediatory efforts seemed to meet with more success. The civil leadership agreed to a cash payment for multiracial French relatives and a generous sum for the debts of the traders.[38]

Four decades later, a Dakota woman named Wiyaka Sinte Win or Tail Feather Woman provided striking evidence that the concept of multitribal persons was still a part of Dakota as well as Ojibwe thought and cultural practice. At an unknown date probably in the late 1870s, Tail Feather Woman experienced a prophetic vision. Its subject matter and the way she encountered a powerful spiritual being say much about the violence and deprivations Dakotas had been enduring since the mid-nineteenth century decades. Though details vary from one narrative to the next in keeping with the fluid nature of oral traditions, Tail Feather Woman received her vision in a time of great crisis. Her village was attacked by American soldiers, and she escaped death or capture by hiding in a lake and breathing through a hollow reed. She stayed hidden in the lake for several days enduring hunger and cold. During this time, she was visited by a powerful spiritual being (often identified in English as the "Great Spirit") who took pity on her for her suffering. The spiritual being gifted her with a new ceremony that featured a large, distinctively decorated drum and accompanying songs, which Tail Feather Woman taught to her community. The community constructed the first drum according to her vision and when they performed the new ceremony, it halted the soldiers' attacks on their village. Subsequent performances of the ceremony also defused confrontations with local American settler-colonists as well as soldiers. Furthermore, the spiritual being informed Tail Feather Woman that the Drum Dance, as the drum and its sacred power came to be called, was meant to shared, "copied and passed on to other tribes." Tail Feather Woman herself was to be the emissary who would travel to other tribes to share her extraordinary vision and its power. Foremost among the tribes who would create a permanent peace with one another through the Drum's power would be the Ojibwes and Dakotas.[39]

Among the many accounts of Tail Feather Woman's travels to other Great Lakes tribal nations, one narrative from the Ojibwe community of Mille Lacs is of special interest. It reveals additional information about the ongoing importance of multitribal persons even as Great Lakes Native peoples were increasingly confined to Reservations and their traditional cultures were becoming ever more invisible to non-Natives. Significantly, the narrative also repeats the themes of interconnection between Ojibwe and Dakota societies. In this telling, which was recorded by the amateur anthropologist Fred K. Blessing, Tail Feather Woman first began the work of sharing her vision with other tribes by traveling to the Ojibwe village of Mille Lacs. With its many Dakota-descended Wolf Clan Ojibwes, Mille Lacs was an obvious place for Tail Feather Woman to begin her prophetic journey. At Mille Lacs she would find relatives, people of Dakota ancestry to welcome her, provide her with a place to stay, and sponsor her as she revealed her vision to other community members. This was indeed what happened. Tail Feather Woman and an escort of "warriors" sent word of their impending visit and their gift of a drum and ceremony. When they reached Mille Lacs, the Dakota visitors were met by a village leader named Mazomanie, a member of the Wolf Clan and himself of partial Dakota heritage. The visiting Dakotas stayed at their relative Mazomanie's village for much of the summer, "teaching [their hosts] the songs and ceremonies" that accompanied what Ojibwes would call "the Sioux drum." The visitors engaged in a variety of other activities too, giving gifts to prominent Mille Lacs leadership families and joining the larger Ojibwe community in "social" dancing and drumming. The Mille Lacs Ojibwes' support of Tail Feather Woman's spiritual message extended beyond the welcome they accorded her at their village. They actively assisted her with the next leg of her journey. A number of Mille Lacs villagers, likely members of the Wolf Clan, accompanied Tail Feather Woman as she continued her travels to more distant Ojibwe communities in Wisconsin, to facilitate introductions and, in Blessings' words, "to act as interpreters." The ability of these Ojibwes to translate for the Dakota-speaking Tail Feather Woman suggests that they were bilingual, and thus retained one of the most important skills multitribal persons could possess. As probable members of a multitribal kin-group, they were optimally positioned to act as mediators, introducing Tail Feather Woman to the several Native communities with whom she eventually shared her vision.[40]

The examples of Zhaagobe, an individual multitribal and multiethnic person who mediated in treaty negotiations involving his multiple kin-groups, and the Wolf Clan Ojibwes of Mille Lacs who traveled with and interpreted for their Dakota relative Tail Feather Woman, reveal two different ways in which multitribal persons acted in tribally centered political and cultural life. In each instance, multitribal persons acted as mediators between groups of persons whom Native peoples conceptualized as unalike, but the circumstances that brought these unalike groups together differed greatly. Zhaagobe's mediation at the Treaty of St. Peters placed him in a familiar setting that involved political negotiations between a Native people and a European-descended political power, the United States. These were the sorts of interactions with Native peoples that Americans were most familiar with, and they had long relied on the mediating and interpreting abilities of persons whom they frequently described, as they did Zhaagobe, as "half breeds." As Zhaagobe's explanation of his multiple heritages indicates, however, this identification did not represent the way he saw himself, nor did it fully encompass the several types of inclusion he was able to claim. The Ojibwes gathered at the St. Peters treaty presumably also understood him this way, since his actions as a boundary-crossing mediator were predicated on his multiple identities as both Ojibwe and multiracial French.

Not surprisingly, the larger collectivity of persons of multiple heritages who bridged the boundaries of tribes and ethno-national groups was far less visible to non-Natives despite appearing at political negotiations those non-Natives considered quite important. The actions of Ojibwes and Dakotas in creating permanent new multitribal kin-groups such as the Wolf and Water Spirit Clans went almost completely unrecognized by non-Native observers, with the seeming exception of the bicultural and multiracial William Warren. And yet, such multitribal groups persisted and continued to act as mediators and interpreters in meetings between tribal communities. On the occasions when multitribal persons drew the attention of Anglo-Americans, the latter usually misunderstood the nature of actions by multitribal persons and appeared unaware of the significance of their multitribal heritage. For instance, when Anglo-American settler colonists in eastern Minnesota and western Wisconsin heard the news of Tail Feather Woman's plans to travel to other Native communities to spread the word of her vision, they expressed alarm that she was accompanied by "warriors." They displayed no recognition that her escort was composed in part of multitribal Dakota-descended Wolf Clan Ojibwes. Of far more concern was the idea that Native men (presumed to be "Sioux") were traveling through the woodlands unbeknownst to Americans and on business of their own. Where Zhaagobe's supposed race was mentioned as a noteworthy piece of information in the treaty journal, the disparate party accompanying Tail Feather Woman was collapsed into a mass of undifferentiated (and menacing) Native males.[41]

As the nineteenth century progressed, Ojibwes themselves would struggle with imposed identities based on racial categories that were translated using terms such as full blood, half breed, and mixed blood. The remarks of Ojibwe witnesses testifying in the early twentieth century White Earth Reservation investigation indicate that acceptance of these constructs was a lengthy, uneven, and deeply contested process. That constructions of Native identity became entangled in the schemes of lumbermen, bankers, and local businessmen to gain illicit access to Ojibwe timber and other resources only worked to further obscure any American understanding that Ojibwes retained very different conceptions of social belonging and social difference, let alone the potential of kinship ties to bridge the two. Yet, individual witnesses such as Jack Porter and Ain-dus-o-ge-shig still insisted that Indigenous constructions of personhood in all their boundary-crossing complexity more accurately represented tribal realities than Anglo-American attempts to assign identities according to new racialized categories. Porter's recollections of Ginoozhens as an Ojibwe, a Dakota, and a Francophone half breed represented one variant of this social complexity, while Ain-dus-o-ge-shig's descriptions of his great-grandfather as "one of those near mixed bloods but not a half breed" attempted to make additional distinctions within the categories Anglo-Americans were collapsing into the single grouping of "mixed blood Indians." Despite American certainty that their categories of "race" were bolstered by scientific evidence of human difference, Ojibwes remained unconvinced. They continued to structure their understandings of difference and sameness according to their own categories. At the same time, if multiethnic and multitribal individuals represented two important types of persons, they did not exhaust Ojibwe or Dakota constructions of human difference and sameness. The following chapter explores Ojibwe views of gender, ethnicity, and norms of masculinity, another series of constructs that were distinctive cultural productions and of far more salience to Ojibwes, and though the evidence is scant, also apparently, to Dakotas, than American notions of "race."

"The Little Crow, A Celebrated Sioux Chief," painted at the 1825 Treaty of Prairie du Chien (Lewis 1836). This Dakota leader's name was probably Cetanwakuwa (Charging Hawk), mistakenly translated as Little Crow. Very probably he was the Dakota leader, along with Wabasha, with whom Kaabemabi and Zhaagobe communicated in 1831 as part of an effort to restore the peace negotiated between the two nations in 1825.
Courtesy of American Indian Histories and Cultures.

"Shing-Gaa-Ba-w'osin [Zhingwaabe Aasin], or the Figure'd Stone," an Ojibwe *ogimaa* at the 1826 Treaty of Fond du Lac (Lewis 1836). At the treaty of Prairie du Chien the previous year, he described his responsibility to select land for the multiracial community belonging to his village at Sault Ste. Marie. *Courtesy of American Indian Histories and Cultures.*

"Jack-D-ba, or The Six [Zhaagobe], A Chippewa Chief," depicts a portrait of the multitribal person, Zhaagobe, who participated in a number of historical events discussed in this work, including the 1837 Treaty of Fort Snelling (Lewis 1836). There is no date on this painting, though it is probable it was painted at the 1826 Treaty of Fond du Lac, which Zhaagobe attended. *Courtesy of American Indian Histories and Cultures.*

"Ta-Ma-Kake-Toke," An Ojibwe Woman, whose name was translated as "The Woman That Spoke First," painted at the treaty of Fond du Lac, 1827 (Lewis 1836). She was recently widowed and carried a mourning bundle as part of an Ojibwe grieving ritual, a cultural practice Americans frequently remarked upon. *Courtesy of American Indian Histories and Cultures.*

"Ma-ko-me-ta, or Bear's Oil," a Menomini leader at the 1827 Treaty of Buttes des Morts (Lewis 1836). As one of several orders of business leftover after the 1825 Treaty of Prairie du Chien was signed, the treaty of Buttes des Morts was held to finalize tribal boundaries between Ojibwes, Menominis, and Ho-chunks in present-day Wisconsin and Michigan. Lewis referred to it in his paintings as the Treaty at Green Bay. *Courtesy of American Indian Histories and Cultures.*

A Winnebago [Ho-chunk] Woman, "Wife of O'Check-Ka, or Four Legs," painted at the 1827
Treaty of Buttes des Morts (Lewis 1836). The presence of elder women, such as the
"Wife of O'Check-Ka," was of political importance to Native nations, but was routinely
misinterpreted by Europeans and their North American descendants.

Courtesy of American Indian Histories and Cultures.

"A View of the Butte des Morts Treaty Ground with the Arrival of the Commissioners Gov. Lewis Cass and Col. McKenney," 1827 (Lewis 1836). In addition to hosting the multitribal treaty, a Menomini leader named Grizzly Bear also described Buttes des Morts as the site of his former village and home to a multiracial French community.

Courtesy of American Indian Histories and Cultures.

[Jean Baptiste] Richardville, "The Head Chief of the Miami tribe painted at the Treaty of Fort Wayne, 1827" (Lewis 1836). While sometimes viewed as a controversial figure, the Miami Head Chief J. B. Richardville participated in a number of efforts to retain tribal lands by placing them in the hands of private tribal individuals of multiracial heritage.

Courtesy of American Indian Histories and Cultures.

Na-She-Mung-Ga, A Miami Chief, also "painted at the Treaty of Fort Wayne" in 1827, does not seem to have been recorded as signing the treaty itself (Lewis 1836).
Courtesy of American Indian Histories and Cultures.

"Sun-A-Get [Zanagad] or Hard Times, A Pottawatomie Chief, at the Treaty of Massinnewa [Mississinewa]," 1827 (Lewis 1836). Interestingly, Zanagad does not appear to have signed this treaty. Though Lewis sometimes painted individuals who were not treaty signatories, it is also possible that he misheard the name and it remains unrecognizable among the treaty's signers.

Courtesy of American Indian Histories and Cultures.

Chapter 4

Working like a Frenchman

Ojibwe Discourses of Masculinity, Labor, and Ethnicity

One chilly morning in early February 1837, an Ojibwe man named Maangozid, or Loon's Foot, was chopping wood for the small Protestant mission located at Fond du Lac village on the westernmost tip of Lake Superior in present-day Minnesota. Although Maangozid had enjoyed a position of leadership within the Fond du Lac tribal community for many years, he had recently suffered significant political reverses. Humiliated by the community's refusal to acknowledge him as their *ogimaa*, or premier civil leader, Maangozid had withdrawn from village life, seeking solace in an intensive exploration of the Christian religion and lifeway advocated by the resident missionary, Edmund F. Ely. Maangozid's work as a woodcutter was in fact an important component of the reordered gender roles that the missionaries, stern Calvinists affiliated with the Boston-based American Board of Commissioners for Foreign Missions (ABCFM), demanded of Ojibwe males. Maangozid, wearing a pair of Ely's cast-off "Pantaloons," had further heightened the difference between himself and other Ojibwe men first by his labor and now by his change of dress. His brother Inini approached him and expressed deep distress. He was pained to see his kinsman reduced to such poverty, Inini continued, and summed up Maangozid's overall debased condition with a culturally specific epithet. "[H]e called me a Frenchman," Maangozid told Ely later the same day.[1]

Ely attached little significance to the words that troubled Maangozid. He focused instead on his sole male convert's continued expectation for reciprocal sharing of food and other acts of social solidarity that Ojibwes esteemed, and the missionaries were determined to eradicate. Yet Maangozid's concern was far more important than the young missionary realized. Encapsulated within the construct of the "Frenchman" that had distressed Maangozid were profound Ojibwe beliefs about masculinity, gender-appropriate male labor, and the power of labor to create different male social identities. The type of work a man performed and the circumstances under which he performed it revealed his ethno-national identity, either as a member of an Indigenous nation such as the Ojibwes, or as a Frenchman, the only Europeans seemingly singled out for this invidious comparison. The reasons why Frenchmen had become the Ojibwe representation of degraded male labor appear to have been rooted in a series of historical events beginning in the middle of the eighteenth century with the French defeat in the Seven Years' War. French subordination to the British had entailed not just political domination but economic exploitation in the fur trade, where Ojibwes observed that the trade's elite of partners and clerks increasingly became Britons or at least English-identified while the laboring force remained majority French. In the decades following the war, Ojibwes expanded their con-ceptualizations of their longtime military and political allies to acknowledge this new social and economic reality. The Frenchman, though he might still be an ally, now also worked for wages for one of the fur trade companies under the often harsh supervision of another man, a condition Ojibwes perceived as deeply exploitive and antithetical to their own ways of working. So demeaning was wage labor under such conditions of subordination and dependency that Ojibwe men who labored under similar circumstances risked becoming such subordinated Frenchmen themselves. This was both the clear implication of Ini-ni's remark and the cause of Maangozid's consternation.

Ojibwe men's conviction that Frenchmen were degraded by their fur trade labor represented more than a memorialization of a bitter military and political defeat. It was also an Indigenous critique of British and later Anglo-American colonialism employing culturally specific gendered constructs. Ojibwe men articulated their concerns about the continued political, social, and economic autonomy of their communities using this distinctively gendered language. In deprecating the French, however, Ojibwe men did not, as might be expected, disparage Frenchmen as having become effeminate or as performing women's work. Their critique of the French was intra-gender; it compared the behavior of Frenchmen in opposition to other men, namely themselves. This perception of Frenchmen as debased in comparison to other men rather than women cre-ates an opportunity to acknowledge and explore Ojibwe understandings of gen-der beyond the well-known binary of male and female. Ojibwe men's discourse concerning masculinity further underscores the fact that, while Ojibwes and Europeans both understood gender as an important category of social identity, the specific ideas and practices that comprised their constructions of gender differed significantly. In the 1830s, moreover, as Ojibwes confronted mounting political pressure from the American government for a major land cession, they also encountered American missionaries, whose efforts to transform Ojibwe people into farmers who owned land as private property attacked the foundations of nearly every aspect of tribal life and culture. In the context of these dual assaults, the gendered symbolism of the demeaned, dependent Frenchman took on new urgency as a vehicle for political criticism.

By the early decades of the nineteenth century, the Ojibwes of the western Great Lakes had had long knowledge of and experience with the French. Their Anishinaabemowin-speaking ancestors had first encountered French Jesuit missionaries (and their military escorts) reconnoitering the shores of what would come to be called Lakes Huron and Superior in the 1640s. At that time, these ancestral communities were in the process of creating new collective tribal social identities, one of which would become known to outsiders as Ojibwes. Over the course of the seventeenth century, the process of social formation unfolded on Native terms, facilitated by mutually intelligible languages and shared understandings of kinship as a foundational organizing principle. By the last three decades of the seventeenth century, when fur traders such as Nicolas Perrot joined missionaries in venturing regularly to localities in the Great Lakes country, a self-conscious Ojibwe polity had coalesced. Its component villages created alliances and traded with the French. During these years, Ojibwes also began their long involvement in the fur trade, pursued initially on Native terms that conceptualized exchanges of goods as embedded in a series of inseparable political and economic acts and expectations. Also central to successful exchanges was the creation of kin-based alliances, which in the Great Lakes country involved the widespread marriage of French men into Indigenous communities. The resulting kin ties also knit extended family groups together over long distances, as Ojibwes moved away from the tribal place of origin at Baaweting, or Sault Ste. Marie as the French called it, in response to the upheavals and opportunities of fur trade colonialism.[2]

In the earliest years of their acquaintance with the French, numerous Algonkian-speaking peoples, including the Ojibwes, Odawas, Potawatomis, Meskwakis (or Foxes), Sauks, Algonquins, and Menominis gave a name to the European newcomers. Collectively, these nations called the French Wemitigoozheg (Wemitigoozhe in the singular). Dating from the seventeenth century, this designation appears to be the oldest ethnonym Algonkian-speaking peoples applied to the French. An early mention of it dates from the 1680s or 1690s, recorded by the French military officer, explorer, and linguist Louis-Armand de Lom d'Arce, Baron de Lahontan, who was assigned to several locations in the Great Lakes country during those decades. Lahontan included Algonkian-language words for "the French" and "the Country of the French" in the dictionary he compiled as part of his two-volume work *Nouveaux Voyages de Mr. le Baron Lahontan dans l'Amérique Septrionale.*[3]

Despite (or perhaps because of) its antiquity, the exact meaning of Wemiti-goozheg defied later efforts at translation. The word's root, *mitig,* clearly denoted wood. Both Natives and non-Natives offered interpretations of the word, their explanations revealing much about the cultural differences and historical experiences that would shape their analyses of the enduring ethnonym. Professional linguists working at the turn of the twentieth century, most of whom were non-Native and English-speaking, proposed translations that emphasized the ways in which the French used wood differently than did Native peoples, with the implication that these uses were so technologically advanced that Native peoples commemorated them in the name they gave the first Europeans they encountered. Anthropologist and editor of the 1907 *Handbook of American Indians North of Mexico,* Frederick Webb Hodge, demonstrated this line of reasoning, rendering the Ojibwe word (spelled with the diacriticals of the day as "wemitigoshi") as meaning "people of the wooden canoes."[4]

Contemporaneous Ojibwes offered other translations. In the mid-nineteenth century, an elderly Ojibwe woman from eastern Minnesota told a petty trader named James H. Van Nett that "the first Frenchman she ever saw" "was building a trading post." While the unnamed woman also noted that the French built their posts "out of oak logs," she expressed no awe at this technological feat. Though this manner of construction did explain "the way the Frenchman came to get his name of Way mit ig oshe," the unnamed elder added this observation as an after-thought. Of more significance to her was the fact that when she first encountered the French, they were involved in the activity that had brought them to Ojibwe country in the first place, namely trading. Trade also figured prominently in the recollections of another elder named Naawagiizhigokwe, or Susan Bolin, a Mississauga woman from the community of Skugog, Ontario. Naawagiizhigokwe, who spoke an eastern form of the Ojibwe language, worked as a consultant with the linguistic anthropologist Alexander F. Chamberlain in the 1880s. In response to Chamberlain's question about the origins of the word Wemitigoozheg, Naawagiizhigokwe replied that she "thought it meant 'he carries a trunk or box,'" adding that the name "was evidently given to the early French traders." [5]

Ojibwes bestowed other, more alliterative names on the French too, much as they did with their own constituent kin groups. They called the Crane Clan the Passinouek, for instance, a word meaning "echo maker" and referring to the crane's clear, far-carrying voice.[6] In a similarly indirect fashion, they referred to the distinctive headgear and bodily posture of the French. "[S]end here the traders that wear a hat and place their hands upon their hips," Flat Mouth of Leech Lake urged in 1836, contrasting the recently arrived Americans unfavorably with the fondly remembered Frenchmen, who by the nineteenth century had become the standard by which all subsequent European-descended traders were judged. Exactly when Ojibwes began using this inferential name is not clear, but evidence from the lower Mississippi Valley, the other region of French colonization in North America, indicates that such descriptions of the French were in existence by the early eighteenth century. In the 1720s, Southeastern Native peoples were depicting the French in pictographs in strikingly similar terms, with "their arms upon their haunches . . . to distinguish them from Indians." While this distinctive posture "was never done amongst them[selves]," Southeastern Native peoples had "observed the French make use of this attitude frequently." As Flat Mouth's words make clear, Ojibwes also explicitly connected the hands-on-hips posture to the fur trade; the distinctive French stance had become the crucial physical attribute differentiating them from other traders of other nations. Frenchmen and trade became closely linked in Ojibwe experience and thought, enduring, as Flat Mouths' words indicate, well into the nineteenth century. [7]

Although the unintended consequences of engaging in trade would be numerous, Ojibwes became French allies and, by extension, trading partners. At the turn of the eighteenth century, their representatives participated in the Great Peace of Montreal of 1701, a "spectacular grand council," in the words of historian Heidi Bohaker, at which the French, their Indigenous allies, and the Six Nations Iroquois Confederacy sought to ratify a peace negotiation so complex it was literally a decade in the making. Along with two dozen other Native nations, Ojibwes joined the Great Peace, solidifying an expansive alliance grounded in Native understandings of the interconnections between alliance and exchange. A key geopolitical objective of the 1701 alliance, shared by tribes and the French alike, was to contain the growing British presence in eastern North America. [8] Ojibwes would remain French allies as the imperial rivalry between France and Britain accelerated over the first half of the eighteenth century, and they would witness the final military defeat of the French at the hands of the British in the Seven Years' War (1756–1763). More memorable still, they would watch the French evacuation of their North American colonies, which took local form in the Great Lakes country in the ritualized transfer or reoccupation by the British of formerly French forts at such places as Michilimackinac and Detroit.[9]

While the French defeat and expulsion as a sovereign power from North America would unleash political tumult lasting more than three decades, in other less acknowledged, less legible ways, the French remained an important presence in their former colonies. In no place was this more evident than in the fur trade, which continued to operate first under the British and later the American regimes but did so following the practices and protocols cocreated by Native nations and the French in the seventeenth century. Though initially resistant to this Indigenously inflected form of exchange, the British and the Americans would each learn that they could best insure a peaceful, profitable trade in furs by embedding economic exchanges in a larger Native context of making or renewing political relationships. The British might disdain the French as a conquered enemy and the Americans might deprecate their ambiguous racial identity, but it quickly became clear to the newly dominant colonial powers that they needed French knowledge, French skill, and French workmen if they were to profit from one of North America's most lucrative extractive commodities. As the decades passed, financial control of the fur trade passed into British and then American hands and men of English-speaking heritage came to dominate the higher ranks of the trade's employees, but most of the workforce, especially those who traveled to and lived in Native villages, remained French. Calling themselves *voyageurs*, or travelers, they continued to self-identify as ethnic Frenchmen after the withdrawal of French sovereignty from North America. French remained their first language and they embraced a distinctive Canadian French culture. Even many voyageurs of multiracial heritage drawn from the local fur trade towns that developed throughout the Great Lakes country in the eighteenth century continued to maintain a French identity, although as discussed in chapter 3, this might not be the only identity they understood themselves to inhabit. Significantly, Ojibwes also recognized that these men remained Frenchmen. They continued to refer to the Canadian French as Wemitigoozheg and they continued to link the Frenchmen conceptually as well as practically with the trade in furs.[10]

While the fur trade was predicated on a series of Native conceptions of alliance and exchange, it was also a European commercial endeavor, organized around the class hierarchies, labor regimes, and socioeconomic practices of preindustrial early modern Europe. This was particularly important in shaping the organization and control of fur trade labor. From the first trading ventures begun in the 1690s, fur companies constructed their work forces according to the series of profoundly unequal European class relations between men who were described as "masters" and those called "servants." The companies themselves were viewed as property-owning entities who, like the seigneurial landowners they imitated, exercised substantial control over the landless men whom they hired for wages. These latter men were literally described as servants; they signed contracts binding themselves to a trading company as its indentured servants. Their work contracts, or indentures, also stipulated wages and covered a specified time period, usually one year. These deeply unequal labor arrangements of masters and servants would prove extremely durable, continuing to shape the labor regimes and social practices of the fur trade well into the nineteenth century.[11]

France's successor regimes, Britain and the United States, continued to utilize these labor systems, giving tribal peoples the impression that the trade had not changed in its essentials with the passage of years and the transfers of colonial power. This seeming air of stability belied the volatility of the fur trade itself in the decades following the Seven Years' War. British and American firms competed fiercely among themselves and with each other while continuously expanding the trade itself west and north across the continent in search of new sources of fur-bearing animals. However, because western Ojibwe villages continued to be profitable even as the epicenter of the trade passed them by, trading companies continued to send outfits to such Ojibwe villages as Fond du Lac, Sandy Lake, and Leech Lake. This enduring presence of traders and their labor forces added to Ojibwes' perceptions of the trade as an unchanging representation of European-descended colonial societies. At the same time, the trade's distinctive social and labor relations exhibited the features of those European-descended societies that most troubled Ojibwes. Each spring, as traders returned to villages such as Fond du Lac, commanding their subordinate voyageur labor forces, Ojibwes could observe a rank-based society in operation and draw what conclusions they would.[12]

Ojibwes, particularly men, regarded the status hierarchies of the fur trade with undisguised contempt and disgust. The rigid division of male labor was all-pervading and highly visible, both in the trade itself and in the fur trade communities that developed near tribal villages. Moreover, it was given daily expression in all forms of work whether undertaken at trading posts, during travel, or at other work sites. A fundamental distinction both shaped the trade's labor force and graphically displayed the unequal relations of power between men. The elite did not perform manual labor. They never engaged in such tasks as paddling or portaging canoes, constructing buildings, planting fields or fishing to subsist at a trading post. Such physical toil was the work of the voyageurs. Only under dangerous and exceptional conditions when everybody had to pull together quickly—to unload a canoe that was foundering on rocks, for instance—would a trader or clerk engage in such labor. These departures from the established rules in times of crisis only reinforced the norms by calling attention to the extreme circumstances necessary for the usual standards to be momentarily breached.[13]

Numerous other social practices further reinforced the unequal statuses of individual fur trade employees. Interactions between members of the elite and the voyageurs were characterized by an assumption of command on the part of the former and deep deference on the part of the part of the latter. Beyond such power-inflected daily interactions, the elite simply lived better, and their comfort was once again insured by the labor of the voyageurs. The trade's elite allotted themselves better shelter while traveling. They slept in tents, which the voyageurs erected for them, then the voyageurs had to make what shelter they could beneath an overturned canoe. The elite had more food, and usually had a designated "cook" or "man" who prepared it for them. An American Board missionary remarked during one lean time at the Ojibwe village of Fond du Lac that the trader caught two fish in his nets. The trader had one fish for his dinner; his men split the other one. The trade's elite, and elite passengers such as missionaries, were carried across streams on the backs of the voyageurs rather than being expected to get wet fording by themselves. Similarly, their baggage was carried for them on portages. Appalling as Ojibwes found these various practices, a final fur trade practice struck Ojibwes as the very essence of humiliating subordination. The voyageurs depended on the traders for their food. They were issued rations on a daily or weekly basis. Many had no containers in which to receive their portions of flour and were forced to accept it "in their pocket handkerchief or hat."[14]

These evidences of the weakness and dependence of the French voyageurs struck Ojibwe men with special force. Two of the most important characteristics defining Ojibwe masculinity were personal autonomy and the ability to be self-sufficient, to feed oneself and one's kin. Success at self-support, especially as hunters, also signaled that an Ojibwe man had established reciprocal ties with powerful spiritual beings, demonstrating a second, even more important, level of personal independence. Hunting was thus a powerfully charged spiritual act as well as an important subsistence practice. Ojibwe men approached hunting with deep respect, offering tobacco and prayers to the spirits of the animals they would hunt. The cultural significance of hunting radiated into other aspects of Ojibwe life. Since most men hunted with relatives, hunting both created and demonstrated the solidarity of kinfolk. Hunting was also a marker of adulthood. A youngster's first kill marked an important transitional moment.[15] Families invited relatives and honored elders to a ceremonial feast to celebrate this step toward self-sufficient adulthood. An occupation with deep roots in both the spiritual and material worlds, hunting was, as historian Heidi Bohaker has observed, "inextricably bound" to Ojibwe "conceptions of acceptable masculinity." By contrast, French dependence on fur traders for subsistence signaled not only their military defeat, but also revealed their profound spiritual weakness. Taken together, these multiple reverses gave another disturbing level of meaning to the political changes sweeping the Great Lakes country.[16]

In this context of political and spiritual defeat, other behaviors of the Frenchmen, especially the voyageurs, greatly perplexed Ojibwe men. Albeit grudgingly, Ojibwe men did admire aspects of voyageur culture and comportment. Voyageurs embraced a rugged masculinity that Ojibwe men also esteemed, including such personal traits as bravery, daring, physical strength, and endurance. Men of both groups celebrated their ability to make light of hardship and face danger with resourcefulness and calm. Among themselves, voyageurs possessed a boisterous, roughhousing work culture that contrasted conspicuously with their deferential behavior toward their fur trade superiors. There was much competitive fraternization and rivalry between young Ojibwe men and the generally youthful voyageurs. Physical competitions between them were frequent, with canoe races particularly favored because of their impromptu nature and quite probably also due to their unacknowledged subversive quality. In the warmer summer months Ojibwes and voyageurs would encounter one another frequently in their various travels around the lakes and canoe races provided a perfect opportunity to inject excitement and diversion into the tedium of waterborne travel. Spontaneous races, undertaken while performing the other work of propelling a canoe, were often unsanctioned by traders or other authorities.

While not open defiance of authority, they nonetheless quietly destabilized the usual relations of power, doubtless to the satisfaction of both voyageurs and Native men. In 1820, as the Cass expedition departed Detroit at the start of its journey to the Mississippi River, Henry Schoolcraft witnessed such a canoe race between "the French voyageurs and the Indians." Among the latter were several Ojibwes recruited to act as guides and hunters on the first leg of the trip. Schoolcraft viewed the race as an opportunity to make a cultural appraisal of two societies, contrasting the Native men, whose "expertness" was in "sudden and short exertions," with the Frenchmen, whose "superiority" was in "labours long continued." His own interest in ethnographic comparison notwithstanding, Schoolcraft recognized something of the other meanings the race held for its participants. For the contestants, he noted, it was a "trial of skill" between men who viewed themselves as members of different nations. What Schoolcraft did not recognize was that Ojibwe men such as these hunter-guides struggled to reconcile the spirited, raucous behavior of the Frenchmen who competed with them, singing to keep the time of their canoe strokes, with the subordinated position of these same men as dependent fur trade laborers. Some Ojibwes, concerned about American intentions in the western Great Lakes, noted that the Frenchmen's submissive demeanor toward their fur trade superiors extended to representatives of the United States' expeditionary forces. This unsettled Ojibwes who detected in Cass, Schoolcraft, and their military escort expectations that Ojibwes would treat them with similar deferential subservience.[17]

Ojibwe conceptions of the French remained nothing if not complicated. Even as they regarded Frenchmen as pitifully subordinated to the British and later Americans, Ojibwes participated frequently in activities marked by solidarity and comradeship with the French. Many of these acts of camaraderie involved situations similar to the competitive masculinity of canoe racing. Rather than emphasizing inter-ethnic competition, however, they focused on collaboration between Ojibwes and Frenchmen. In the spring of 1835, ABCFM missionary Edmund F. Ely described such an event, a game of "the Ball," or lacrosse, at the community of Fond du Lac. Frenchmen "from the fort," he wrote in his journal, "have been playing with the Indians this P.M." Ely's use of the conjunction 'with' as opposed to a word such as 'against' suggests the cooperative spirit animating the game. Unlike canoe races, the players did not divide into nationality-based teams. Furthermore, the French players honored the martial temper of the game, which Ojibwe men played attired for war in a breechcloth and moccasins, by wearing only "their shirts and bare legs." These items of dress performed multiple roles. The shirts signaled the Frenchmen's continuing commitment to European notions that linked civility to clothing and, significantly, nudity to savagery. These ideas were in turn partially subverted by the bare legs, a gesture of commonality toward Ojibwes' views on appropriate male attire. The fact that many Frenchmen knew how to play lacrosse further suggests the deeper kin-based connections they had with Ojibwe villages where they might have initially learned the rough game from relatives and friends.[18]

A second, more somber form of intercommunity solidarity existed between Ojibwes and Frenchmen, revealing itself in rituals surrounding death, funerals, and grieving. While games or sporting competitions also provided opportunities to diminish intercommunity tensions, such solidarity-building was often subsumed in the general excitement of a canoe race or a hard-fought game of lacrosse. In a world where deaths were frequent, often violent or due to inexplicable injuries or illnesses, funeral rites brought the two communities together to mourn while allowing Frenchmen to pay culturally appropriate respects to their Ojibwe allies. The ABCFM missionaries documented numerous instances of intercommunity participation in funerals and rituals of grieving and remembrance. William Boutwell, a missionary who also accompanied Schoolcraft's 1832 journey to Lake Itasca, described an event on that journey when the expeditionaries arrived at the Ojibwe village of Cass Lake as the funeral was being conducted for an Ojibwe man recently killed by the Dakotas. "Our voyageurs each procured some tobacco," Boutwell wrote. Revealing their familiarity with the ritual, the boatmen waited until "after the dance began," at which time they "presented their tobacco . . . to the widow." A year later in 1833, when Boutwell was stationed at LaPointe, he observed that at the end of the maple sugar-making season, when Ojibwe families returned to the village, they brought newly made maple sugar which they placed on the graves of their kinfolk. Families often celebrated the sugar-making season, which marked the first intensive food-producing activity after the lean times of winter, and the festivities included remembrances of the dead. In another inclusive gesture, Ojibwes also "invite[d] the Frenchmen to go and eat" from the offerings of the new maple sugar, thus joining in commemorations of the lives of the deceased.[19]

The sharing of food and remembrances of the dead also contained Ojibwe acknowledgments of their long political relationship with the French nation. Although as a political sovereign and military ally the French were only a memory by the 1830s, Ojibwes facing the pressures of Anglo-American settler-colonialism wistfully recalled the French alliance of the eighteenth century.

"Our fathers always said they would love to see the French from France again," the Leech Lake Ojibwes assured the French-born scientist Joseph N. Nicollet when he traveled through Minnesota territory in 1836 on an expedition funded by the United States to map the upper Mississippi River. Though he established cordial ties with the Leech Lakers, Nicollet made clear he was not a representative of the French government, and Ojibwes unhappily concluded their old ally would not be returning to aid them in restoring more equitable relationships between themselves and the other nations of the Great Lakes country. The excitement generated when an unexpected *"Frenchman of the olden time"* turned up in Ojibwe communities in 1836 is nevertheless instructive. The eagerness of tribal leaders to hold formal councils with Nicollet and present him with calumets and other gifts symbolic of reanimating an alliance indicated that Ojibwes continued to think of their erstwhile allies in political terms. Ojibwes understood the nation of France still existed "beyond the sea" and continued to hope that they might be able to reanimate a political relationship with their old ally.[20]

Even before Nicollet's visit raised their hopes, Ojibwes often evoked their enduring alliance with the French in an Indigenous context laden with political significance. The French were referenced and incorporated into funeral observances for tribal leaders and their kinfolk. In 1833, Bizhiki, the elderly premier civil leader at La Pointe, spoke to the French as political allies at the funeral of one of his adult sons. "I wish to put up a flag at the grave," he said, "to tell the Frenchmen that a chief is dead." Significantly, Bizhiki also sent word to another important regional political figure, the American Indian agent at Sault Ste. Marie, informing him of his son's death and describing his son as an Ojibwe leader. [21] In a second instance, the coffin of a grandson of the Leech Lake war leader Big Cloud "was borne to the grave by the Frenchmen." Big Cloud, who sought to strengthen his ties with the fur traders at Leech Lake, used his grandson's funeral to demonstrate his intentions, once again by casting the Frenchmen in their role as allies.[22]

Despite the range and variation in their interactions with the men they called Frenchmen, Ojibwes found little to admire or emulate in French society and culture, particularly as they observed it in North America. When it suited their purposes, Ojibwe leaders such as Flat Mouth described the French as "being the first to discover us" and "showing us how to use the ax and the rifle." Introducing metal versions of the stone, wood, and bone tools that they had already invented for themselves did not put Ojibwes in awe of French technological or intellectual ability, however. Flat Mouth's droll allusion to the French showing Ojibwes how to use axes was meant to suggest precisely this, to be an acknowledgement to his Native audience that his words were intended to cajole the French into following a particular course of political action rather than to accurately represent historical events. Not even the Europeans' game-changing metal weapons technology persuaded Ojibwes that the men from beyond the sea were their intellectual or social betters. In the same vein, Ojibwes dismissed American claims that they were destined to colonize the Great Lakes country either by virtue of their defeat of the British in the War of 1812, or because of their distinctive way of living that featured Protestant religious traditions and a socioeconomic system based on private land ownership, hierarchic gender relations, and sedentary agriculture. Such a lifestyle might suit Americans, Ojibwes remarked on numerous occasions, but the American "religion, mode of life, and learning" were "to them . . . of no use." Expanding upon this observation, Ojibwes made clear they did not think their own way of living would be enhanced by the changes the Americans advocated. The American way of living "would not make them anymore successful in hunting and fishing."[23]

This Ojibwe self-assurance surprised numerous Americans in the early decades of the nineteenth century. William Keating, the official chronicler of Stephen H. Long's 1823 expedition to reconnoiter the St. Peter's River, was disconcerted to learn that Ojibwes "have a high opinion of themselves." "Some Indians are represented as supposing themselves to hold a rank in creation inferior to that of a white man," Keating continued, but "this is certainly not the case with the Chippewas [Ojibwes]." On the contrary, Ojibwes "consider[ed] themselves as created for the noblest purposes." Their creator, they informed Keating, had intended that they "should live, hunt, and prepare medicines and charms." As further evidence of this astonishing attitude, Keating cited "a common expression" which Ojibwes used "when anything awkward or foolish is done, Wemetegogin gegakepatese [Wemitigoozhe gagibaadizi]." Keating translated the phrase to mean "[a]s stupid as a white man," which certainly proved his point about Ojibwe confidence, yet the phrase's meaning is more complex than he evidently realized. The first Ojibwe word in Keating's transcription is clearly "Wemitigoozhe," or "Frenchman," making the phrase specific to a particular nationality rather than, as Keating apparently assumed, a blanket racialized comment applied to all European-descended peoples. Certainly when Ojibwes employed this phrase they were expressing disdain for many of the elements of the European civilizations they had been exposed to, but the insult's ethnic specificity once more reflected how Ojibwe observations of the French continued to shape their perceptions of later European-descended populations, including the Americans. The French remained Ojibwes' initial point of reference and comparison when they evaluated other colonial and settler-colonial arrivals in the Old Northwest.[24]

Given their disdain for the types of labor performed by Europeans (and their North American descendants) in contrast to their own "noblest" of pursuits, it is not surprising that Ojibwe men centered their critiques of these European-descended societies on work, paying particular attention to the conditions under which it was performed. Ojibwes had first observed European labor in the context of the stratified and coercive work environment of the fur trade. The plainly unequal divisions of labor between traders and voyageurs made a deep impression on Ojibwes, initially attracting their attention then eliciting their condemnation. Most Ojibwe labor was gendered but within the broad categories of female-gendered and male-gendered labor there was little specialization. Hierarchies between men such as those exhibited in fur trade society simply were not present in subsistence-oriented Ojibwe society. Though there were certainly variations in individual levels of skill, all women and all men performed essentially the same array of tasks.[25]

Certain gendered tasks were particularly valued and considered iconic representations of masculinity and femininity, however. Men's work as hunters was such labor; it epitomized the male role in provisioning and supporting their kin groups, much as ricing and gathering wild foods did for women. Yet hunting labor extended beyond simply supplying the animal protein in Ojibwe diets. Ojibwes regarded men's hunting labor and women's gathering labor as paired and collaborative endeavors. While most forms of labor were strongly associated with one or another gender, they also displayed subtle forms of gender collaboration. Wild rice harvesting, for instance, was historically female gendered work. Women organized the labor of the harvest, setting the work rhythms and performing the various processes of sheaving, threshing, parching, and winnowing the grains. However, the specialized wooden threshing tools, called *bawa' iganaakoon,* that women used to knock the grains from the rice stalks were personalized, hand-crafted for individual women by the men of their families.[26] Ojibwes conceptualized such gendered but collaborative labor as jointly creating the tribal subsistence. They described the practices of this mutually supportive gendered labor using phrases such as "to make a living." Understood in this way, hunting was not just important as an expression of idealized masculinity, it was also a crucial element in constructing and sustaining the Ojibwe social world. If Ojibwe men abandoned hunting to become farmers, that social world rooted in gendered, balanced cooperation would collapse. What would replace it, Ojibwes feared, was a world in which they had become, like the Frenchmen, subjugated to the Americans.[27]

Ojibwes continued to esteem hunting beyond all other forms of masculine labor in the seventeenth and eighteenth centuries, during which time they encountered European colonists and their descendants. Concern whether other forms of labor were appropriate for men seem to have intensified, however, as Ojibwes navigated the political and social upheavals of the late eighteenth and early nineteenth centuries. North America's colonial landscape was radically reconfigured by the Seven Years' War, and in the postwar world Ojibwes encountered the French not just as their longtime allies but as a subjugated minority in a British colonial state. Ojibwes had always been aware of the subordination of the voyageurs to the fur trade's elite of traders and clerks; in the aftermath of the British victory in 1763, the trade increasingly came to reflect the new colonial hierarchy of power defined by nationality. The elite became mostly British or British-identified, while the French were largely confined to the ranks of the laboring men, the voyageurs. Ojibwes coming of age in the decades after the 1760s would perceive the French, not as powerful allies, but as vanquished laborers whose very work, and indeed, whose national language, were emblematic of their subjugation. While it is unclear exactly when the insulting expression "working like a Frenchman" entered Ojibwe speech, the years after the Seven Years' War suggest themselves as a pivotal moment when such a concept might have developed as Ojibwes and other Great Lakes Native peoples reckoned with the fur trade's postwar changes and continuities.[28]

Though the origins of the phrase "to work like a Frenchman" remain obscure, the expression was much in evidence during the early decades of the nineteenth century. Frenchmen continued to compose the majority of the fur trade's workforce and work relations in the trade remained as hierarchic as before. The symbol of the "Frenchman" as a man defeated and subordinated to an enemy, compelled to labor for wages and behave with subservience toward those who paid him, persisted as a daily lived reality as well. An incident recorded in 1839, in which an Ojibwe man named Buanens [Bwaanens] refused to perform specific kinds of labor for the American Board missionary Edmund Ely, offers important insights into Ojibwe men's understandings of what constituted acceptable masculine work. In conversation with Ely, Bwaanens revealed that Ojibwe men had developed clearly defined standards for the work that they would perform as opposed to other labor which they regarded as fit only for "Frenchmen." Bwaanens also indicated that Ojibwes recognized that the forms of labor involving non-Natives were historically contingent and thus subject to change. Ojibwe men monitored their own behavior to insure they would continue to comport themselves appropriately and thus retain their independence from the several foreign nationalities dwelling in their midst by the early nineteenth century. Much like Maangozid in the chapter's opening anecdote, Bwaanens had also been called out for his recent actions. Where it was Maangozid's brother who admonished him, members of the larger Fond du Lac village community reproached Bwaanens. "[T]he Indians," he told the missionary, "had been saying to him that he was lowering himself by working for [Ely] like a Frenchman." Newly sensitized by the remarks of his fellows, Bwaanens insisted when he arrived at Ely's mission one April day "[t]hat he was hired to voyage," that is, to work as a boatman, a form of labor that Ojibwe men deemed acceptable. He was taken aback to discover Ely expected him "to be working about [the] house." Labor such as this, especially when undertaken in the culturally alien space of the missionary's non-Indigenous "dwelling House," was outside the range of what Ojibwes judged to be acceptable masculine work. Moreover, Ely had indicated that he would be providing "direction" himself, a situation too much like a fur trader overseeing his voyageur workforce for Bwaanens' comfort. Under circumstances such as these, Bwaanens would indeed feel himself to be working like a Frenchman. Standing in the front room of Ely's house, Bwaanens further clarified that acceptable male labor was also contingent upon the physical space in which the work was performed. Ely had engaged a third person to hire Ojibwes to transport his goods to a new mission location, and Bwaanens objected that the contractor "who hired him did not tell him any thing about working *here*," that is, within the house itself.[29]

Bwaanens' refusal to perform work in and around a non-Indigenous household space was echoed in the one known instance of another tribal nation besides Ojibwes employing the concept of the Frenchman as degraded laborer. In the 1840s, Yanktonais Dakotas associated with the Catholic Little Prairie Mission near present-day Chaska, Minnesota, used a similar epithet. Like Ojibwes, they drew on the older practices of the fur trade elite of traders and clerks, who employed servants to do menial household work. Despite its location in and around a household compound, which might seem to be a female-gendered space, the labor performed was distinctly gendered as masculine, as Father Anthony Godfert, a priest at the mission, made clear. To do their own proselytizing labor effectively, Godfert wrote, the missionary priests needed "a man who could look after our material wants, such as to accompany the priest, do the cooking, take care of the horse, [and] cultivate the garden." Furthermore, the Dakotas understood the presence of such a household manservant to be a marker of status within a European-descended hierarchy and lost respect for missionaries who did not have a Frenchman as a laborer. Godfert quoted an unnamed Dakota leader as saying to him "Man of the Great Spirit, how is it that you work? Why have you not a Frenchman at your service?"[30]

The fact that both Ojibwes and Dakotas carefully distinguished between the labor appropriate for their own men and the labor performed by Frenchmen points to a second, largely unacknowledged reality. Men of both tribal nations did, in fact, hire on to work for fur traders and later, missionaries and other non-Native individuals. In doing so, Ojibwe men once again took care to contrast themselves to Frenchmen, while once more making no reference to the gendered labor of women. As before, the comparison that they drew was intragendered, an evaluation among men of labor performed by men. Many of the tasks of fur trade laborers in fact overlapped with those of Ojibwe men, among them fishing, canoeing, and portaging. Because of these similarities, context became all-important. Working with one's relatives and friends in circumstances Ojibwes understood as characterized by mutuality and egalitarianism was unproblematic. When one worked under the command of another man, who assumed a position of overt, coercive authority, one's own personal and political subordination was on display. As the remark of Inini to his brother Maangozid suggests, one's ethnicity might even change, transforming from the independence that characterized Ojibwe men to the craven dependence that marked the Frenchmen.

Not surprisingly, given their keen awareness of the circumstances under which their own labor for traders (and other non-Natives) overlapped with that of Frenchmen, Ojibwe men also routinely sought to distance themselves from the French by the types of work they undertook. They selected tasks that utilized their widely admired and culturally valued skills as hunters and woodsmen, abilities Europeans and their descendants were notoriously believed to lack. They accepted work as guides and hunters, messengers, mail carriers, and packers at portages as well as brief stints as boatmen. Such tasks were short term assignments and, in a further effort to distance themselves from the Frenchmen and in particular their dependence on yearly wage contracts, Ojibwe men demanded lump sum payments when the specified task was completed. They also refused to accept "in kind" payments or credits with a trading post in exchange for such work, insisting instead on cash in hand. [31] They maintained other literal forms of distance as well. When traveling in company with fur traders, Ojibwe workers camped separately, if possible on the other side of a river from the traders' camp. Most importantly, perhaps, for drawing the distinctions between themselves and the Frenchmen, Ojibwe men provided their own food, mainly, of course, by hunting.[32]

Still other aspects of their hired labor continued to distinguish Ojibwe work from that of men who relied for their entire subsistence on wage work. In addition to accepting jobs that emphasized their uniquely masculine skills as hunters and woodsmen, Ojibwe men sought work that could be carried out as part of a man's ordinary round of subsistence activities. An Ojibwe man at Fond du Lac planning to visit relatives at the village of Leech Lake, for instance, might act as mail carrier, transporting letters to the Leech Lake trader and the resident missionary. Or, if an Ojibwe family was traveling from the village of LaPointe on Lake Superior to the village at Yellow Lake on the St. Croix River, the father might agree to guide a party of missionaries who were also traveling to Yellow Lake. Missionaries often complained of their guides bringing their families along, apparently never recognizing that for the guides, the family's travels were paramount and only incidentally were they assisting the missionaries.[33]

When working for traders or missionaries, Ojibwe men also made it plain that they were not subordinates who could be ordered about. Guides, for instance, asserted their independence by refusing to work at a pace determined by others. Edmund Ely and William T. Boutwell discovered this to their chagrin when they hired an Ojibwe man and his teenage son to guide them on their trip from LaPointe to Yellow Lake. Each morning, Ely complained, the guides ate a "leisurely" breakfast before "anything was said concerning our proceeding on our Journey." Ely and Boutwell's efforts one morning to rush their guides backfired and the guides threatened to abandon the missionaries in the woods. It took two hours of negotiating in the missionaries' limited Ojibwe to persuade the guides to continue. Ely for one learned a valuable lesson about Ojibwe work culture. "It does no good to attempt to *drive* an Indian," he confided in his diary.[34]

The arrival in the 1830s of American missionaries intensified an endemic debate about appropriate labor and masculinity that had existed in Ojibwe, and apparently also Dakota, communities dating back several generations. Ojibwe experiences with the fur trade and its majority French laboring force had given rise to their initial constructions of appropriate and inappropriate masculine labor, which they articulated through ethno-national difference. The ABCFM missionaries unknowingly stoked this existing controversy with their efforts to transform Ojibwe men into wage-earning members of an agricultural society based on private land ownership. Whereas most Ojibwe men, like Bwaanens, carefully monitored their own actions, refusing to engage in certain forms of labor as part of their effort to retain an appropriate manly independence, others caused great community concern because they explored the missionaries' Christian religious teachings, including the mandated changes in masculine work roles and labor practices. A second family intercession like the one initiated by Maangozid's relatives further reflected the Ojibwes' long-standing conception of the problem of appropriate male labor. At the same time, community reaction to the Christian conversion of this second villager, a young man named Madweweyaash, reflected mounting Ojibwe concern at the presence of Americans in the western Great Lakes region. Intensely aware of American past actions respecting other tribes, and deeply disapproving of the cultural changes the missionaries advocated, Ojibwes also reconsidered whether the missionaries were the disinterested parties they claimed to be or whether they were the "forerunner of the Americans."[35]

Ojibwes had good reasons for concern. The second intervention occurred almost exactly one year after Wisconsin and Minnesota Ojibwes had negotiated the July 29, 1837, Treaty of St. Peters, their first substantial land cession treaty with the United States. Though most of the land alienated was in Wisconsin, a tract in Minnesota extending from the St. Croix River to the Mississippi was also sold. Ojibwes living in the St. Croix River valley as well as those at Fond du Lac just to the north of the land cession, who utilized resources and traveled within the ceded land, were gravely concerned. There was widespread suspicion among them that the ABCFM missionaries residing in some of their villages were "Agents of Am[erican] Govt," and had colluded in the land sale. [36] This controversy was especially intense at Fond du Lac, where Ely's initially unwitting involvement in a village leadership struggle had made him a particularly suspect figure. In the charged atmosphere that lingered in the months after the treaty's negotiation, Madweweyaash's actions became the subject of deep community concern. [37] For nearly two years he had been engaged in a profound exploration of the ABCFM missionaries' religious teachings. He thoughtfully compared Protestant and Catholic theology and discussed Christian concepts with fellow Ojibwes who had previously converted as well as with Edmund Ely.

Ultimately, he declared his belief in the tenets of the missionaries' New England-inflected Protestantism. He had, in the delighted words of Ely, "found the Saviour." Because the ABCFM missionaries expected complete cultural transformation would follow on the heels of Christian conversion, they persuaded Madweweyaash and his wife to move their home near Ely's mission, away from Fond du Lac village proper "in order to begin to live like civilized people." At Ely's insistence, Madweweyaash also began to wear Anglo-American style clothing.[38]

Members of the community made their disapproval known shortly after Madweweyaash adopted American attire. He was ridiculed by his peers, other young Ojibwe men who "laugh[ed] at him in his new costume." Madweweyaash sought to walk a middle path, however, insisting on his Christian convictions while acknowledging the concerns of his fellow villagers by "tak[ing] Indian dress again." More importantly, he continued to demonstrate a firm allegiance to Ojibwe conceptions of appropriate male labor. He participated in the wild rice harvest, an important food-gathering activity in which the cooperative labor of women and men was prominently featured. Significantly, he also continued to hunt for subsistence, evidence of his own awareness of the centrality of hunting to Ojibwe masculinity. Madweweyaash's ongoing commitment to traditional Ojibwe male labor pointedly distinguished him from Maangozid, whose earlier embrace of Christianity and performance of unacceptable labor had worried both his own family and the village at large. Yet as the months passed, Madweweyaash did eventually begin to make the kinds of cultural changes that alarmed his fellow villagers. By the spring of 1838 he was engaging in paid labor for Edmund Ely, cutting wood and fishing to supply the mission family. It was at this point that his father arranged for a meeting with "some of the principal men" of the village.[39]

The respected elders who "assembled at his father's lodge" to speak with Madweweyaash minced no words. They opened the discussion by voicing their objections to the types of labor the young man was performing. "'The Indians do not like to see me work,'" Madweweyaash informed Ely the following day. Ely recorded this blunt remark in his journal, adding the words "i.e. hired out to labor" in parentheses to the initial entry. Ely's qualification of the sort of labor Madweweyaash was describing is perhaps even more significant than he knew. The Ojibwe language spoken in the western Great Lakes in the early nineteenth century contained several words that differentiated between various types of labor. After almost two hundred years of exposure to European-derived forms of labor, Ojibwes had fashioned nuanced verb forms to illuminate the crucial distinctions between work they did for self-support and the hired labor performed for others under coercive circumstances. The verb *nind anoki,* "I work, I labor, I act," generally reflected a sense of self-directed labor, but the closely related verb, *nind anokia,* "I make him work, I put him to work," indicated coercion and inequality of social condition. Another verb, *nind anokitas,* meant "I work for myself," while *nind anokitawa* meant "I work for him." The noun *Anôkitagan* further underscored the implications of forced work for another person; it translated as "hireling" or "servant."[40] The elders' use of the verb "to work for hire" was thus already freighted with cultural significance. By using it, they made clear to Madweweyaash that his labor for hire was inherently problematic. It could never be construed as acceptable work for Ojibwe men.

Madweweyaash seems to have anticipated this type of objection. This is not surprising, given the controversy within Fond du Lac village over the missionaries' close connections to the American state and the Ojibwes' growing apprehension that the larger sociopolitical goals of the Americans were to "get possession of a little land, then claim much & finally drive the Indians away entirely." In this context, the assaults on traditional Ojibwe men's work appeared as the first shots fired in the American campaign "to do with [Ojibwes] as they had done to other Indian nations." Madweweyaash tried to assure the elders that his relationship with Ely was not what it seemed, that it was founded in egalitarian practices. "I told them I was hired, but yet we worked in each other's fields," he explained. The village leadership was unconvinced. "You can kill animals," they replied, this time directly referencing the emblematic labor of hunting that most defined Ojibwe masculinity. Such socially valued labor stood in direct opposition to the coerced wage work of the French voyageurs, whose subjugation had become the metaphor for the fate Ojibwes strove to avoid. The elders also raised the troubling parallel between the missionaries' policies of providing food and clothing to Ojibwe men in exchange for their labor and the fur traders' longstanding practice of issuing weekly rations to their French workers. Frenchmen enacted their defeat and dependence every time they accepted those rations. Ojibwe men like Madweweyaash came dangerously close to acquiescing in a similar subordination when they worked for the missionaries in exchange for food and clothing. Working together in one another's fields did not change the fact that subjugation was inherent in any Ojibwe acceptance of hired labor for others, the principal men emphasized. At a time when Americans treated for their lands, Ojibwe men had to stand firm in support of traditional cultural practices if they hoped to avoid the fate of the Frenchmen. The elders concluded their talk with a final admonition couched in cultural comparisons of acceptable and unacceptable behavior. "[W]e had rather have you hunt than work!" they told Madweweyaash.[41]

The elders' advice to Madweweyaash that he pursue hunting rather than hired labor recapitulated a series of Ojibwe understandings about the nature of the social, political, and economic world they inhabited in the early nineteenth century. By this time Ojibwes had observed Europeans for close to two centuries, gaining much from their involvement in the fur trade and their alliance with the French but also seeing much to concern them. The repercussions of the French defeat in the Seven Years' War continued to reverberate through the Ojibwe world in the first decades of the nineteenth century as they confronted an aggressive and increasingly powerful United States bent on territorial expansion. If the dependent fur trade laborer was always a politically charged symbol reminding Ojibwes who they were and who they were not, that symbolism only became more compelling as Ojibwes confronted the region's first settler-colonial power. The symbolic figure of the Frenchman, though still associated with the fur trade and its draconian labor regime, had by the early nineteenth century gained another disquieting political dimension. As American officials negotiated for a land sale and American missionaries demanded Ojibwe men perform wage labor under the very conditions that had previously separated them from dependent Frenchmen, the expression "to work like a Frenchman" took on heightened significance. The labor of Frenchmen now represented the future that Americans envisioned for Ojibwes. Toiling for wages under the supervision of another male, unable even to feed themselves, Ojibwes would literally embody their subordination to the Americans as the defeated French had been forced to do.

Yet as Ojibwe men contemplated the degraded labor of Frenchmen, they drew no parallels to the work of Ojibwe women. Ojibwe society possessed a gendered division of labor, but Ojibwes did not construct it based on hierarchic power relations between men and women. Instead, Ojibwes emphasized gender complementarity, viewing the gendered labor of women and men as coequal components that together comprised a whole. This Ojibwe emphasis on mutuality was evident even in those forms of labor such as ricing or hunting where the work itself was associated with, and mainly performed by, one gender or another. In this context, Susan Sleeper-Smith's *Indigenous Prosperity and American Conquest; Indian Women of the Ohio River Valley, 1690–1792*, offers an astute elaboration of the differing gendered impact of settler colonialism on Native men and women. As Sleeper-Smith documents, eastern Great Lakes Native women's labor abundantly fed and sheltered tribal villages even in the most perilous years of warfare and contestation in the eighteenth century, providing cultural and societal continuity as well as nourishment. Several decades later in the early nineteenth century, Ojibwe women were still able to provide for their families and communities. Their emblematic gendered labor was not threatened in the same ways that Ojibwe men experienced, underscoring the intra-gendered specificity of the danger posed by Frenchmen's labor. Ojibwe men's work was imperiled, but not because they were being forced to change their own most meaningful labor for work they socially constructed as properly belonging to women. It was the coerced labor of other men that represented the peril that Ojibwe men confronted.[42]

Facing the challenges of an aggressive new settler-colonial power in the Great Lakes region, Ojibwe men redeployed an image of the French that they had earlier developed to depict fur trade labor relations, reconceptualizing it to fit the new realities of the early nineteenth century. The Ojibwe reconfiguration of the Frenchmen stands as an example of transformations in Native intellectual traditions generated from within Native communities, an instance of Native knowledge production. Simultaneously, the changes Ojibwes made to their imagery of the Frenchman also widens the lens on Native constructions of gender. It moves beyond the usual emphasis on male-female binaries to consider other ways gender could be comprehended and mobilized in societies where it was configured differently than in the societies of Europeans and their North American descendants. Ojibwe men's creation of an intra-gendered symbol that served to critique men other than themselves provides an example of how such gendered constructs might be imagined. The unique historical circumstances of coercive fur trade labor relations, ongoing rivalries between competing European colonial powers, and the emergence of the United States as a new settler-colonial nation all contributed to the intellectual environment in which Ojibwe men constructed the Frenchman as a potent yet malleable symbol of what they were not and must not become.

Although Americans often noted Ojibwe men possessed a sense of personal and national superiority and occasionally recorded epithets that contrasted Ojibwe men with Frenchmen, their overall preoccupation remained what they perceived as Ojibwe male and female gender roles and relations. As the United States gained greater ascendancy in the Great Lakes country, Ojibwes would find themselves confronting very different expectations of the behavior of men and women. The final chapter of this work explores how two Ojibwe-descended people negotiated changing gender expectations in the middle decades of the nineteenth century at a time when American occupation of the Great Lakes country grew into more of a daily lived reality. Their experiences also involved very different encounters with the emerging racialized identities that Anglo-Americans sought to fasten upon Native and multiracial persons. Each would discover that gender intersected with race in ways that disadvantaged both men and women of color but fell much more heavily on women.

Chapter 5

Navigating the Changing Racial Landscapes of the Great Lakes Country

The Lives of William Whipple Warren and
Matilda Aitken Warren Fontaine, 1822–1857

On June 24, 1847, William Whipple Warren and Matilda Aitken Warren of the town of LaPointe, Wisconsin Territory, experienced an act of racialized and sexualized brutality the likes of which they would never have believed possible. In a town where the fur trade still dominated the economy and social life was still structured according to the fur trade's class and ethnic hierarchies, William and Matilda, the well-educated, English-speaking children of Anglophone traders, were indeed members of the elite. However, they were also multiracial, of Ojibwe, French, and English descent, a fact that had gained new meaning by the 1840s as Anglo-Americans ever more fervently defined "race" as a series of embodied, unchanging, and bounded identities. Physical characteristics such as skin color became newly important in defining one's race, while other cultural attributes, such as education, religion, and occupation, mattered far less. More ominously, one's newly racialized identity also became the definitive factor in determining one's relationship to the American nation. A "white" racialized identity meant social inclusion and privilege, including protection under American laws. An identity as a person of color, in contrast, meant exclusion and dispossession. Anglo-Americans who arrived in the Great Lakes country from eastern states in ever greater numbers in the 1830s and 1840s often viewed as anomalous and threatening those persons they regarded as of "mixed" race. To the great bewilderment and dismay of multiracial persons, Anglo-Americans often treated them as subordinates who had to be violently taught their place in the

American racial order. Yet racialized categories remained fluid and contingent in the Great Lakes country, as they did in other regions of North America where intermarriage had long flourished. People like William and Matilda, who expected their cultural orientation not their phenotype to determine their identity, would find themselves navigating unknown and unpredictable waters in the 1830s and 1840s. They endured acts of violent injustice, yet they also successfully challenged both the Americans' discourses of racialization and their smug predictions that Native peoples would disappear, vanishing from American society as they supposedly disappeared from its landscapes. Predictably, William and Matilda's lives were powerfully shaped by gender, yet each by their actions ensured the ongoing survival of Native peoples in the Great Lakes country.

As a young couple, Matilda and William made their home at the town of LaPointe. An old and cosmopolitan place, LaPointe was home to an Ojibwe community of such significance that it was prominently featured in tribal origin narratives. Its colonial history was also of long duration; French expeditionaries made note of the Native community as early as the 1640s. Fittingly, given the town's long association with the fur trade, its first semipermanent European residents were not missionaries but the explorer-traders Radisson and Groseilliers, who established a winter base camp on nearby Chequamegon Bay in 1660 while they fanned out across the hinterland to trade. The community subsequently weathered imperial warfare, the French trade ban of the early eighteenth century, the replacement of the French colonial regime with the British at the end of the Seven Years' War and, most recently, the arrival of the Americans, whose numbers grew steadily in the years after the War of 1812. By the 1840s, its character as a fur trade hub remained, but the town of LaPointe was also becoming an outpost of the American state in disruptive new ways. It had been designated an outpost of direct American colonial domination in the late 1820s, when a subsidiary office, or Subagency, of the larger Chippewa Agency headquartered at Sault Ste. Marie, Michigan, was located at LaPointe. In 1831, in no small part because a modest, European-style town already existed at LaPointe, the interdenominational American Board of Commissioners for Foreign Missions (ABCFM) selected it as the site of a substantial Protestant mission. As Ojibwes, Odawas, Menominis, Ho-chunks, and other Native peoples of the western Great Lakes began to sell land to the United States, LaPointe also saw an influx of venturesome Anglo-Americans who sought to exploit the region's natural resources. They began commercial lumbering and fishing operations and often dabbled in the petty mercantile trade with Native peoples. Each of these undertakings involved illegal liquor sales to Native individuals.

Reflecting this long history of Native and European interaction, William and Matilda understood themselves as part of the community of multiracial persons who lived in the Great Lakes country and embraced a collective ethnic identity. When speaking French, they called themselves "Bois Brulés." Reflecting the influx of English speakers to the region, initially British subjects and more recently, Anglo-Americans, this population increasingly spoke English, employing "Half Breeds" as a synonym for "Bois Brulés." Significantly, and in keeping with Matilda and William's own self-identity, they did not view their multiracial heritage as incompatible with an identity as "whites," based on their social, economic, and cultural orientations. Following time-tested strategies of incorporating foreigners that were as old as the fur trade, the multiracial population of LaPointe continued to absorb newcomers, utilizing old practices such as marriage while developing new ways to create ties with Americans through mutual membership in Protestant churches and employment by the Indian Agency. William, widely regarded as one of the region's most fluent and accurate bilingual speakers of Ojibwe and English, was in fact employed as a US Government Interpreter. While aware of the socioeconomic changes occurring at LaPointe, the Warrens were sheltered by their elite status within the town's class hierarchy. They experienced few of the economic, political, and social dislocations that accompanied the American assumption of power. The events of June 24 took them completely by surprise; little in their lives up to that point had prepared the young couple for what happened. [1]

Matilda Warren was in her home at LaPointe on that day, nursing her ten-month-old daughter, Cordelia. With her were several extended family members—three of her husband's sisters, Charlotte, Sophia, and Julia Warren, who ranged in age from sixteen to ten, and two male houseguests: Michel DuFault, a cousin of her husband, and Henry Blatchford, an Ojibwe-descended convert to Protestant Christianity and the interpreter at the ABCFM mission at LaPointe. Matilda's husband was not initially present when James P. Hays, the Indian subagent stationed at La Pointe and William's superior officer in the military-inflected nomenclature of the US Indian Office, entered the house. Hays was, in Blatchford's words, "under the influence of Liquor." He proceeded to embrace the resistant Matilda, rip her clothing "in several places," choke her, and try to strike her "for resisting his attempts." According to a second eyewitness, Michel DuFault, Hays ignored the fact that Matilda had "her child at the Breast and "embrac[ed] with all his might the mother," threatening to smother the child in the process. Matilda succeeded in repulsing Hays, however, after which he turned to her young sisters-in-law, "chasing" them and "tearing the[ir] dresses." At this point William returned to the house and tried to defuse the horrific situation, "remonstrating" with Hays on his "shameful conduct" and appealing to him to behave "as a gentleman and an officer of Govt." Hays responded by summarily firing William, taking "pen and ink to discharge him." Hays then staggered from the house ostensibly to mail the letter of dismissal. In reality, he continued on the drunken binge that had been going on for over two weeks and would continue for a third. The Warren family was left distraught and shaken, Matilda, no doubt, most of all. [2]

The days that followed were full of frantic activity. Most immediately, the family that William and Matilda supported—their two children, William's three sisters, and a niece—faced homelessness and impoverishment. Their only source of income was William's salary and they lived in a house provided by William's now-former employer, the American government. As they scrambled to pack their belongings and find temporary lodgings, Matilda and William also struggled to understand what had happened to them. Hays's violent assault on Matilda and her young sisters-in-law, with its implicit assumption that they were sexual prey based on their racialized status as women of color, forced the Warrens to confront unsettling realities about the nature of the American occupation of LaPointe. Their own high social rank, respectability, and cultivation of ties with the newly arrived American population should have served to prevent such an attack. So too should William's frequently expressed identification as an American which he claimed as a birthright because his father was an American citizen and seconded by the fact of his government employment. That none of this evidence of membership in LaPointe's elite mattered was deeply troubling. Hays's intemperance and his position as William's immediate superior officer only compounded the problem.[3]

Just as the sexual assault on Matilda revealed that Indigenous women were being racialized in ways that made them newly vulnerable to violent attacks, subsequent events also expose the gendered differences in the ways William and Matilda responded to the experience. Their understandings were complex, since they lived and functioned, sometimes simultaneously, in three cultural milieus. The first was the fur trade society in which they were raised; the second, which increasingly intersected with the first, was the Anglo-American world to which they were exposed through their schooling, residence in towns like LaPointe, and William's employment by the Indian Office. The third, which exercised a powerful influence on the first, was the society and culture of the Ojibwe people, among whom they had relatives and among whom they frequently lived. William's reactions and observations are more easily accessible, as several his writings survive. Matilda's thoughts are far less knowable. None of her correspondence is known to exist, nor is she quoted, nor are her thoughts described in the writings of others. Yet in their actions as well as William's writing, the young couple revealed their abilities to operate in differing cultural environments, deploying gendered skills from one or more of their cultural backgrounds as the situation warranted as they dealt with the assault and the loss of their home and livelihood. At the same time, it is critical to exercise caution in reconstructing and analyzing events and not be deceived by William's greater prominence due to his extant written correspondence. When writing to American officials William presented himself in ways that accorded with early nineteenth century Anglo-American cultural and social norms. This had the effect of, among other things, rendering Matilda almost invisible, while also implying she took no part in salvaging the family from their predicament. There is great irony in this, for the first act taken by the Warrens appears to have been initiated by Matilda in the days immediately following June 24. While William utilized his American-style proficiency as interpreter and clerk to write letters to American officials protesting his firing and seeking reinstatement to his job, Matilda employed skills that generations of Native and Native-descended women had carefully cultivated. Drawing on her kinship network, she sent word to her father, William A. Aitken, a former American Fur Company trader who operated an independent trading post in the Minnesota Territory along the Mississippi River at a small settlement called Swan River south of the town of Little Falls. Not only did she secure a place for the family to stay, but William also apparently received assurances of temporary employment at his father-in-law's establishment while the family got back on its feet.[4]

The Warrens also enjoyed considerable support within the LaPointe community. Sexual assaults on Indigenous women seem to have been increasing as greater numbers of Americans arrived in the town, and the attack on a woman such as Matilda, who was of high social status and locally understood to be "white," only heightened the anxiety of the region's inhabitants. Ojibwes, for it was women locally constructed as Ojibwes who bore the brunt of these attacks, very likely approached William in the days after June 24 to express their concern and inquire into the family's well-being. A number of European-descended residents, appalled by Hays's alcoholic rampages, had already written complaints to federal officials; they advised William to do likewise. William also had the support of members of the American national government, particularly territorial officials. As a U.S. Interpreter, and a highly valued one at that, William was a federal government employee. At the urging of some of his allies, William wrote to protest his dismissal to Wisconsin territorial governor Henry Dodge, the official who was both William's and James Hays's superior. William also collected the affidavits of Michel DuFault and Henry Blatchford, the two male eyewitnesses to Hays's sexual assaults, and enclosed them in his letter to Dodge. He crafted that letter with great care, revealing his own familiarity with the nuances of Anglo-American culture, especially its growing commitment to gender-based separate spheres that relegated women to the private domestic world of the home while men occupied the rough-and-tumble public sphere of business, commerce, and politics. William also positioned himself within a culture of elite masculine professionalism, framing the confrontation with Hays as an issue to be resolved dispassionately by rational gentlemen and minimizing the assault (and its explicitly sexual nature) on his wife and sisters.[5]

William Warren commenced his letter by describing himself as a "young man endeavoring to bear a good name." Reflecting his nine years' education in religiously oriented, progressive, educational academies in upstate New York, he identified himself with what he understood to be an American elite composed of educated, public-spirited men of republican virtue and respectability. "I owe it to my good character," he added, to protest his unwarranted dismissal. After establishing that he did not act from base or vengeful (or merely "personal") motives, William emphasized that his concern stemmed from the larger political effects of Hays's actions. The subagent's behavior, he declared, was "most pernicious to the interests of the Government." Positioning himself as a knowledgeable, on-the-ground Indian Office employee, William warned that Hayes "[b]y his conduct of late . . . has lost the respect of both whites and Indians." The precise conduct that had lost Hays local respect was left unspecified and William was similarly discreet in describing why he had chided Hayes "[f]or most shamefully abusing my family and insulting strangers under my roof." Once more William deployed American constructions of appropriate behavior, this time calling forth ideologies of gender and class. He represented himself as an upright citizen whose patriarchal prerogatives had been unconscionably violated. By implication, of course, such a citizen was male. As such a gendered citizen of the American republic, William claimed not only the growing ideology of whiteness as his defense; he harked back to the language of political equality originating in the Revolutionary era. A male citizen could expect to be secure in his home and in his ability to protect his dependents. "Every man rich and poor alike is protected by the good laws of our country," William observed. In this male-centered telling of events, Matilda Aitken Warren was cast as a victim, but she was simultaneously minimized, almost to the point of erasure. Hays's attempted rape and whatever trauma or injury she might have suffered were framed not as physical attacks on Matilda's person but as assaults on William's honor and masculine privilege.[6]

At this point, the Warrens' personal difficulties collided with a larger series of unforeseen events. The American national government, anticipating the Wisconsin Territory would soon apply for statehood, sought to negotiate a series of treaties containing removal provisions with the territory's several Native nations, among them Ojibwes, Ho-chunks, and Menominis. Plans had been underway since the previous winter of 1846–47 to convene a treaty council with the Ojibwes of the Wisconsin and Minnesota territories to be held during the summer of 1847, but the effort had been fraught with problems and delays. On June 17, 1847, Commissioner of Indian Affairs William Medill, fearing something was amiss, wrote to Henry Rice of the Minnesota Territory. Rice, a fur trader and land speculator, had been involved in the initial plans for the series of regional removal treaties. He had also recently concluded such a cession-and-removal treaty with the Wisconsin Ho-Chunks. Medill asked the ambitious trader to join the commission at LaPointe to ensure the Ojibwe treaty came to fruition. By a remarkable coincidence, Rice met William Warren on the road as Rice was traveling east and William was making his way west. "I met him on his way to the Mississippi," Rice said of William, indicating that the Warrens were traveling in the direction of Matilda's father's trading post at Swan River. Rice also learned the reason for William's departure, of Hays's assault on Matilda, and that William had lost his job. Realizing that the LaPointe Subagency now lacked a qualified interpreter just as treaty negotiations were about to commence and "knowing that his [William's] service would be indispensable [sic]," Rice "brought him back to [LaPointe]." The two men arrived at LaPointe on June 30 where they would remain for several weeks.[7]

In all likelihood Matilda Warren, with five youngsters in her care, continued the journey of over four hundred miles to Swan River, leaving William to return to LaPointe with Henry Rice.[8] Precisely where Rice and the Warrens met on their respective travels to and from LaPointe is unclear, though it would appear that they were quite close to the fur trade town. William Warren was in LaPointe as late as June 28, when he collected the affidavits of Blatchford and DuFault. Since he and Henry Rice returned to LaPointe on June 30, it would appear the Warrens had left to begin their long journey on the 29th and encountered Rice the same day. The Indian agent Hays had remained in LaPointe, still binge drinking, for several days after his sexual assaults on Matilda and William's younger sisters on June 24, which surely provided a powerful additional incentive for the women of the Warren family to continue once they commenced their journey. Matilda was also fully capable of such a voyage. She had traveled by canoe and on foot between Ojibwe villages and her father's fur trade posts since her early childhood, so the trip to Swan River would not have been beyond her experience or abilities. William would not join the family at Swan River until sometime in mid-August. His role in negotiating what came to be the 1847 Treaty of Fond du Lac would occupy all of July and the early days of August. At the treaty's conclusion, he returned once more to LaPointe to seek medical treatment for an injury he had received the preceding winter. The annuity payments for two treaties previously negotiated in 1837 and 1842 with the Ojibwes were also scheduled for late August, and William returned to LaPointe for these payments. Matilda very probably spent the summer months establishing the family's new household at Swan River. In creating and sustaining a household for her family, Matilda would once again have performed the types of respected labor that Ojibwe and Ojibwe-descended women considered emblematic of their gender. In particular, women worked to acquire the ability to provision their families. This underappreciated activity involved close observation of seasonally available land- and water-based food resources as well as developing preservation, storage, and cooking techniques that allowed women to provide daily food for their kinfolk as well as demonstrate their generosity by gifting food to other households. Perhaps such familiar and valued work also afforded Matilda a degree of solace and renewed self-esteem in the wake of Hays's assault.[9]

While Matilda settled the Warren family at their new home in Minnesota, William and Henry Rice took stock of the inauspicious situation at LaPointe. Subagent Hays had disappeared for parts unknown about June 27, apparently taking with him the subagency's official books and papers. No preparations for the treaty council had been made because Hays, in Rice's contemptuous words, had "been beastly intoxicated for three weeks." Furthermore, the treaty commissioners were late in arriving. On August 5 when the head commissioner, General Isaac A. Verplanck of Batavia, New York finally reached LaPointe, he had his

own tale of miscommunication and mishaps. His attempts to obtain information from the Indian Office about departure dates and travel times to the Wisconsin Territory had gone unanswered and he brought the additional news that
the second commissioner, Charles A. Mix, the knowledgeable long-time clerk
in the Indian Office, had fallen seriously ill at Detroit and would be returning
to Washington once he was well enough to travel. Between them, Verplanck,
Rice, and William Warren hurriedly set about preparing to host a major treaty
council with important Ojibwe leaders representing some twenty communities from both the Wisconsin and Minnesota territories. They began by hiring
such necessary local personnel as messengers and voyageurs and purchasing
"canoes, tents [,] provisions for the [treaty] party [and] provisions for the Indians." Although William had been fired as U.S. Government Interpreter, Verplanck hired him temporarily as "Interpreter for the U. States in Treaty." Their
preparations begun, Verplanck and Warren set out in mid-July for Fond du Lac,
an Ojibwe village and the site of an American Fur Company trading post where
they had determined to hold the treaty negotiations. Located at the western
end of Lake Superior, Fond du Lac was two to three day's travel by canoe from
LaPointe, barring inclement weather. Henry Rice remained behind to escort
Wisconsin Ojibwe leaders who were gathering first at LaPointe before making
the trip to Fond du Lac.[10]

While William Warren was engaged with the treaty negotiations, his letter detailing Hays's behavior worked its way through official channels, reaching
Washington, DC, coincidentally on August 2, 1847, the date that the Treaty of
Fond du Lac was concluded. Henry Dodge, the Territorial Governor of Wisconsin to whom William had initially written, had forwarded the letter with its
accompanying affidavits to William Medill, the Commissioner of Indian Affairs,
adding his own blunt assessment of the seriousness of subagent Hays's alcoholism. Hays was "frequently intoxicated," Dodge wrote, and "when in that state
[he] looses [sic] his senses." Testily, Dodge reminded the Commissioner that
Warren's letter was not the first time the Indian Office had received complaints
about Hays's behavior. "[S]everal respectable gentlemen whose veracity can be
relied on" had previously reported the subagent's uncontrollable drinking. He
closed his letter with the curt recommendation that Hays "should be removed
from office." While Dodge's remarks reveal that Warren's complaints were not
the first to be lodged against the subagent, the graphic contents of the affidavits
may have pushed Medill into finally launching an investigation of Hays. Such
an investigation was, apparently, on some level already being contemplated. On

July 21, Hays had learned through another Indian Office employee, William Richmond, the Indian Superintendent of the neighboring state of Michigan, that "representations unfavorable to my conduct and habits had been made to [the Indian] Department." A month later, Richmond notified Hays that he would soon be arriving at LaPointe to "make enquiries concerning certain complaints preferred against you." The helpful Richmond further assured Hays that he would share "all the facts and information in my possession," and that the subagent would have "the opportunity for any explanation or defense you may wish to make."[11]

Hays wasted no time in responding to the charges. Although Indian Office officials considered his most egregious offence to be his absence from his post when Commissioner Verplanck arrived to negotiate with the Ojibwes, Hays recognized that the more damaging issues were the accusations of public drunkenness and "abusing the wife and family of Mr. Wm. W. Warren." A member of a wealthy, respected, and politically influential early-settler family in western Pennsylvania's Venango County, Hays had long struggled to control his alcoholism. His appointment as Indian subagent was a desperate effort to relocate him to a place where he had no access to liquor undertaken by his brother, Alexander, and his father, General Samuel Hays, who had recently completed a term in the 28th Congress of 1843–44 and would have been aware of the patronage possibilities of the Indian Office. Under the Trade and Intercourse Acts, the United States had committed itself to preventing the introduction of alcohol into unorganized territories where Native peoples still lived on unceded tribal lands. A seemingly isolated spot like LaPointe in the western Great Lakes must have appeared an ideal environment to a beleaguered family from the eastern United States. Free of alcoholic temptation, Hays and his family hoped he could master his cravings and rehabilitate his reputation. Hays especially needed to demonstrate his newfound social respectability to reclaim a position of privilege as a member of a socially and politically prominent family. Hays crafted a letter that, like Warren's, drew on cultural tropes and popular assumptions common in 1840s Anglo-America. Yet where Warren invoked the ideals of the early republic with its admonitions of Christian responsibility toward strangers and assertions that personal character rather than inherited social rank determined one's respectability and moral worth, Hays embraced an identity as a member of a permanent landowning upper class, a "gentleman." Affirming the same long-standing popular associations between wealth and moral probity that William rejected, Hays insisted that high-ranking men like himself possessed inborn

qualities that placed them above suspicion of bad behavior. Throughout his letters defending his conduct, Hays repeatedly implied his gentlemanly character
and high social rank.[12]

Hays began his defense by manipulating language and selectively utilizing
facts to diminish his culpability. Responding first to "[t]he charge of abusing Mr
Warrens family," Hays disguised the fact that he had committed violent sexual assaults on Matilda Warren and at least two of William's younger sisters
by describing the charge as one of mistreating undifferentiated family members.[13] Ignoring the affidavit of Henry Blatchford, the literate, bilingual interpreter at the ABCFM mission who penned his own statement, Hays focused on
the shorter, less detailed affidavit of Michel DuFault. This artful framing thus
suggested there was only one eyewitness to his assaults on the Warren women.
He characterized DuFault as "a half breed boy," and "an inmate of Mr Warrens
family," stressing DuFault's unreliability on account of his youth, his race, and
his dependent position in the Warren household. Claiming he had never seen
the DuFault affidavit, which appears improbable given Richmond's willingness to hand over all the documents in the case, Hays denied direct knowledge
of the charges against him. "I . . . know not what it [the affidavit] contains or
in what the abuse consisted," he declared, further disguising his drunken violence against four Native-descended women. He attempted to further discredit
DuFault's testimony by implying that William Warren had had an additional
opportunity to put words in the mouth of "the boy" because Warren had interpreted when the French-speaking DuFault appeared before a local justice of
the peace to swear his affidavit. Having thus reframed the issues involving the
Warren family in ways that minimized his own misdeeds, Hays simultaneously
reasserted his class position, while subtly linking class with race by his identification of DuFault as a "half breed." [14]

As he attempted to substitute his narrative of the encounter at the Warren
family home for William's letter and affidavits, Hays further utilized the act of
composition and letter-writing stylistics to signal his class status (and by implication the privileges that should go with it) in subtle but meaningful ways. He
adopted a supercilious tone; composed lengthy, complex sentences; and employed
British rather than American spellings for several words to suggest an advanced,
hence upper-class, education. He belittled Richmond as a social inferior, scold-
ing the Michigan Indian Superintendent for his failure to ask LaPointe's elite,
by which he meant its newly arrived Anglo-American elite, for their opinions
on the validity of Warren's charges. "Such is my character here," Hays claimed,

that if Richmond had "seen proper to make inquiries of any or all [persons] of respectable standing who have known me," Warren's allegations would have been dismissed as unworthy of consideration. After rebuking Richmond for conducting such an inadequate investigation, Hays then condescended to help. "I shall endeavour [sic] to procure the statements of such persons as may be known to you and cognisant [sic] of the manner in which I have always treated Mr W and his family & transmit them herewith," he wrote. Hays had in reality already acquired letters testifying to his good character from several members of LaPointe's American elite, among them the superintendent of the ABCFM mission, a second missionary at the institution, and a government farmer. Not only were these men upright representatives of American settler society, but they also shared Hays's understanding of how class, race, and gender privileges converged to shield elite white men from the consequences of their actions. The three American newcomers all made note of Hays's high rank and described his treatment of the Warren family as "gentlemanly." Each also referred to the subagent using the respectful if old-fashioned honorific "Esquire," which Sherman Hall, the mission superintendent also used to address the Indian Agent Henry R. Schoolcraft. In attesting to Hays's good character, Hall went so far as to exonerate the subagent, giving it as his "opinion that Mr. Hays had no criminal intention in any of his conduct towards Mrs. W."[15]

Reassured, perhaps, by the endorsements he received from LaPointe's Anglo-American elite, Hays turned his attention to discrediting William Warren. Once again, he attempted to shift the narrative to privilege his own point of view, providing only partial answers and reframing questions to obscure facts or imply contrary meanings. Although Richmond had made it clear that he was charged with investigating several complaints made against Hays by a number of individuals, Hays insisted that the only person who had filed a complaint was William Warren. "If you have also taken the trouble to examine into the origin of the charges made against me," Hays again chided Richmond, "you will I am convinced have found that they all emanate from the same source." Far more disturbing was Hays's treatment of the charge that he had been under the influence of alcohol when he fired William Warren. Continuing to avoid any discussion of the Blatchford affidavit, the frankest and most detailed statement of his drunken condition on the day he fired Warren, Hays told a lie. "If anyone states that I was intoxicated at the time I gave the notice to Mr Warren," he declared, "he states an untruth."[16]

By dismissing or obfuscating the most serious charges against him, however, Hays found himself hard-pressed to provide a defensible reason for firing a man widely regarded as "the best Interpreter in the country." Based on a conversation the two men had had while they were visiting Ojibwe villages in the early winter of 1847 to gauge the amount of support for the upcoming treaty, Hays attempted to prove Warren was disloyal to their mutual employer, the United States government. As proof, he offered Warren's conjectural remarks about what he might do if faced with a particular ethical dilemma. Such hypothetical speculations hardly amounted to conclusive proof, however, and Hays had no further evidence to offer of Warren's alleged disloyalty. Interestingly, Hays did not introduce Warren's multiracial heritage as a means to discredit him, as he had done with Michel DuFault. Warren's social and cultural orientations—his style of dress and comportment, his English-language fluency, and his education in academies in the United States—were so unmistakably perceived as "American" at LaPointe and in Washington that Hays may have realized such a line of attack would not be credible. Although he never referred to Warren's race, one can perhaps glean in Hays's accusations of Warren's disloyalty to the United States a level of animosity toward a well-educated multiracial man who claimed both an American identity and a social equality that Hays was not prepared to grant him. Hays's attempt to have Warren fired from his job as an American government employee clearly had its roots in his desire to retaliate against the man who had not been cowed by his assertion of class privilege and had instead brought serious criminal charges against him. Hays's efforts to discredit Warren can further be read as an attempt to refuse—on the basis of a racialized identity that foregrounded phenotype over cultural orientation—Warren the inclusion within the United States and the equal treatment under its laws that he claimed.[17]

Ultimately, it would be the political tumult and intrigue surrounding the negotiation of the 1847 Treaty of Fond du Lac and not Hays's vengeful efforts, that would cost William Warren his job. As official interpreter and unabashed ally of the treaty commissioners, Warren earned the special enmity of the powerful American Fur Company (AFC). He enthusiastically supported head commissioner Verplanck's objective to negotiate a treaty "without fraud," "without presents," and "without providing for the debts claimed by the Fur Company." The proverbial ink was still drying on the treaty's manuscript pages when the "Lepointe gentlemen," in Verplanck's dry phrase, commenced their counterattack. Seasoned traders were dispatched to Washington to lobby members of Congress to oppose ratification of the treaty and local operatives orchestrated a letter-writing campaign at the late August annuity payments, held at LaPointe about three weeks after the treaty commissioners had concluded their work and disbanded. A small group of Ojibwes, whom Verplanck characterized as among the less-influential leaders present at the treaty, complained of fraud and coercion in the negotiations and in the signing procedures. These "seven Indians" criticized the poor quality of the interpretation and, while naming no names, alleged that an interpreter had threatened them, warning them that they would lose their annuities if they refused to sign the treaty. Despite Warren's best efforts, which included letters of support from commissioners Verplanck and Rice, the AFC's clout in Washington proved too formidable. The company scuttled Warren's attempts to win reinstatement as US interpreter. At this point, with the treaty completed and the annuity payments over, Warren concluded there was nothing left for him at LaPointe. He accepted an offer from Henry Rice to clerk at the latter's trading post and moved to Crow Wing, a town located on land that would in a few short years be formally organized as the Minnesota Territory. A cheerful, optimistic person, Warren remembered being driven from LaPointe, his birthplace and home of his mother's Ojibwe and French relatives, with uncharacteristic bitterness. "I have seen hard times," he wrote to his cousin George Warren two years later in 1849, "Dire necessity amid a host of enemies drove me from my birth place to pitch my tent among strangers."[18]

Although William considered himself unjustly forced to abandon LaPointe, the family's move to Crow Wing ended up being quite fortuitous. In 1847, Crow Wing was a small outpost located at the confluence of the Mississippi and Crow Wing Rivers. Fur traders had periodically established posts at this crossroads dating at least as far back as the mid-eighteenth century, but it assumed new importance for Americans after the 1837 Treaty of Fort Snelling. By this treaty the Ojibwes ceded a tract of land on the eastern side of the Mississippi, placing Crow Wing on the border between American national territory and the remaining unceded Ojibwe homeland. Anticipating the money to be made by establishing a store or trading post so near the lands of a tribal nation that received annuity payments, traders such as Henry Rice began to congregate along the river in the years following the 1837 treaty. William and Matilda Warren rented a good-sized building at Rice's trading compound and began the task of reassembling their lives. In addition to William's work as a clerk and interpreter for Rice, the Warrens opened a boarding house, "accommodating all comers" in the building they rented. Rice's unmarried workmen also took their meals with the Warrens and, William reported proudly, when an American military fort was constructed about six miles downriver in 1848, soldiers "come most every day for the sake of getting a good meal." Within a year William was feeling he had recouped the family's financial losses and could look forward to a new level of economic stability. "[W]henever he writes," Henry Blatchford observed, "the theme of his letters is telling about being so well off." Still further evidence of returning normalcy occurred in May 1848, when Matilda gave birth to the couple's third child.[19]

William's ongoing concern with ensuring the family's financial security, which loomed especially large in his correspondence in the years just after the family's forced departure from LaPointe, obscures as well as reveals. Reflecting the social practices of his day, which strictly separated the public world of men from the private world of women, William seldom spoke of Matilda in his letters, except in the most prosaic and conventional of terms, as when he wrote in March 1849 that "My wife and children and the girls [his sisters] have enjoyed good health." He also employed the patriarchal convention of subsuming the entire family's activities under his own singular pronoun. "I have got to keeping a Boarding house at this place," he informed his cousin George in that same year. Such comments leave the impression that Matilda took no part in supporting the family, which was certainly the middle class aspirational ideal, but it is contradicted by information that is known or can be inferred about her. In the days immediately following Hays's assaults on her and her sisters-in-law, it was Matilda who likely moved the family to her father's Swan River trading post. She apparently maintained the household at Swan River largely by herself while William spent much of July, August, and September away from home, initially engaged in the work of negotiating the 1847 treaty, and subsequently returning to LaPointe for medical treatment and to attend the annuity payments. Since the couple's third child was born May 20, 1848, Matilda likely conceived in late August 1847, indicating William was able to visit the family at Swan River at least occasionally. Nevertheless, his many trips over the summer months would have left the daily provisioning and care of the family to Matilda.[20]

Once the family moved to Crow Wing, Matilda's work in support of the household was even more important, though again it went largely unrecognized and is revealed only in glimpses in the surviving historical records. Nonetheless, much can be inferred from those brief mentions. William's comment that he was keeping a boarding house completely ignored the significant amount of skilled knowledge and routine physical labor that Matilda brought to that family enterprise. Of his own contribution to the meals offered at the boarding house, William wrote that he had "been able to go about hunting this spring for ducks and fish" and could thus "set a good table for my Boarders." Absent from this remark is any acknowledgement of the work that transformed a newly shot duck into a dinnertime entrée. That labor, subsumed under the trivializing label of "cooking," involved cleaning, plucking, and butchering animal carcasses, plus knowledge of fire-making and maintaining the appropriate cooking temperatures for the several foods being prepared simultaneously at an open hearth. Extensive familiarity with the wild or "country" foods of the region would also have allowed Matilda to provide vegetables, greens, and the all-important staple wild rice to supplement boarding house menus that otherwise would have run heavily to potatoes and dried legumes. As a young girl, Matilda had absorbed much of this knowledge of the land's resources from her own mother. While at the Mackinaw boarding school she had added a variety of European-derived skills to her repertoire, including baking bread using wheat flour and yeast and the construction, washing, ironing, and mending of European-style clothing. In addition to the daily labor of running the household, Matilda doubtless also educated William's two younger sisters, Charlotte and Sophia, who still lived in the family, in what Anglo-Americans called the arts of housewifery. Caring for a family of seven people, one a newborn, plus accommodating fluctuating numbers of daily diners (as many as fifteen on some Sundays) certainly attests to Matilda's skill at household management. Such "women's work" was undervalued and often invisible in the Anglo-American world, but it is important to pay attention to the significance of Matilda's land-based knowledge and provisioning skills. The Warren family's new economic stability was grounded in Matilda's specific Indigenous women's knowledge as well as her considerable physical labor on behalf of the family.[21]

The family prospered in other ways as well. Utilizing his knowledge as a cultural insider, William began to write the essays about Ojibwe history and culture for which he would ultimately be remembered. His first piece, a partial reply to an extensive ethnographic questionnaire circulated by the Office of Indian Affairs, was probably submitted to the *Minnesota Pioneer* by Henry Rice, to whom the initial request for information had been sent in 1848. First published in the September 6, 1849, edition of the paper, it garnered sufficient interest that the *Pioneer*'s editor, D. A. Robinson, published an expanded version of the article in December, acknowledging William's authorship. Encouraged by the positive reception of his first written work, William would publish additional articles while embarking on his most ambitious project, a book-length history of the Ojibwes based on oral narratives and interviews that he conducted with Ojibwe elders and political leaders.[22] In the half-decade following the family's move to Minnesota Territory, he developed a reputation as a literary figure and knowledgeable public intellectual who was unafraid to take controversial positions respecting Native issues, especially as they involved Ojibwes. He was a frequent contributor to newspaper debates and participated in territorial politics, serving one term in 1851 in the newly organized territorial legislature as a representative from Benton County.[23]

In all his public-facing activities, William Warren continued to describe himself as an Ojibwe "Half Breed," an identity that reflected the long regional history of intermarriage and extended families whose expansive webs of kinfolk crossed the boundaries of tribe, ethnicity, and nation. In many ways, however, he was a unique intellect, a product of a lived experience that differed substantially from those of most multiracial French-descended persons in the western Great Lakes. A devout Protestant rather than a Catholic who had spent six years living in New York State while attending school and had worked in both formal and informal capacities as an interpreter between Ojibwes and Americans, Warren had a great deal more familiarity with the United States and a northern variant of its culture and society than most multiracial men of his time. He thought deeply about how Ojibwes and "their half-breed relations" would face a future certain to be dominated by the United States. His opinions are thus of particular interest as he navigated changing definitions of social identity in the 1840s and 1850s, by which time Americans had reimagined "race" as an unchanging, physically embodied identity, replacing the older understandings founded in cultural orientation and nationality. Warren regarded Ojibwes and Half Breeds as significantly different from one another in most aspects of their societies—their economic organization, political institutions, cultural practices, and, critical to his mind, their religious beliefs and traditions. Nonetheless, precisely because he inhabited a social world where kinship bridged seemingly bounded categories, he also believed them to be connected by "the strongest ties" of kin.[24]

The expansiveness of Warren's reflections is further demonstrated by his willingness to think beyond the affective ties of kinship to consider another, more material bond that united these two social collectivities. Both Ojibwes and their Half Breed relatives were united by what Warren described as "our common interest" in the Ojibwe land base. Although Half Breeds and Ojibwes gained their subsistence in different ways, both relied on the land's resources. His close association with American government officials, traders, and land speculators convinced Warren that the United States was going to continue its colonial expansion into the western Great Lakes and both Ojibwes and Half Breeds were going to need to make difficult economic, social, and political changes as a result. Along with other young, western-educated Half Breeds, including several of his cousins on both the Warren and Cadotte sides of his family and his friend Henry Blatchford, William strategized to ensure that treaties would be negotiated "in a manner which will conduce best for the interests of the Indians as well as our own." As these young Indigenous intellectuals conceived of the future of their related peoples, treaties would not just provide an equitable distribution of land; they would be the foundation upon which Ojibwes and Half Breeds would build an ongoing place for themselves as modern people in the modern world. They were not unique in this respect, as is revealed by the recent work of Christina Snyder on the Choctaws and other tribal nations who sent their sons to the first federal boarding school, the famed Choctaw Academy. Located at Great Crossings, Kentucky, the school, which accepted only young men, operated between 1825 and 1848, graduating over six hundred Native youth. Well-versed in a body of canonical western knowledge, these young men crafted a series of arguments that disputed the new Anglo-American constructions of Native peoples as racialized inferiors incapable of social adaptation or change.[25]

While William's thinking echoed that of other Native intellectuals with its commitment to adaptation and modernity, it reflected the unique circumstances of western Great Lakes Ojibwes and Half Breeds. While Warren foresaw dramatic changes for both, he predicted different trajectories for the two groups of relatives. Ever optimistic, his fervent belief in the transformative power of Christianity assured him that Ojibwes would ultimately transition to a version of American agrarian society that would bring them spiritual and physical comforts previously unknown to them, while allowing them to adapt to the challenging times of the mid-nineteenth century. As might be anticipated, he accepted the Enlightenment-influenced social-evolutionist theory that "savage" Native societies could not survive when placed in proximity to superior "civilized" societies, like that of the United States. Much as he admired aspects of Ojibwe culture, Warren firmly believed that Ojibwes too needed to adopt American "civilization" or they would perish, a sentiment that was only strengthened as he witnessed the growing numbers of American emigrants to the western Great Lakes and experienced the disruptions caused by their presence. Ojibwes "are fast degenerating under the influence of contact with the whites," he wrote soberly in 1849. He placed particular emphasis on equitable treaties that provided solid, culturally specific economic foundations and recognized the differing needs and skills of Ojibwes and Half Breeds. Ojibwes needed a "guaranteed" land base with a "perpetual annuity" to provide the all-important funding necessary for "their eventual civilization." In this protected state, the younger generations would convert to Christianity, the first and most important adaptation to William's mind, then with the passage of time would come to accept the several other components that composed Anglo-American culture and society.[26]

While Warren believed that Ojibwes would gradually adopt such hallmarks of "civilized" life as "living by agriculture, owning farms, and stock, living in houses and professing the religion of the whites," his vision of the future for Half Breeds was markedly different. Half Breeds had already adopted "civilized" institutions and practices. The very social-economic and cultural attributes that Ojibwes needed to accept, Half Breeds, he felt, had already made their own. They were committed to a market economy and recognized private property, especially in landholding. They had long been practicing Christians (Matilda was a devoted Catholic and William was far more tolerant of Catholicism than many Anglo-Americans). Since Half Breeds met the criteria of "civilized" persons, Warren believed they needed no period of tutelage like their Ojibwe relations. They were ready to take their place as American citizens. He pointed to his own success as a writer and public intellectual to argue that multiracial men could prosper and gain acceptance in Anglo-American society. His experiences in Minnesota territory after the family's forced departure from LaPointe convinced him that American society was open to men like himself. "I have come to this country, poor, humble, and sick. By good conduct & perseverance I have gained many strong friends and popularity among the whites and the Indians," he wrote to his cousin George in 1850.[27]

At the same time, William also developed a wider view of Ojibwe-descended persons that encompassed diasporic populations. In 1850, he reached out to the emergent Métis Nation of the Red River region of Manitoba, proposing they "come and live on the American side." "[W]e look upon you as brothers," he wrote to the "Half Breeds of Red River." He invited them to join the American "Chippeway [H]alf Breeds" so "that we might one day be as one body and act in such a manner for our general welfare." Reflecting his usual optimism along with a commonly expressed nineteenth-century American disdain for the continued British presence to their north, he encouraged the Canadian Half Breeds to "become American Citizens." The United States was "a free government" and "will protect you," he explained, contrasting this advantageous situation to colonial governance in western Canada, where the Hudson's Bay Company "rules your country" while its "traders . . . govern you." The "united vote" of the Half Breeds, he assured the Red River people, would guarantee them a secure future in the democratic United States where their political participation would protect and advance their social and economic interests. Tellingly, he also enclosed with his letter a copy of the "Constitution" that the American Half Breeds had written for themselves. While they noted that they "[a]ccept[ed] US law," the "Half Breeds [of] Lake Superior and [the] Mississippi" also laid out forms of local self-governance with a "chief" and an elected "12-person council." William, it seems, was imagining a kind of ongoing local Indigenous sovereignty. Given the long-standing regional logic of assigning racial identities based on cultural orientation and personal attributes, Half Breeds were already "whites." It seems probable that William expected Ojibwes would become "whites," too, once they adopted the "teachings of civilization." Taken together these several populations of Native-descended persons, much-Americanized yet still retaining such important cultural practices as consensus-based local governance, could remain a politically important force in Minnesota and Wisconsin, able to insure their future as equal voting participants with Anglo-Americans.[28]

From the vantage point of the early 1850s, William imagined a future in which the linked kin groups of Ojibwes and Half Breeds would ensure their continued survival through strategic adaptations to the demands of the Anglo-American colonial nation-state. Had he lived, he would likely have continued to advocate for the future of the peoples he regarded as his own, but William was not destined to enjoy a long life. He had never regained his health following the accident he suffered in the winter of 1846–1847. On June 1, 1853, returning from New York City where he had gone to seek medical treatment and locate a publisher for his master work, *The History of the Ojibway People,* William died of a probable pulmonary hemorrhage at the home of his sister Charlotte Warren Price in St. Paul. He was twenty-eight. Either while he was on his homeward journey or shortly after his death, Matilda gave birth to their fourth child, a girl, whom William never saw.

Matilda, now a widow with four children to support, would face a rapidly changing world. The composite societies of the western Great Lakes, knitted together by families of multiple tribal, national, and ethnic origins, would come under increasing assault in the Minnesota Territory as the 1850s progressed. The official organization of the Minnesota Territory by the United States occurred in 1849 and by 1853, the year of William's death, an economic boom was well underway. An emigrant American population surged, as a wave of largely male settler-colonists descended on the territory, anticipating impending statehood and eagerly seeking opportunities to make money. Intent on land speculation or launching profitable logging operations, the newcomers felt no obligation to treat Native peoples with honesty or consideration and were no respecters of fur trade society's cultural norms and practices. Matilda herself confronted the new Anglo-American majority's construction of whiteness as founded in racial purity rather than nationality and cultural orientation. Her subsequent experiences also exposed the gendered component of the new racialized construction of whiteness, revealing how profoundly the combination of race and gender disadvantaged Native and Native-descended women in ways they had not been previously either in Ojibwe or fur trade societies.[29]

At some point after William's death, Matilda formed a new relationship. This union seemed to reflect fur trade mores rather than those of Anglo-Americans, for the couple did not seek a marriage ceremony performed by a clergyman before they began cohabiting. Such informal "custom of the country" marriages had been common throughout the fur trade era, with trade employees and Indigenous and Indigenous-descended women establishing mutually advantageous but not necessarily permanent relationships. The clergy, beginning with the French, pressured European men to wed their wives in indissoluble Christian rites and many did so, but customary marriages were nonetheless widely recognized as legitimate unions by both the Native and fur trade communities. Matilda's parents had first entered into such a "country marriage," and were remarried when Matilda was seven years old by William M. Ferry, a Protestant clergyman who operated a boarding school on Mackinac Island that Matilda and several of her siblings attended. Matilda would thus have been familiar with country marriages and with the community expectations that accompanied them. It was assumed, for instance, that when couples separated, the men would provide some support to former wives and, more especially, to their children.[30]

Matilda's new relationship generated interest among men who had known William, among them former fur traders who had settled in the territorial capital of St. Paul. A new arrival to Minnesota named Sam Abbe was rumored to be the father of the child Matilda bore in 1856. Rather than acknowledge his relationship with Matilda, however, Sam flouted fur trade norms and abandoned Matilda along with his newborn child. In 1857, he returned to New

England where he married an Anglo-American woman, the sister of one of his business partners, and brought her back to Minnesota. To the beleaguered fur trade elite of St. Paul, Sam Abbe's treatment of Matilda Warren not only underscored their declining political and economic power, but it also challenged their symbolic class power. These former traders had long considered themselves the arbiters of "whiteness," while simultaneously policing female sexuality for their own benefit. As the daughter of the Scottish-born fur trader William A. Aitken and widow of William Warren, Matilda was a member of the elite, and that class status should have protected her from exploitation by a man like Sam Abbe. Instead, she experienced the Anglo-American double standard of sexual behavior as it uniquely affected and disadvantaged women of color. Ten years earlier at LaPointe, Matilda's ambiguous racial identity had made it easier for the small newly arrived Anglo-American elite to rally to the defense of another high-ranking white American man who attempted to rape her. The fact that the powerful former fur traders at St. Paul defended her must be placed in the context of the traders' declining economic and political clout and their nostalgia for the old free-wheeling days when the trade was booming, and they might themselves have cohabited (and fathered children) with Indigenous women. Framed as "the widow Warren," Matilda represented the older fur trade-centered society that was under attack from the incoming mass of Anglo-Americans, and they came to her defense. Yet there were limits to their comprehension of Matilda's predicament. While they constructed her as a vulnerable and grieving widow and denounced Sam as a bounder who took advantage of her, they nonetheless cast her as a passive symbol. As a woman, perhaps particularly as an Indigenous woman, they believed she possessed no power of her own.[31]

As in the case of the assault by James Hays, none of Matilda's own words or thoughts appear to have survived. Once more she found herself the subject of a narrative that centered on yet evaded mention of both her sexuality and her racial identity. She was yet again constructed as a victim in a discourse that rendered her even more invisible and silenced than she had been in her husband's earlier letters. Yet just as her actions in the years after the 1847 assault revealed her personal resourcefulness and her central importance in stabilizing the family economically after their hurried departure from LaPointe, her actions in the years after William's death can be reexamined and reinterpreted to focus on Matilda, rather than on the depictions of the nostalgic and self-interested fur trade elite. Such a recentering immediately suggests a different, more nuanced narrative than the moralistic tale of Matilda as a grieving widow hoodwinked by an unscrupulous adventurer. Sam Abbe was not the only one who relocated, although his movements were well known and often discussed. Matilda also traveled. At some point before September 21 when the 1857 Minnesota territorial census placed them at the Gull Lake Ojibwe Reservation, Matilda had transported her five children to the Agency headquarters, home to a small community of slightly less than two hundred people. Matilda and William had lived there in 1849–1850 during the year that William was employed as the US Government Farmer, so when Matilda returned in 1857, it was to a familiar place with family members to greet her. William's surviving brother, Truman, lived at the Agency headquarters, as did several of her siblings. Thus, another interpretation of Matilda's behavior suggests itself. Perhaps Matilda had acted first, initiating the breakup of the marriage. Perhaps Matilda, in fact, had left Sam.[32]

Several reasons might have prompted Matilda to return to Gull Lake. Most obviously, as a widow with young children and few means of earning a living, she may have sought the security and support of extended family members congregated on the Reservation. At the same time, her efforts to behave in culturally appropriate ways by establishing a union with one of the American newcomers, had been painfully unsuccessful. Matilda's failed relationship stood in such contrast to William's personal experiences that Matilda may have radically reconsidered her options in the new American-dominated society of Minnesota. William had navigated the tumultuous new world of Anglo-American state-building in Minnesota with his usual buoyant optimism, certain that multiracial Half Breeds would take their place as a political constituency within it. Matilda's assumption that the American newcomers would continue to be absorbed into the existing social relations did not prove correspondingly true. In ways neither of them had likely anticipated, their experiences with the emerging American social order were shaped by their genders. William's focus on obtaining political power within the new American state involved a decidedly masculine definition of inclusion based on citizenship, voting rights, and political participation. Moreover, his acceptance of the American political system reassured Anglo-Americans that Half Breed males would adapt to American social norms and practices, shedding their foreignness.

Matilda's behavior, while perfectly appropriate in the context of fur trade society, offered no such reassurances. Her expectation that newcomers could be incorporated into the regional society through its kin networks emerged from the fluid culture of the fur trade world. Involving women, families, and reproduction, that culture was far less legible or comprehensible to Anglo-Americans and far more open to ethnocentric misinterpretation. The multiracial community's marital practices formed a case in point. In important ways they differed from those of mid-nineteenth century Anglo-Americans, especially when it came to women's sexuality. Where Matilda saw her actions and her sexual behavior as thoroughly within the norms of respectability, Sam was far more likely to regard her willingness to cohabit with him without a marriage ceremony as proof of her immoral, dissolute character; she was the kind of woman with whom he could form a temporary liaison and abandon when it suited him. Matilda's multiracial identity was newly problematic as well. Where multiracial women had been sought-after as spouses of European and American men in earlier decades, the new influx of Anglo-Americans committed to racial constructions based on a supposed racial purity were often deeply ambivalent about multiracial women. Rather than viewing women like Matilda as suitable mates because of their Anglo-American cultural orientation as well as their European ancestry, multiracial women were more likely to be constructed as tainted, their sexual purity suspect along with their racial ambiguousness. When Sam refused to behave as Matilda anticipated he would, especially after she had given birth to their child, she drew a very different lesson than William had about how the new Americans were going to behave and how successful the incorporation of multiracial persons into the American polity was likely to be. She voted with her feet, taking her children and returning to tribal land where cultural traditions associated with older composite societies endured and the American state's presence was far more tenuous. Matilda would not be alone in this decision. The 1850s and 1860s were chaotic decades for Minnesota Ojibwes and their multiracial kinfolk. They endured further land sales, coerced and in a few cases forcible removals to new Reservations, mounting social turmoil, and political conflict leading to violence. In these difficult times, numerous other multiracial people, seeking stability and a familiar social and cultural environment, would make the decision to move to remaining tribally reserved lands.

Matilda would dwell on tribal lands for the rest of her life. She lived at the Gull Lake Reservation agency community until July 1868 when she joined several members of William's family, including Truman, Charlotte, Sophia, and their spouses and children, as part of the first contingent of Ojibwes and their multiracial kinfolk to move to the White Earth Reservation. Newly created with considerable fanfare, White Earth was to be the future home and an assimilationist showcase for all Ojibwes living in Minnesota. Opportunities for wage work for women, especially women with young children, were few at both Gull

Lake and White Earth Reservations. There is also evidence to suggest that Matilda was not a fluent speaker of English, which would have further limited her economic prospects to such low-paid traditionally female labor as providing domestic services. Nonetheless, she seems to have played to her strengths. Drawing on her previous experience, she took in boarders and occasionally found work as a seamstress, once again employing the Indigenous women's skills that had helped to sustain her family since she and William had first moved to Crow Wing in 1847.[33]

Despite the promises of cultural familiarity, economic assistance, and federal protection of the remaining reserved land bases, Reservations brought challenges of their own. Increasingly the American state came to regard Native nations as subject to their jurisdiction and imposed a colonial status upon the Indigenous polities that they had formerly recognized as politically independent. Depicting Native peoples as wards of the state, and thus as minors without legal rights, the United States also assumed control of Reservation resources, installed its own governing regimes, and oversaw numerous aspects of Reservation social, educational, and religious life. Yet, as Native Studies scholar Jean O'Brien, herself a White Earth Ojibwe, has recently observed, Ojibwes and Ojibwe-descended kindred who found themselves propelled to Reservations in the late nineteenth and early twentieth centuries nonetheless made localities such as White Earth into their homes. They did not "vanish," despite considerable American rhetoric proclaiming the imminent disappearance of North America's Indigenous nations. Instead, they found new ways to earn their living. They imbued the new Reservation's spaces with meaning and its landscapes with memories. Matilda participated in these processes. She created extended family households in which she raised her own children, a number of grandchildren, nieces, nephews, and several seemingly unrelated orphaned or uprooted youngsters. As adults, her three youngest children clustered their homes around hers, and the families of Charlotte and Sophia, who had spent much of their childhoods with Matilda and William, often resided nearby.[34]

The Indigenous women's work of sustaining and provisioning families and kin groups that Matilda had found meaningful and important throughout her life remained a crucial component of the process of remaking White Earth Reservation into an Indigenous place despite the imposition of the American colonial apparatus. As Ojibwes and their multiracial kin transformed the Reservation into their new home, women applied their general land-based knowledge to the specific land- and waterscapes of White Earth, identifying where various plants grew and where good ricing lakes were to be found. As American policymakers focused most of their attention on Ojibwe men, seeking, as always, to transform them into farmers, women's work was often overlooked. Their gathering of wild plants and their planting of small fields that Americans could dismiss as "gardens" raised few alarms about inappropriate gendered labor in the minds of Indian agents or missionaries. Yet such food production supported families as people first arrived at White Earth and continued to contribute to food stores in ensuing years. Gradually, Ojibwes and their multiracial kin came to think of the White Earth Reservation as a home place. Families might have come from elsewhere and families and individuals might frequently travel away from the Reservation for work or military service or to visit relatives, but White Earth became the place they were from and to which they would return. Developing that sense of belonging was in no small measure enabled by women. Their long-standing work of sustaining tribal families and their understanding of kinship as expansive and incorporative provided a foundation upon which Ojibwes at White Earth and elsewhere imagined new, often difficult, but ultimately enduring Indigenous futures.[35]

Conclusion

From time out of mind, Great Lakes Native peoples had engaged in political and diplomatic relations with one another using a discourse of kinship as the central mode of communication. Based in a somewhat universalized version of eastern Woodlands kinship structures, the Customs of All the Nations, as the discourse was called, were nonetheless elastic and flexible, capable of expressing a great range of ideas about political power and social relations between polities. Statuses of both equality and hierarchy could be affirmed as well as challenged using mutually understood terms such as grandfathers and grandchildren, elder and younger brothers, and uncles and nephews. Not only did this shared language make metaphoric meanings clear to all participants, the kin-based language of the Customs also linked political activity to the most foundational constructs in Great Lakes tribal societies, signifying to tribal representatives that their political actions were mutualistic endeavors among relatives, peoples with shared interests. This purposeful framing of political relations within the construct of kinship helped to naturalize political activity and avoid spontaneous angry or provocative words that could derail negotiations or deteriorate into warfare. References to kinship also inferred the appropriate reciprocal behavior between relatives and the commonly accepted obligations and responsibilities of kin toward one another. Strangers could also be transformed into relatives by intermarriage or adoption, making the theory of kinship into a literal practice. The conceptualizations that underwrote the Customs reflected bedrock tribal ideals and cultural practices. Their deployment in everyday acts of communication foregrounded the primacy of kinship and reciprocal relations between genders in creating tribal societies and by extension alliances between tribal polities. When Great Lakes Native polities encountered Europeans beginning in the sixteenth century, they would utilize the kin-inflected language and practices of the Customs of All the Nations to frame their initial diplomatic encounters and subsequent relationships with these newcomers.

As the Customs were recorded in English translations, however, their language appears to privilege masculinity, depicting its many kin relationships as those between superior and inferior male relatives. This privileging appeared normal and typical to the French, Dutch, and British, the major European regimes who began colonization efforts in northeastern North America in the early sixteenth century. They attempted to appropriate the diplomatic discourse of the Customs, deploying what they understood as its patriarchal hierarchies in pursuit of their own colonial projects. A language of domination, they thought, would be a first step toward the subjugation of Native peoples. Unfortunately, they badly misunderstood the Customs. Believing that male dominance and female subordination were universal human social norms, they interpreted Native labor practices, which were gendered, as evidence of the gender hierarchy they assumed they would find. They minimized the political significance of Native women as peacemakers, and seldom realized that Native peoples assigned different but equally necessary political responsibilities along gender lines. They also completely misconstrued the many references tribal speakers made to the ranked pairing of women and children. Rather than recognizing women and children as an elder/junior duality comparable to those of uncles and nephews or grandfathers and grandchildren, Europeans and their North American descendants assumed the phrase "women and children" referred to the same category of dependents in Native societies that it referenced in their own. They thus possessed only a partial understanding of the significance of the Customs and the social relations of power in which the Customs were embedded. They would continue attempting to bend the Customs to reflect their own interpretations and objectives, of course, but lacking a full understanding of the Indigenous intellectual foundations of the Customs, their efforts met with minimal success.

If Native constructions of social hierarchies founded in distinctions between age and youth rather than in gender baffled Europeans, their American descendants were similarly perplexed. Americans would also attempt to manipulate the discourse of kinship, but because they possessed the same cultural biases and assumptions as their British predecessors, they were also unable to wrest control of the discourse from Native peoples. By the latter half of the eighteenth century, however, several long-term historical developments would induce Anglo-Americans to try once again to shift the discursive terms of the Customs of All the Nations. As part of a lengthy intellectual transformation in their thinking about human social difference, fueled in great measure by their growing commitment to for-profit agriculture using enslaved labor, American perceptions of the significance of "race" began to change. As they increasingly viewed human beings as racialized subjects, European-descended Americans began trying to alter the language of diplomacy to reflect the new significance they accorded to hierarchic racialized identities. They introduced a racialized vocabulary into the Customs of All the Nations, referring to themselves as "white," while describing Native peoples as "red." These terms had existed previously, as had the third major racialized construct, "Black," but Americans began to give new emphasis to certain aspects of the meaning of "race." Races were not fluid and variable categories any longer; they became immutable and bounded. Physically embodied differences, most notably skin color, took on new significance. No longer was the color of one's skin one element among many that could determine one's racial identity; now it became the ultimate defining hallmark of one's race. In addition, just as skin color was now fixed, cultural practices, intellectual aptitudes, and even personal characteristics were reimagined as innate to different racialized groups. Finally, and unsurprisingly, these races were ranked, with "whites" at the top and "Blacks" at the bottom.

Despite growing American acceptance of the newly rigidifying racial hierarchy in the latter half of the eighteenth century, the older forms of claiming identity would endure in the Great Lakes country. "White" Americans from the eastern seaboard states, many of whom came from northern states with relatively little racial diversity, would begin emigrating into the old French pays d'en haute in the two decades after the American Revolution. During these decades, they would encounter the distinctively multiracial French colonial population. Though many Anglo-Americans, newly aware of their own racialized "white" identity, were already disparaging multiracial persons by this time, the older markers of whiteness still mattered. Americans could not help but notice that the Great Lakes French populace possessed obvious European attributes. They wore European-style clothing, built European-style houses, and worked at European occupations. They spoke, and some were literate, either in French or English, and they proclaimed their adherence to the oldest of the western European Christian traditions, Catholicism. They were also the essential interpreters, mediators, and facilitators of interactions between the incoming Americans and the still-numerous Native polities of the region. Their seeming commitment to the basic tenets of a European religious and cultural tradition was deeply reassuring to the first Anglo-American settler-colonists. The whiteness of the French, based on their cultural characteristics, seemed certain.

That assurance would give way to ambivalence over the next several decades. Several factors were responsible and among the most important was the dramatic shift in American national policy toward Native nations. In the wake of the Northwest Indian Wars, American elected officials and policymakers reassessed the wisdom of expensive, frequent wars against Native polities. They determined on an alternative strategy of buying Native land and forcing the now-landless Native community to remove from American national territory to new lands west of the Mississippi River, often over the course of several years. The new federal Indian policy hardly secured an end to warfare in the region (Native coalitions and the United States would fight in the War of 1812, among other conflicts), but it anticipated an end result that would remain the same whether a tribe negotiated a land sale during a peaceful encounter or at the conclusion of a war. In keeping with the developing goals of a settler-colonial nation, nearly all treaty negotiations involved a sale of land with the eventual expectation of complete Native removal from American territory.

It would be in the context of the numerous treaty negotiations with the region's Native nations that American views of the multiracial French would begin to change. Faced with American demands that they sell their tribal homelands, Native collectivities experimented with ways to hold onto at least some of their lands by transferring parcels to their multiracial kinfolk. They insisted that their multiracial kin be included in treaty provisions and deeded valuable lands into the hands of multiracial relatives who were members of tribal leadership lineages. Americans did not recognize these tribal efforts for the land-retaining strategies they were. Similarly, they misinterpreted Native discourse about multiracial persons as relatives who belonged to known tribal kin groups and lived in specific communities. Even as their own ideas about race and racialized identities were shifting, Americans remained convinced that their society's constructions of kinship, which they viewed as religiously sanctioned, represented the ideal all humans should emulate. They could not comprehend that tribal strategies to create kinship ties across national and ethnic boundaries had been purposefully developed as socio-political practices for creating alliances and enabling intertribal amity.

When tribal negotiators pressed for the inclusion of multiracial French kinfolk in treaty provisions, Americans did not recognize a tribal strategy at work. They dismissed the frequent assertions by tribal leaders and spokespersons that select multiracial French persons were "our children, the half breeds" and "our half breed relations." Instead, reflecting the growing American unease with multiracial persons in general, since their very presence challenged the supposed ironclad boundaries between "races," Americans downplayed the cultural whiteness of the multiracial French, emphasizing instead their transgressive racial heritage. Steadily ignoring tribal insistence that certain multiracial persons were in fact relatives, Americans manipulated their own descriptive categories to emphasize that the connections between Native peoples and the multiracial French were based only in common biological descent, not kinship ties. In this iteration, the French possessed "Indian blood," a designation that reinforced the construct of racialization as an inherited category. As Americans increasingly adopted racialized thinking, however, they became less able to recognize the realities Native speakers articulated in council meetings and treaty negotiations. They continued to employ their appropriated version of the kinship language of Customs of All the Nations, confident that Native peoples had also come to accept these conceptualizations. Yet careful reading of Native speeches, even in translations of varying degrees of accuracy, makes it clear that Native peoples were not acceding to a racialized hierarchy in which they were the subjugated red children of a white American father. Nor had they abandoned the idea that kinship ties could transcend boundaries of ethnicity and tribal nation to create political alliances.[1]

Native words and actions, at treaty negotiations and in other contexts, reveal the depth and complexity of their thought about kinship, and shed special light on Indigenous categories of persons whose kinship ties allowed them to act as intermediaries across tribal and ethno-national lines. The Ojibwe war leader Zhaagobe, who drew American attention at the 1837 Treaty of Fort Snelling, was such a person. Of Ojibwe, Dakota, and French heritage, he possessed exceptional abilities to mediate in difficult political situations where the tactful diplomacy of a relative helped insure a successful outcome. Persons whose actions were not as high-profile as Zhaagobe's were similarly important in the delicately balanced Indigenous context of Ojibwe and Dakota relations. Such a person was Ginoozhe, or Jack Porter, also of Ojibwe, French, and Dakota heritage, whose presence in the Ojibwe village of Fish Lake, Minnesota, protected the community from attacks by Dakotas because they would not harm the relative who also dwelled there. Ginoozhe and other multitribal individuals were remembered by the generation of Ojibwe elders who testified at the White Earth disenrollment hearings in the early twentieth century. Such persons, even when recognized by Americans, were not fully appreciated. Yet their presence serves as a reminder that Native ways of knowing and living in the world, as exemplified by the actions of multitribal persons, existed at the same temporal moment that Native nations were interacting with Americans. Indeed, as the travels of the Dakota holy woman Wiyaka Sinte Win, or Tailfeather Woman, across northern Minnesota and Wisconsin escorted by multitribal Wolf Clan Ojibwes demonstrates, Great Lakes Native peoples, both women and men, continued to pursue their own social and political objectives long after Americans thought all such independent activity had ended. They utilized their own political protocols and continued to privilege ties of kinship as the vehicle by which intertribal dialogue and negotiation were undertaken.

The existence and political importance of multitribal and multiethnic persons by no means exhausted tribal conceptualizations of categories of human beings. Tribal peoples continued to construct their own culturally distinctive understandings of social difference and sameness in ways that reveled the significance of gender as well as kinship. Examples once again drawn from the experiences of Ojibwes and Dakotas reveal another type of person—the Frenchman—a category understood in terms of an intra-gendered critique of Indigenous men's experiences with Europeans and their North American descendants. Initially a negative assessment of the labor hierarchy of the fur trade, Ojibwe men, and very probably Dakota men as well, expanded the figure of the Frenchman to address their perceptions of the new threats posed by the Americans. The earlier Indigenous critique of fur trade labor relations was reformulated to identify and reject the new forms of dependence that Ojibwes and Dakotas detected in American efforts to buy tribal lands, forcibly remove Native peoples, and radically alter Indigenous constructions and practices of gender.

That tribes recognized how American policies harmed them and mounted their own culturally resonant critiques of American settler colonialism serves as an important corrective to the still prevalent belief that Native peoples were helpless in the face of the invasion of North America by successive waves of European and European-descended colonizers. Native ways of reckoning kinship and social belonging endured, although over the second half of the nineteenth century, as the United States grew in size and power and enveloped Native lands within its borders, it exercised significant new forms of coercion over Native peoples. It ceased to regard Native polities as independent nations, replacing its earlier view with a settler colonialist interpretation of Native collectivities as conquered "Indian tribes," stateless aboriginal persons whose cultures were denigrated as "barbaric" or "savage" and whose political language and decision-making practices were dismissed as "primitive." By the 1870s and 1880s, Americans were redefining Native peoples as colonial subjects lacking American citizenship or political standing at law. They ignored the variety and complexity of Native experience, as exemplified in the lives of William and Matilda Aitken Warren. Instead, they imagined Native peoples as an undifferentiated mass of primitive racialized subjects, who lacked such long-prized Anglo-American virtues as a commitment to private land ownership and a Christian religious tradition. Under the guise of "civilizing" Indigenous peoples, they developed policies designed to appropriate Native lands and resources (most notoriously, perhaps, via the Dawes Allotment Act of 1887) while assimilating Native individuals into the work force of the American nation-state. They sought to break apart tribal collectivities and undermine Indigenous forms of leadership and governance. Native youth were to be educated in boarding schools distant from their home communities where they could be stripped of their cultural heritages and taught the menial skills that would insure their absorption into the lowest levels of the nation's wage economy.

Racialized constructions of Native peoples were integral to these policies as white Americans remained firmly committed to racial hierarchy and white supremacy. Over the last two decades of the nineteenth century, these racialized identities became painful realities for Great Lakes Native communities, as they did elsewhere in North America. The identification of tribal members became the prerogative of the American state, not tribal kin groups or tribal collectivities. An individual's degree of "Indian blood" became the standard for inclusion or exclusion from tribal membership, now a bureaucratic procedure divorced from tribal conceptions of social belonging or understandings of the boundary-crossing abilities of kin ties. Native peoples might reject the relevance of these decisions at the familial or local level, but they nonetheless shaped many aspects of tribal life, as is evident in the testimony of Ojibwe individuals in the White Earth disenrollment hearings of the early twentieth century. Most damaging of all, racialized identities based on blood quantum became deeply divisive issues within tribal communities in the Great Lakes country and across the United States. They remain controversial in many Native communities to this day.

The twentieth century would bring dramatic changes to Native life in the United States, beginning in the 1930s with the Indian Reorganization Act of

1934, which sought to reverse the most draconian of the assimilationist policies of earlier decades. Despite these efforts, the colonial legacy of racialized "blood"-based identities remained the externally imposed standard by which tribal membership was determined. It received renewed emphasis in the years following World War Two when the United States became more socially and politically conservative and members of Congress, many from states with substantial Native populations, attempted to liquidate (or "terminate" in the language of the day) all Reservations to force assimilation on Native peoples. Yet the mid-century decades between the 1960s and 1980s, often termed the Red Power era, galvanized a cultural renewal among Native peoples, the results of which are ongoing. Fueled by Native activism and the larger Civil Rights movement as well as by Supreme Court decisions acknowledging forms of tribal sovereignty that had been long ignored, the years since the mid-twentieth century have seen the remarkable resurgence of all aspects of tribal cultures, from language reclamation to spiritual practice to renewed interest in historic foodways. In this context, it is not surprising that Great Lakes tribal nations would revisit the issue of tribal identity and social belonging and imagine new ways in which Indigenous governance might be practiced.

An example with direct connection to this study is the recent endeavor of the White Earth Nation (WEN), formerly the White Earth Chippewa Reservation, which in 2007 began the intensive process of writing a new tribal constitution. Their years' long effort to reimagine themselves as a nation has been expertly described by Native Studies scholar, Jill Doerfler, in her book *Those Who Belong: Identity, Family, Blood, and Citizenship among the White Earth Anishinaabeg* (2015).[2] As the title suggests, the issues surrounding tribal belonging formed important elements of the larger nation-building project. Doerfler details a process of self-education as constitutional delegates and ordinary tribal individuals engaged in the work of developing new, more representative forms of governance and tribal inclusion. As part of the process, they studied the extensive testimony generated by the White Earth disenrollment hearings, which preserved the perspectives of so many ancestral kinfolk. They were struck by the elders' rejection of racialization and their emphasis on the kin-based nature of tribal belonging. Ojibwes in the 1910s spoke from a position of weakness as colonized subjects encapsulated by the United States, but they nonetheless insisted on the legitimacy of their ways of knowing. Their resolve inspired their descendants to reimagine a new form of tribal belonging that reflected earlier kin-based understandings rather than the externally imposed definitions of identity founded in the fiction of divisible "Indian blood." The process was not smooth, as indeed, nation-building seldom is, but on November 19, 2013, citizens of the White Earth Nation voted by a wide margin of almost 80 percent to accept a new constitution that eliminated the blood quantum requirement. In its place, the citizenry opted for lineal descent, once more grounding tribal identity and belonging in Ojibwe understandings of kinship and family.

Notes

Introduction

1. "Treaty of 3 August 1795, at Greenville," *American State Papers: Indian Affairs*, 2 vols. (Washington, DC: Gales and Seaton, 1832), 1:562–83 (hereafter cited as ASP: IA). For the larger context of the Northwest Indian Wars of the 1790s, see Colin G. Calloway, *The Victory with No Name: The Native American Defeat of the First American Army* (Oxford: Oxford University Press, 2015). Helen Hornbeck Tanner, ed., *Atlas of Great Lakes Indian History* (Norman: University of Oklahoma Press for the Newberry Library, 1987), 69–73, provides concise chronological descriptions and a helpful table of the armed clashes that characterized the trans-Appalachian border region between the 1770s and the 1790s.

2. The cooperative relationships that existed between human kinfolk were echoed in the social composition of all other communities of living beings, from the Other Than Human persons (whom Europeans and their descendants sometimes called "spirits"), to animal and plant communities, to collectivities of other human beings who identified themselves as members of tribal polities other than their own. An insightful recent analysis of Algonkian-speaking Great Lakes peoples that recognizes the alliances between these multiple communities is Heidi Bohaker, *Doodem and Council Fire: Anishinaabe Governance through Alliance* (Toronto: University of Toronto Press, 2020).

3. See Alan Taylor, "Captain Hendrick Aupaumut: The Dilemmas of an Intercultural Broker," *Ethnohistory* 43 (Summer 1996): 446, for the English-language reference to the Customs of All the Nations. To indicate the significance of this phrase, which is, after all, a translation of an unknown Indigenous expression in an unknown Indigenous language, it has been written throughout this work using capital letters to mark its exceptional nature.

4. "Journal of the proceedings at the Treaty held by Govr Cass and Col. McKenney with the Indians at the Butte des Morts [*sic*] near Green Bay—1827," Treaty of 11 August 1827, 28, roll 2, National Archives and Records Administration, Record Group 75, Microcopy T494 (hereafter cited as NARA, RG 75, T494).

5. Michael Witgen, *An Infinity of Nations: How the Native New World Shaped Early North America* (Philadelphia: University of Pennsylvania Press, 2012); Patrick Wolfe, "Settler Colonialism and the Elimination of the Native," *Journal of Genocide Studies* 8, no. 4 (2006): 387–409. Also, Wolfe, *Settler Colonialism and the Transformation of Anthropology: The Politics and Poetics of an Ethnographic Event* (London: Cassell, 1999).

6. James C. Scott, *Domination and the Arts of Resistance: Hidden Transcripts* (New Haven, CT: Yale University Press, 1990). The full title of the treaty's minutes is "Minutes of a Treaty with the Tribes of Indians called the Wyandots, Delawares, Shawanese, Ottawas, Chippewas [Ojibwes], Pattawatamies, Miamies, Eel River, Kickapoos, Piankeshaws, and Kaskaskias, begun at Greenville, on the 16th day of June, and ended on the 10th day of August, 1795" (hereafter cited as "Minutes"), ASP: IA, 1:564–83. The treaty "Minutes" state that the negotiations concluded on August 10, but three supplementary documents are appended indicating that two additional meetings occurred that related directly to finalizing the treaty. Interestingly, the Treaty as it appears in Kappler, *Indian Affairs, Laws and Treaties*, gives its concluding date as August 3. See "Treaty with the Wyandot," at Greenville, Northwest Territory, 3 August 1795, in Charles J. Kappler, comp. and ed., *Indian Affairs, Laws and Treaties* (Washington, DC: Government Printing Office, 1904), 39–45.

7. "Speech of Wayne," 16 June 1795 ("brush," kindling fire), "Speech of New Corn," 17 June 1795 ("good work"), "Minutes," ASP: IA, 1:564.

8. Speech of New Corn, 23 July 1795 ("my young men, women and children"), "Minutes," ASP, IA, 1:564; Aw ban aw bee quoted in "Record of the proceedings," Treaty of 16 October 1826 on the Wabash River, 895, roll 1, NARA, RG 75, T494. See also Bohaker, *Doodem and Council Fire*.

9. Speech of Mash-i-pi-nash-i-wish, 23 July 1795 ("whites"), "Minutes," ASP: IA, 1:572; Speech of Wayne, 24 July 1795 (British and French as American predecessors), "Minutes," ASP: IA, 1:573; "Treaty of 3 August 1795, at Greenville" ("in possession of French people," "Indians"), ASP: IA, 1:563; Masass quoted in Speech of Wayne, 30 July 1795 ("what will become of French?"), "Minutes," ASP: IA, 1:578. For a recent history of the Three Council Fires, see Phil Belfy, *Three Fires Unity: The Anishinaabeg of the Lake Huron Borderlands* (Lincoln: University of Nebraska Press, 2011).

10. Important theorizations in the development of the field of social history, or history "from the bottom up," include George Rudé, *The Crowd in History: A Study of Popular Disturbance in France and England, 1730–1848* (New York: John Wiley and Sons, 1964); Eric J. Hobsbawm, *Primitive Rebels: Studies in Archaic Forms of Social Movement in the Nineteenth and Twentieth Centuries* (New York: W. W. Norton, 1965); Hobsbawm and Terence Ranger, *The Invention of Tradition* (New York: Cambridge University Press, 1983); E. P. Thompson, "The Moral Economy of the English Crowd in the Eighteenth Century," *Past and Present* 50 (1971): 76–136; Jesse Lemisch and John K. Alexander, "The White Oaks, Jack Tar, and the Concept of the Inarticulate," *William and Mary Quarterly*, 3rd series, 19 (1972): 109–34; Herbert Gutman, *Work, Culture and Society in Industrializing America: Essays in American Working-Class and Social History* (New York: Knopf, 1976); Sterling Stuckey, "Through the Prism of Folklore: The Black Ethos in Slavery," *Massachusetts Review* 9 (summer 1968): 407–37; Jesse Lemisch, The American Revolution Seen from the Bottom Up," in *Toward a New Past: Dissenting Essays in American History*, ed. Barton J. Bernstein (New York: Vantage Books, 1969), 3–45. The phrase "history from the bottom up" is taken from this last essay. The classic historical articulation of gender as an analytical category is Joan Wallach Scott, "Gender, a Useful Category of Historical Analysis," *American Historical Review* 113 (December 1986): 1053–75, while important Native perspectives on the feminist practice of Native history include Maile Arvin, Eve Tuck, and Angie Morrill, "Decolonizing

Feminism: Challenging Connections between Settler Colonialism and Heteropatriarchy,"
Feminist Formations 25 (Spring 2013): 8–34; Renya Ramirez, "Race, Tribal Nation, and
Gender: A Native Feminist Approach to Belonging," *Meridians* 7, no. 2 (2007): 22–40;
Mishuana R. Goeman and Jennifer Nez Denetdale, "Native Feminisms: Legacies, Inter-
ventions, and Indigenous Sovereignties," *Wicazo Sa Review* 24, no. 2 (2009): 9–13.

11. William Whipple Warren, "History of the Ojibways, Based Upon Traditions
and Oral Statements," *Minnesota Historical Society Collections* 5 (1885): 3–394. Peter
Jones, *The History of the Ojebway Indians, with Especial Reference to Their Conversion
to Christianity* (London: A. W. Bennett, 1861); also *The Life and Journals of Kah-ke-wa-
quo-na-by (Rev. Peter Jones), Wesleyan Missionary* (Toronto: A. Green, 1861); George
Copway, *The Traditional History and Characteristic Sketches of the Ojibway Nation*
(London: C. Gilpin, 1850); also *The Life, History and Travels of Kah-ge-ga-gah-bowh
(George Copway), a Young Indian Chief of the Ojebwa Nation, a Convert to the Christian
Faith, and a Missionary to His People for Twelve Years; with a Sketch of the Present State
of the Ojebwa Nation, in Regard to Christianity and Their Future Prospects,* 2nd ed. (Philadelphia: J. Harmstead, 1847); Andrew J. Blackbird, *History of the Ottawa and Chippewa
Indians of Michigan; A Grammar of Their Language, and Personal and Family History
of the Author* (Ypsilanti, MI: Ypsilantian Job Printing House, 1887). Blackbird did not
include his Indigenous name in the title of his work but provided it in his first introduc-
tory remarks.

12. James Joseph Buss, *Winning the West with Words: Language and Conquest in
the Lower Great Lakes* (Norman: University of Oklahoma Press, 2011); Susan Sleeper-
Smith, *Indigenous Prosperity and American Conquest: Indian Women of the Ohio River
Valley, 1690–1792* (Chapel Hill: University of North Carolina Press for the Omohundro Institute of Early American History and Culture, 2018); Brenda Child, *Holding Our
World Together: Ojibwe Women and the Survival of Community* (New York: Viking Penguin, 2012), Heidi Kiiwetinepinesiik Stark, "Marked by Fire: Anishinaabe Articulations
of Nationhood in Treaty Making with the United States and Canada," *American Indian
Quarterly* 36 (Spring 2012): 119–49. See also Rob Harper, *Unsettling the West: Violence
and State Building in the Ohio Valley* (Philadelphia: University of Pennsylvania Press,
2018); John P. Bowes, *Land Too Good for Indians: Northern Indian Removal* (Norman:
University of Oklahoma Press; 2016); Colin G. Calloway, *The Victory with No Name: The
Native American Defeat of the First American Army* (New York: Oxford University Press,
2015); Michael A. McDonnell, *Masters of Empire: Great Lakes Indians and the Making of
America* (New York: Hill and Wang, 2015); Stephen Warren, *The Worlds the Shawnees
Made: Migration and Violence in Early America* (Chapel Hill: University of North Car-
olina Press, 2014); Michael Witgen, *An Infinity of Nations: How the Native New World
Shaped Early North America* (Philadelphia: University of Pennsylvania Press, 2012).

Chapter 1

1. Molly Brant quoted in Alan Taylor, "Captain Hendrick Aupaumut: The Dilemmas
of an Intercultural Broker," *Ethnohistory* 43 (Summer 1996): 446. The names of Native
persons are inconsistently and variously spelled in written documents. Where possible,
throughout this work they have been recorded in the currently accepted double-vowel
orthography. To indicate the significance of the phrase the Customs of All the Nations,

a translation from an unknown Indigenous expression, it is capitalized throughout this work.

2. Shinguabe Wossin [Zhingwaabe Aasin] quoted in "Journal of the Proceedings of the Commissioners at the Treaty with the Chippewas on Lake Superior," Treaty of 5 August 1826 at Fond du Lac, 838, roll 1, National Archives and Records Administration, Record Group 75, Microcopy T494 (hereafter cited as NARA, RG 75, T494); Tarhe quoted in "Journal of the Proceedings of the Commissioners appointed to Treat with the North West Indians at Detroit," Treaty of 8 September 1815, 0219, roll 1, NARA, RG 75, T494; Speech of La Bay, 0240. For the elder brother/younger brother relationship of the Ojibwes and Odawas, see "Journal of the preceedings of a Treaty between the United States and the United Tribes of Pottawottamies, Chippeways and Ottowas," Treaty of 14 September 1833 at Chicago, 0068, roll 3, NARA, RG 75, T494; for the Delawares as grandfathers, see "Minutes of a Treaty, with the tribes of Indians called the Wyandots, Delawares, Shawanese, Ottawas, Chippewas, Pattawatamies, Miamies, Eel River, Kickapoos, Piankeshaws, and Kaskaskias, begun at Greenville, on the 16th day of June, and ended on the 10th day of August, 1795," in "Treaty of Greenville. Communicated to the Senate, December 9, 1795," *American State Papers: Indian Affairs*. 2 vols. (Washington, DC: Gales and Seaton, 1832) (hereafter cited as ASP: IA), 1:564 (Potawatomis acknowledge Delawares as grandfathers); 565 (Ojibwes acknowledge Delawares as grandfathers); 569 (Shawnees acknowledge Delawares as grandfathers). For a brilliant recent treatment of the contested uses of kin terms involving Delawares and the Six Nations Iroquois, see Gunlög Fur, *A Nation of Women: Gender and Colonial Encounters Among the Delaware Indians* (Philadelphia: University of Pennsylvania Press, 2009), 160–98. Another excellent discussion of Iroquois kin terms and power relations they encoded is Jane T. Merritt, *At the Crossroads: Indians and Empires on a Mid-Atlantic Frontier, 1700–1763* (Chapel Hill: University of North Carolina, 2003), 157–58, and especially 198–231. A perceptive examination of kin metaphors and Native manipulation of them from another region of North America is Raymond J. DeMallie, "Touching the Pen: Plains Indian Treaty Councils in Ethnohistorical Perspective," in Frederick C. Leubke, ed., *Ethnicity on the Great Plains* (Lincoln: University of Nebraska Press, 1980), 32–53. The famed Covenant Chain of the Iroquois employed much of the language of the Customs of All the Nations, but was not synonymous with it. See Fur, *A Nation of Women*, Merritt, *At the Crossroads*. The most detailed treatments of Iroquois diplomacy and its metaphors remain Francis Jennings, *The Ambiguous Iroquois Empire: The Covenant Chain Confederation of Indian Tribes with English Colonies from its Beginnings to the Lancaster Treaty of 1744* (New York: W. W. Norton, 1984) and *Empire of Fortune: Crowns, Colonies and Tribes in the Seven Years War in America* (New York: W. W. Norton, 1988), see also "Glossary of Figures of Speech in Iroquois Political Rhetoric," in Francis Jennings, ed., William N. Fenton, joint ed., Mary A. Druke, assoc. ed., David R. Miller, research ed., *History and Culture of Iroquois Diplomacy: An Interdisciplinary Guide to the Treaties of the Six Nations and Their League* (Syracuse: Syracuse University Press, 1985).

3. Fur, *A Nation of Women*; see also Gunlög Fur, "'Some Women Are Wiser Than Some Men': Gender and Native American History," in *Clearing a Path: Theorizing the Past in Native American Studies*, ed. Nancy Shoemaker (New York: Routledge, 2002), and the pathbreaking studies in Mona Etienne and Eleanor Burke Leacock, eds., *Women and Colonization: Anthropological Perspectives* (New York: Praeger, 1980).

4. Fur, *A Nation of Women*; Merritt, *At the Crossroads*; also see the discussion of Shawnee concepts of gender in Stephen Warren, *The Worlds the Shawnees Made: Migration and Violence in Early America* (Chapel Hill: University of North Carolina Press, 2014), especially 6–7, for discussion of the gendering of life-giving and life-taking persons. See also the deeply insightful analysis of women as embodying peace and peace-making on the southern plains in Juliana Barr, *Peace Came in the Form of a Woman: Indians and Spaniards in the Texas Borderlands* (Chapel Hill: University of North Carolina Press, 2007). Additional studies that describe eastern Woodlands gender roles and role complementarity include the important early work of Eleanor Burke Leacock, in particular "The Montagnais-Naskapi 'Hunting Territory' and the Fur Trade," American Anthropological Association *Memoir* 78 (Menasha, WI: George B. Banta Co., 1954); "Matrilocality in a Simple Hunting Economy (Montagnais-Naskapi)," *Southwestern Journal of Anthropology* 11 (Spring 1955): 31–47; and "Women's Status in Egalitarian Society: Implications for Social Evolution," *Current Anthropology* 19 (June 1978): 247–75; Susan Sleeper-Smith, *Indian Women and French Men: Rethinking Cultural Encounter in the Western Great Lakes* (Amherst: University of Massachusetts Press, 2001); Margaret M. Caffrey, "Complementary Power: Men and Women of the Lenni Lenape," *American Indian Quarterly*, 24 (Winter 2000): 44–63; Lucy Eldersveld Murphy, *A Gathering of Rivers: Indians, Métis, and Mining in the Western Great Lakes, 1737–1832* (Lincoln: University of Nebraska Press, 2004); Theda Perdue, *Cherokee Women: Gender and Culture Change, 1700–1835* (Lincoln: University of Nebraska Press, 1998); Sarah H. Hill, *Weaving New Worlds: Southeastern Cherokee Women and Their Basketry* (Chapel Hill: University of North Carolina Press, 1997), especially 1–109; Katy Simpson Smith, "'I Look on You . . . As My Children': Persistence and Change in Cherokee Motherhood, 1750–1835," *North Carolina Historical Review* 87 (October 2010): 403–30; for an anthropological overview of women's access to various forms of power in a number of Native societies, see Laura F. Klein and Lillian A. Ackerman, eds., *Women and Power in Native North America* (Norman: University of Oklahoma Press, 1995); also Jane Fishburne Collier, *Marriage and Inequality in Classless Societies* (Stanford, CA: Stanford University Press, 1988).

5. Me-te-a quoted in "Proceedings of the Treaty at Chicago, 19 August 1821," Treaty of 29 August 1821 at Chicago, p. 4, Typescript, Schoolcraft Papers, National Archives, Record Group 75, NIS-203; Flat Mouth quoted in "Proceedings of a Council with the Chippewa Indians," *Iowa Journal of History and Politics* 5 (1911): 429.

6. Fur, *A Nation of Women*, especially 160–98.

7. Fur, *A Nation of Women*; see also Merritt, *At the Crossroads*, for an interpretation that both parallels that of Fur and explores Delaware encounters with Christian missionaries in great depth as well.

8. Merry E. Wiesner, *Women and Gender in Early Modern Europe* (Cambridge: Cambridge University Press, 1993); Mary S. Hartman, *The Household and the Making of History: A Subversive View of the Western Past* (Cambridge: Cambridge University Press, 2004) and, for a more general overview, Renate Bridenthal, Claudia Koontz, and Susan Stuard, eds., *Becoming Visible: Women in European History*, 2nd ed. (Boston: Houghton Mifflin, 1987). In addition to Merritt, *At the Crossroads*, especially 129–66, and Fur, *A Nation of Women*, two exceptional recent historical studies that examine gender comparatively in Native and non-Native societies are Juliana Barr, *Peace Came in the Form of a Woman*, and James F. Brooks, *Captives and Cousins: Slavery, Kinship, and*

Community in the Southwest Borderlands (Chapel Hill: University of North Carolina Press for the Omohundro Institute of Early American History and Culture, 2001).

9. The father/child metaphor has engaged the interest of numerous scholars; the most well-known recent examination being perhaps Richard White, *The Middle Ground: Indians, Empires and Republics in the Great Lakes Region, 1650–1815* (New York: Cambridge University Press, 1991); see also James Axtell, *The Invasion Within: The Contest of Cultures in Colonial North America* (New York: Oxford University Press, 1985); Janet Chute, *The Legacy of Shingwaukonse: A Century of Native Leadership* (Toronto: University of Toronto Press, 1998); Wilbur Jacobs, *Wilderness Politics and Indian Gifts: The Northern Colonial Frontier, 1748–1763* (Lincoln: University of Nebraska Press, 1950); Benjamin Ramirez-Shkwegnaabi, "The Dynamics of American Indian Diplomacy in the Great Lakes Region," *American Indian Culture and Research Journal* 27 (December 2003): 53–77; Michael Paul Rogin, *Fathers and Children: Andrew Jackson and the Subjugation of the American Indian* (New York: Knopf, 1975); and Nancy Shoemaker, "An Alliance Between Men: Gender Metaphors in Eighteenth-Century American Indian Diplomacy East of the Mississippi," *Ethnohistory* 46, no. 2 (1999): 239–63. See also the recent consideration by Merritt, *At the Crossroads*, 214–16. Also Allan Taylor, *The Divided Ground: Indians, Settlers, and the Northern Borderland of the American Revolution* (New York: Alfred A. Knopf, 2006). For an articulation of the father/child metaphor by Native peoples that emphasizes mutuality and alliance rather than hierarchic relationships, see "Speech of Ke way gush cam," in "Proceedings of the Treaty," Treaty of 29 August 1821 at Chicago, p. 21, Typescript, Schoolcraft Papers, National Archives, Record Group 75, NIS-203.

10. Gregory Evans Dowd, *A Spirited Resistance: The North American Indian Struggle for Unity, 1745–1815* (Baltimore, MD: Johns Hopkins University Press, 1992); James Joseph Buss, *Winning the West with Words: Language and Conquest in the Lower Great Lakes* (Norman: University of Oklahoma Press, 2011).

11. For conditions leading to renewed profitability of chattel slavery, see Ira Berlin, *Many Thousands Gone: The First Two Centuries of Slavery in North America* (Cambridge, MA: Harvard University Press, 1998); Allan Gallay, *The Indian Slave Trade: The Rise of English Empire in the American South, 1670–1717* (New Haven, CT: Yale University Press, 2002); Robbie Ethridge and Sheri M. Shuck-Hall, eds., *Mapping the Mississippian Shatter Zone: The Colonial Indian Slave Trade and Regional Instability in the American South* (Lincoln: University of Nebraska Press, 2009); Sven Beckert, *Empire of Cotton: A Global History* (New York: Alfred A. Knopf Publishers, 2014); for changing perceptions of "race," see Ariela J. Gross, *What Blood Won't Tell: A History of Race on Trial in America* (Cambridge, MA: Harvard University Press, 2008); Ivan Hannaford, *Race: The History of an Idea in the West* (Baltimore, MD: Johns Hopkins University Press, 1996); Reginald Horsman, *Race and Manifest Destiny: the Origins of American Racial Anglo-Saxonism* (Cambridge, MA: Harvard University Press, 1981), 98–138, 189–207; Audrey Smedley, *Race in North America: Origin and Evolution of a Worldview* (1993; repr., Boulder, CO: Westview Press, 1999), 169–200; for the role of science in defining and "proving" the existence of race, see William Stanton, *The Leopard's Spots: Scientific Attitudes toward Race in America, 1815–1859* (Chicago: University of Chicago Press, 1960); George M. Fredrickson, *The Black Image in the White Mind: The Debate on Afro-American Character and Destiny, 1817–1914* (New York: Harper and Row, 1971);

see also Robert E. Bieder, *Science Encounters the Indian, 1820–1880: The Early Years of American Ethnology* (Norman: University of Oklahoma Press, 1986) for a work that examines how the emerging and supposedly scientifically-based discipline of ethnology was shaped by the race-based ideas about Native Americans held by its practitioners. For a thorough debunking of the scientific "proof" of race and of the racial inequality it supposedly proves, see Stephen Jay Gould, *The Mismeasure of Man*, rev. ed. (New York: W. W. Norton, 1995).

12. "Journal of the Proceedings," Treaty of 19 August 1825 at Prairie du Chien, 727 ("Fox Chief"), 728 (Shingwaabe Aasin), roll 1, NARA, RG 75, T494; "Journal of the Proceedings" Treaty of 5 August 1826 at Fond du Lac, 0839 (Big Marten, or "Gitshee Waabizhaas" [Gichi Waabizheshi]), roll 1, NARA, RG 75, T494. For a persuasive evaluation of the construct of Native peoples as "red" people, see Nancy Shoemaker, "How Indians Got To Be Red," *American Historical Review* 102 (June, 1997): 625–44, and her longer work, *A Strange Likeness: Becoming Red and White in Eighteenth-Century North America* (New York: Oxford University Press, 2004); see also Alden T. Vaughan, "From White Man to Redskin: Changing Anglo-American Perceptions of the American Indian," *American Historical Review* 87 (October, 1982): 917–53, and Nicholas Hudson, "From 'Nation' to 'Race': The Origin of Racial Classification in Eighteenth-Century Thought," *Eighteenth-Century Studies* 29 (Spring 1996): 247–64.

13. "Journal of the proceedings of the Council held with the Winnebagoe Indians, at Green Bay by Govr Cass & Colonel Menard, Commrs," Treaty of 25 August 1828 at Green Bay, 140 (Spotted Arm), 146 (Quash-quam-may), and 131 (White Crow), roll 2, NARA, RG 75, T494; LeGros quoted in "Record of the proceedings of His Excellency Lewis Cass, His Excellency James B. Ray, Gen. John Tipton, Commissioners appointed to treat with the Indians owning lands in the State of Indiana, in the year 1826," Treaty of 23 October 1826 with the Miamis, appended to the 16 October 1826 treaty with the Potawatomis at the Wabash River, 0887, roll 1, NARA, RG 75, T494. As can be seen from these speeches, tribal nations often attended councils and their representatives participated in the discussions when they were not the principal group with whom the United States wished to negotiate.

14. "Journal of the Proceedings," Treaty of 19 August 1825 at Prairie du Chien, 0724 (Clark quoted), roll 1, NARA, RG 75, T494; "Journal of the proceedings at the Treaty held by Govr Cass and Col. McKenney with the Indians at the Butte des Morts near Green Bay—1827," Treaty of 11 August 1827 at Butte des Mortes (with "Chippewas, Menominis and Winnebagos"), 0030 (McKenney quoted); 0044 (McKenney identified as speaker), roll 2, NARA, RG 75, T494.

15. Porter quoted in "Journal of the preceedings of a Treaty between the United States and the United Tribes of Pottawottamies, Chippeways and Ottowas," Treaty of 26 September 1833, 0063, 64, roll 3, NARA, RG 75, T494. On changing gender roles in early nineteenth-century American society, see Jeanne Boydston, *Home and Work: Housework, Wages and the Ideology of Labor in the Early Republic* (New York: Oxford University Press, 1990).

16. Que-we-shan-shez [Gwiiwizhenzhish] quoted in "Proceedings of a Council with the Chippewa Indians," *Iowa Journal of History and Politics* 5 (1911): 420; Flat Mouth quoted in Martha Coleman Bray, ed., *The Journals of Joseph N. Nicollet, A Scientist on the Mississippi Headwaters, with Notes on Indian Life, 1836–37* (St. Paul:

Minnesota Historical Society Press, 1970), 117. For the British and French as wearing hats, and an indication that tribal nations other than Ojibwes and Odawas may have employed the hat-wearer identifier, see "Minutes of a Treaty, with the tribes of Indians called the Wyandots, Delawares, Shawanese, Ottawas, Chippewas, Pattawatamies, Miamies, Eel River, Kickapoos, Piankeshaws, and Kaskaskias, begun at Greenville, on the 16th day of June, and ended on the 10th day of August, 1795," in "Treaty of 3 August 1795, at Greenville, "Minutes of a Treaty," 1:571, "Speech of Little Turtle," 22 May 1795, ASP: IA.

17. William Whipple Warren, "A History of the Ojibways, Based Upon Traditions and Oral Statements." Minnesota Historical Society *Collections*, 5 (1885): 31–32 (Odawa), 32 (Potawatomi), 195 ("Shaug-un-aush") (hereafter cited as MHS *Collections*); Frederick Baraga, *A Dictionary of the Ojibway Language* (St. Paul: Minnesota Historical Society Press, 1992), 2:163 ("Jaganash"), 194 ("Kitchimokoman"); John D. Nichols and Earl Nyholm, *A Concise Dictionary of Minnesota Ojibwe* (Minneapolis: University of Minnesota Press, 1995), 1:124; 2:174. Also see Alexander F. Chamberlain, *The Language of the Mississagas of Skugog* (Philadelphia: MacCalla and Company, 1892), 59, for a nineteenth century Anishinaabeg explication of the name Kichimokomaan, which makes clear the connection to American weaponry. Chamberlin's consultants stated that "Kitcimo'komen," (in Chamberlin's orthography), "literally signifies 'big knife,' [and] is said to have been given on account of the 'swords' of American soldiers." The ethnonym appears widespread among tribal communities self-identifying as Anishinaabeg, but by no means all Algonkian-speaking tribal nations employed it. The Shawnees, for instance, did not, according to Chief Ben Barnes of the Shawnee tribe. Personal Communication, 27 September 2019.

18. The Potawatomi Prophet quoted in "Journal of the Proceedings," Treaty of 8 September 1815 at Detroit, 241, roll 1, NARA, RG 75, T494; Baraga, *A Dictionary of the Ojibway Language*, 2:4 (*Abiitan*), 73 (*Bemiged*). At least one of these words, *abiitan*, retains its nineteenth century meaning in present-day Ojibwe; see Nichols and Nyholm, *A Concise Dictionary of Minnesota Ojibwe*, 1:3.

19. "'Statement Made by the Indians': A Bilingual Petition of the Chippewas of Lake Superior, 1864," John D. Nichols, ed., The Centre for Research and Teaching of Canadian Native Languages (London: University of Western Ontario, 1988), 10–11, 14–15, 17–18, and *passim* 19–28. Erik M. Redix, *in The Murder of Joe White: Ojibwe Leadership and Colonialism in Wisconsin* (East Lansing: Michigan State University, 2014), provides an insightful recent study of the impact of several mid-nineteenth century treaties negotiated with Wisconsin Ojibwe communities. Fluent in English and Anishinaabemowin, Redix retranslates this bilingual petition to reveal more accurate meanings of important words and concepts. Perhaps not surprisingly, he also makes clear that Ojibwes possessed a far different understanding of their treaties than Americans realized.

20. "Proceedings of the Treaty at Chicago," Treaty of 29 August 1821 at Chicago, 33 (Me-te-a), Typescript, Schoolcraft Papers, National Archives, Record Group 75, NIS-203; "Extracts from Minutes of a Council held at Prairie du Chien," Treaty of 15 July 1830, 257 (Waw-row-csaw), roll 2, NARA, RG 75, T494; "Journal of the preceedings of a Treaty between the United States and the United Tribes of Pottawottamies, Chippeways and Ottowas," Treaty of 26 September 1833 at Chicago, 67 ("Ap-te-ke-zhig"), roll 3, NARA, RG 75, T494.

21. "Minutes of a Treaty," Treaty of 3 August 1795, at Greenville, 1:564 (Potawatomis acknowledge Delawares as grandfathers); 565 (Ojibwes acknowledge Delawares as grandfathers); 569 (Shawnees acknowledge Delawares as grandfathers); 571 (Blue Jacket changes seat); 570 (all remaining quotes), ASP: IA. Significantly, Tarhe and the Wyandots did not regard the Delawares as their grandfathers, but as nephews.

22. Ah be te ke zhick quoted in "Journal of the preceedings," Treaty of 26 September 1833 at Chicago, 68, roll 3, NARA, RG 75, T494. For Ah be te ke zhick and Apte-ke-zhick identified as the same person, see 67, 79, and 100. Possibly this name is "Aabitagiizhig," or Half Sky. See Baraga, *Dictionary of the Otchipwe Language*, 2:4 "abita" or "half," and 2:132 "gijig" or "sky"; see also "aabita" and "giizhig," Ojibwe People's Dictionary, https://ojibwe.lib.umn.edu/. Accessed 2 September 2021. LeGros quoted in "Record of the proceedings," Treaty of 23 October 1826 on the Wabash River, 887 (first two quotes), 889 (final quote), roll 1, NARA, RG 75, T494. See James Joseph Buss, *Winning the West with Words: Language and Conquest in the Lower Great Lakes* (Norman: University of Oklahoma Press, 2011) for the larger context of Miami and Potawatomi history.

23. All quotes from "Journal of the proceedings," Treaty of 11 August 1827 at Butte des Morts, 28, roll 2, NARA, RG 75, T494.

24. "Journal of the proceedings," Treaty of 11 August 1827 at Butte des Morts.

25. Agabe-gijik's words were recorded by the German ethnographer Johann Georg Kohl, who traveled to Lake Superior in the 1850s, described elements of Ojibwe culture, and spoke at length with a number of Ojibwe people. See Kohl, *Kitchi-Gami: Life Among the Lake Superior Ojibway* (1860; repr., St. Paul: Minnesota Historical Society, 1985), 235. Nanabozho's name is given variously as Nenibozo, Nanibush, Menibozo, and Waynibosho. For the cycle of youthful adventure stories, see William Jones, *Ojibwa Texts*, in Truman Michelson, ed., Publications of the American Ethnological Society, vol. 7, parts 1–2 (New York: G. E. Stechert and Company, 1917, 1919), 3–501; for similar spiritual beings in other eastern Woodlands Native cultures, see also "Nanabozho (Michabou, Mieska, Wisakedjak)" in Frederick Webb Hodge, ed. *Handbook of American Indians, Bureau of American Ethnology*, Bulletin 30, pt. 2 (Washington, DC: Government Printing Office, 1910), 19–23.

26. John Tanner, *The Falcon: A Narrative of the Captivity and Adventures of John Tanner* (1830; repr., New York: Penguin Books, 1994), 198; Frederick Baraga, "Chippewa Indians, as Recorded by Rev. Frederick Baraga in 1847," *Studia Slovenica* X (1976): 47, 50 (elders seating); Michael D. McNally, *Honoring Elders: Aging, Authority, and Ojibwe Religion* (New York: Columbia University Press, 2009), 281 (rebuking Ojibwe deacon); Alan Corbiere, personal communication ("older than me"). My thanks also to Cary Miller for the reference to Tanner's story.

27. Edmund F. Ely Diaries, 20 December 1833, box 1, Edmund Franklin Ely and Family Papers, Minnesota Historical Society [hereafter Ely Diaries, Ely Papers] (the woman elder's recollection of shooting stars); see McNally, *Honoring Elders*, for an in-depth discussion of elderhood as an achieved and enacted status.

28. Baraga, *A Dictionary of the Otchipwe Language*, 2:335 (*oshki*); for Ojibwe views of vulnerability of young children, see Sister M. Inez Hilger, *Chippewa Child Life and Its Cultural Background*, Smithsonian Institution Bureau of American Ethnology Bulletin 146 (Washington, DC: Government Printing Office, 1951), 44–46; and Frances Densmore,

Chippewa Customs (1929; repr., St. Paul: Minnesota Historical Society Press, 1970), 53–58. See also Kohl, *Kitchi-Gami*, 235, for parental consternation over a failed vision quest.

29. Bizhiki quoted in "Journal of the Commissioners, "Treaty of 5 August 1826 at Fond du Lac, 840, roll 1, NARA, RG 75, T 494; Flat Mouth quoted in "Interview between the Commissioner of Indian Affairs and the Pillager and Winnepec band of Chippewas on Saturday morning, Feby 17, 1855," in "Transcription of the record of the negotiation and signing of the Treaty of February 22, 1855, made and entered into at Washington, D. C., by and Between George W. Manypenny, Commissioner of Indian Affairs, on the part of the United States, and the chiefs and delegates of the Mississippi, Pillager and Lake Winnibigoshish bands of Chippewa Indians," p. 74, in James F. Sutherland Papers, Minnesota Historical Society.

30. "Journal of the Proceedings," Treaty of 19 August 1825 at Prairie du Chien, 731 (Bayezhig, as "Pie-a-juck"), roll 1, NARA, RG 75, T494; "Diary Kept by the Reverend William Thurston Boutwell, Missionary to the Ojibwa Indians. 1832–1837." 21 July 1832, box 2, William T. Boutwell Papers, Minnesota Historical Society [hereafter Boutwell Diary, Boutwell Papers] (Whitefisher); "Proceedings of a Council with the Chippewa Indians," *Iowa Journal of History and Politics* 5 (1911): 419 (Spruce). For additional tribal speakers acknowledging their youthful years, see Treaty of 19 August 1825 at Prairie du Chien, 728 (Wan-na-ta, a Yankton Dakota spokesperson, who remarked "Altho I am a young man"), and 729 (unnamed "Winnebagoe Chief," who stated "I am but a child"), roll 1, NARA, RG 75, T494.

31. "Journal of the proceedings at a Council held at Green Bay by Col. Stambaugh, U.S. Agent, with the Menominie Indians," Treaty of 8 February 1831 at Green Bay, 455 ("one heart"), roll 2, NARA, RG 74, T494; "Minutes of a Treaty," 3 August 1795 at Greenville, ASP: IA, 1:571 ("one voice"); see also Cary Miller, *Ogimaag, Anishinaabeg Leadership, 1760–1845* (Lincoln: University of Nebraska Press, 2010) for a recent thorough analysis of civil or chiefly leadership, war leadership, and the leadership of religious practitioners.

32. "Minutes of a Treaty," 3 August 1795 at Greenville, ASP: IA, 1:579 (all quotes).

33. Historical analyses of the relationship between civil leaders and war leaders date back to the nineteenth century when William Whipple Warren discussed the two types of leadership and the frequent political rivalry between them in "A History of the Ojibways," 49, 319–20, 376–77. Other nineteenth-century sources also describe rivalries between civil leaders and war leaders. See for instance, William Johnston, "Letters on the Fur Trade, 1833," in J. Sharpless Fox, ed., *Michigan Pioneer and Historical Society Collections* 37 (1909–1910): 189, 190, 202. In the twentieth century, see the anthropological analyses of Harold Hickerson, *The Southwestern Chippewa: An Ethnohistorical Study*, American Anthropological Association Memoir 92 (Menasha, WI: George B. Banta Company, Inc., 1962) and *The Chippewa and Their Neighbors: A Study in Ethnohistory* (New York: Holt, Rinehart and Winston, Inc., 1970), and James G. E. Smith, "Leadership Among the Southwestern Ojibwa," National Museums of Canada, *Publications in Ethnology*, vol. 7 (Ottawa: National Museums of Canada, 1973). More recent historical treatments include Gregory Evans Dowd, *A Spirited Resistance: The North American Indian Struggle for Unity, 1745–1815* (Baltimore: Johns Hopkins University Press, 1992); Michael N. McConnell, *A Country Between: The Upper Ohio Valley and Its Peoples,*

1724–1774 (Lincoln: University of Nebraska Press, 1992); Daniel K. Richter, *The Ordeal of the Longhouse: The Peoples of the Iroquois League in the Era of European Colonization* (Chapel Hill: University of North Carolina Press for the Omohundro Institute of Early American History and Culture, 1992); Laura L. Peers, *The Ojibwa of Western Canada, 1780–1870* (St. Paul: Minnesota Historical Society Press, 1994); Rebecca Kugel, *To Be The Main Leaders of Our People: A History of Minnesota Ojibwe Politics, 1820–1900* (East Lansing: Michigan State University Press, 1998), Gunlög Fur, *A Nation of Women,* 27–42. The statements of village leaders that they could not control their young men are literally found everywhere from treaty journals to the diaries of missionaries and reports of Indian agents; for instance, see "Speech of Shinguaba W'Ossin" in "Journal of the proceedings," Treaty of 19 August 1825 at Prairie du Chien, 0728 ("The Young men are bad & hard to govern"), roll 1, NARA, RG 75, T 494; 19 June 1832, Boutwell Journal, Boutwell Papers, MHS.

34. Aw ba naw bee quoted in "Record of the proceedings," Treaty of 16 October 1826 on the Wabash River, 895, roll 1, NARA, RG 75, T 494. Although these negotiations resulted in separate treaties with Potawatomis and Miamis, the same American commission negotiated both treaties. The journals of proceedings form one document and are filed together in the microfilmed T 494 records under the Treaty of 16 October 1826 with the Potawatomi. For the final versions of both treaties, see Charles J. Kappler, comp. and ed., *Indian Affairs, Laws and Treaties,* vol. 2 (Washington, DC: Government Printing Office, 1904), 273–77 (Potawatomi treaty), and 278–81 (Miami treaty).

35. "Speech of Keeacock Great War Chief of the Socks [Sauks] in "Sauk & Fox Speeches made to the Secy of War," Treaty of 4 August 1824 [no location given], 0570, roll 1, NARA, RG 75, T 494; "Journal of Rev. S. Hall," 6 September 1831, box 1, American Board of Commissioners for Foreign Missions Papers, MHS (originals at the Houghton Library, Harvard).

36. Martha Coleman Bray, ed. *The Journals of Joseph N. Nicollet,* 21 (Flat Mouth); Major H. Day to George W. Manypenny, 26 April 1856, National Archives and Records Service, Washington, DC. Letters Received by the Office of Indian Affairs, 1821–1881. 0008–9 (Hole-in-the-Day), roll 151, National Archives Microfilm Publications, RG 75, Microcopy 234.

37. For tribal speakers invoking the language of pity, see "Speech of Decor ree," "Journal of the proceedings," Treaty of 19 August 1825 at Prairie du Chien, 736, roll 1, NARA, RG 75, T494; and "Speech of Kau-rah-kaw-see-kaw," "Proceedings of the Commissioners for holding a Treaty with the Winnebaygoes and the United nations of the Ottaways, Chippeways and Potawatamies of the Illinois," Treaty of 29 July 1829 at Prairie du Chien, 183, roll 2, NARA, RG 75, T494; see also 181–84 for Native characterizations of the metaphoric kindly father. For Great Lakes tribal openness to social and spiritual ambiguity, see Bruce White, "The Woman Who Married a Beaver: Trade Patterns and Gender Roles in the Ojibwa Fur Trade," *Ethnohistory* 46 (Winter 1999): 109–47. The classic anthropological exploration of Ojibwe (and by extension other Algonkian-speakers) perceptions of malleable categories of being is A. I. Hallowell, *Culture and Experience* (Philadelphia: University of Pennsylvania Press, 1955).

38. For further elaboration of Ojibwe views of the human life cycle with its four ages, see Basil Johnston, *Ojibway Heritage* (New York: Columbia University Press, 1976), *Ojibway Ceremonies* (Toronto: McClelland and Stewart, 1982), and *The Manitous: The*

Spiritual World of the Ojibway (New York: Harper Collins, 1995). Recent explorations of the enslavement of Native peoples complicate a view of Great Lakes Native societies— and the region as a whole—as lacking groups of permanently unfree individuals. See the superb recent treatment of enslavement of both Native and African persons by Tiya Miles, *The Dawn of Detroit: A Chronicle of Slavery and Freedom in the City of the Straits* (New York: The New Press, 2017). See also Christina Snyder, *Slavery in Indian Country: The Changing Face of Captivity in Early America* (Cambridge, MA: Harvard University Press, 2010) and Brett Rushforth, *Bonds of Alliance: Indigenous and Atlantic Slaveries in New France* (Chapel Hill: University of North Carolina Press for the Omohundro Institute of Early American History and Culture, 2012).

39. "Journal of George B. Porter, Governor of the Territory of Michigan and Superintendent of Indian Affairs, on his visit to Green Bay in pursuance of the following Letter of Instructions from the Honorable Lewis Cass, Secretary of War," Treaty of 27 October 1832; 618 ("Great Father knows"), roll 2, NARA, RG 75, T494; "Journal of the preceedings," Treaty of 14 September, 1833 at Chicago, 0076 ("dutiful children"), roll 3, NARA, RG 75, T494; Flat Mouth quoted in "Journal of a voyage from Chippewa Agency to the source of the Mississippi," by Charles E. Flandrau, 26 August 1858, Charles Eugene Flandrau and Family Papers, vol. 23, MHS.

40. Jacqueline Peterson, "Many Roads to Red River: Métis Genesis in the Great Lakes Region, 1680–1815," in Jacqueline Peterson and Jennifer S. H. Brown, eds., *The New Peoples: Being and Becoming Métis in North America* (Lincoln: University of Nebraska Press, 1985), 63. For the history of the Métis Nation and the complications arising from expanding usage of the term *métis*, see Chris Andersen, *"Métis": Race, Recognition, and the Struggle for Indigenous Peoplehood* (Vancouver: University of British Columbia Press, 2014). For the social-cultural patterns that developed in a specific tribal community, see Nicole St-Onge, "Familial Foes? French-Sioux Families and Plains Métis Brigades in the Nineteenth Century," *American Indian Quarterly* 39 (Summer 2015): 302–37.

Readers will note a handful of terms that first appear in text with quotation marks indicating potentially changing usages. Several of the words found in eighteenth and nineteenth century sources use language that strikes contemporary hearers as offensive or biased. Words such as "half breed" and "mixed-blood" fit this category. It is important to place such words in their historic context and recognize that they represent complex and much-contested social realities. Initially these words had few pejorative connotations. Over the course of the second half of the eighteenth century, as European and later American ideas about race shifted, demeaning names for racialized groups were used deliberately as shows of domination.

41. Zhaagobe, as "Sha-go-bai," quoted in "Proceedings of a Council with the Chippewa Indians," *Iowa Journal of History and Politics* 5 (1911): 416; Chandonnet, as "Chandonai," quoted in "Journal of the preceedings," Treaty of 26 September 1833 at Chicago, 0083, roll3, NARA, RG 75, T494. For differing expressions of multiracial individuals' sense of identity, see J. G. Kohl, *Kitchi-Gami*, quoted in Peterson, "Prelude to Red River," 54; William Johnston, "Letters on the Fur Trade," in J. Sharpless Fox, ed., *Historical Collections of the Michigan Pioneer and Historical Society*, 37 (1909–1910): 177; Elizabeth T. Baird, "O-De-Jit-Wa-Win-Wing; Comptes du Temps Passe," box 4, Henry S. and Elizabeth T. Baird Collection, State Historical Society of Wisconsin.

42. "Journal of the proceedings at a Council held at Green Bay by Col. Stambaugh, US Agent, with the Menominie Indians," Treaty of 8 February 1831, 0451 ("our children the half breeds"), roll 2, NARA, RG 75, T494; Marten to Lyman Warren, n.d., 404 ("our half breed relations"), roll 388, NARA, RG 75, M234; Pizhiki (or Buffalo) to Lyman Warren, 5 January 1843, 405 ("grow from my side"), roll 388, NARA, RG 75, M234; Zhingwaabe Aasin, as "Shinguaba Wossin," and Maangozid, as "Mawn-gaw-sid," in "Journal of the Proceedings," Treaty of 5 August 1826 at Fond du Lac, 838 ("my half breeds"), 844 ("live in our hearts"), roll 1, NARA, RG 75, T494.

43. Grizzly Bear quoted in "Journal of George B. Porter," Treaty of 27 October 1832 at Green Bay; 0616, roll 2, NARA, RG 75, T494; Mayaajigaabaw quoted in "Proceedings of a Council with the Chippewa Indians," *Iowa Journal of History and Politics* 5 (1911): 425, 426. For an extended discussion of Ojibwe women's importance in extending kinship ties through marriage, see Heidi Bohaker, *Doodem and Council Fire: Anishinaabe Governance through Alliance* (Toronto: The Osgoode Society for Canadian Legal History and the University of Toronto Press, 2020).

Chapter 2

1. Audrey Smedley, *Race in North America: Origin and Evolution of a Worldview* (1993; repr., Boulder, CO: Westview Press, 2007); Geraldine Heng, "The Invention of Race in the European Middle Ages I: Race Studies, Modernity, and the Middle Ages," *Literature Compass* 8, no. 5 (May, 2011): 315–31; and "The Invention of Race in the European Middle Ages II: Locations of Medieval Race," *Literature Compass* 8, no. 5 (May, 2011): 332–50.

2. "Speech of LeGros" in "Journal &c of Comm[issio]n to Negotiate with the Indians in Indiana, 1826," in "Documents Relating to the Negotiation of the Treaty of October 16, 1826, with the Potawatomi Indians," 889, 890, roll 1, National Archives and Records Administration, Record Group 75, Microcopy T494 (hereafter cited as NARA, RG 75, T494). For the concept and operation of frontier exchange economies, see Daniel H. Usner Jr., *Indians, Settlers, and Slaves in a Frontier Exchange Economy: The Lower Mississippi Valley before 1783* (Chapel Hill: University of North Carolina Press for the Omohundro Institute of Early American History and Culture, 1992).

3. For discussion of the end of the War of 1812 and the start of treaty negotiations, see Helen Hornbeck Tanner, ed., *Atlas of Great Lakes Indian History* (Norman: University of Oklahoma Press for the Newberry Library, 1987), 120–21; also, Treaty of Ghent, 1814, International Treaties and Related Records, 1778–1974; National Archives and Records Administration, General Records of the United States Government, Record Group 11, https://www.nationalarchives.gov. Accessed 21 August 21. For American perceptions of their "first frontier," see Stephen Aron, *How the West Was Lost: The Transformation of Kentucky from Daniel Boone to Henry Clay;* 1996); on the lasting impact of the earliest frontier, see John Mack Faragher, *Daniel Boone: The Life and Legend of an American Pioneer* (1992); for a larger contextualization of the Great Lakes region in several successive imperial struggles, see David Curtis Skaggs and Larry L. Nelson, *The Sixty Years' War for the Great Lakes, 1754–1814* (East Lansing: Michigan State University Press, 2001).

4. Alan Taylor, "Captain Hendrick Aupaumut: The Dilemmas of an Intercultural Broker," *Ethnohistory* 43 (Summer 1996): 446 ("customs of all the nations"). R. David

Edmunds, *The Shawnee Prophet* (Lincoln: University of Nebraska Press, 1985), discusses the aftermath of the War of 1812 from the perspective of the Native peoples of the Great Lakes country; Gregory Evans Dowd, *A Spirited Resistance: The North American Indian Struggle for Unity, 1745-1815* (Baltimore: Johns Hopkins University Press, 1992) places Native movements for political unity and spiritual revitalization in a comparative and analytical context, while John Sugden's biography, *Tecumseh, A Life* (New York: Henry Holt, 1998), offers a deeply researched scholarly examination of the remarkable Shawnee leader.

5. See Tanner, *Atlas of Great Lakes Indian History,* 120-21, for the postwar treaty negotiations; for representative treaties see "Treaty with the Potawatomi," at Portage des Sioux, 18 July 1815; "Treaty with the Piankashaw," at Portage des Sioux, 18 July 1815; "Treaty with the Teton [Lakota]," at Portage des Sioux, 19 July 1815; "Treaty with the Sioux of the Lakes," at Portage des Sioux, 19 July 1815; "Treaty with the Sioux of St. Peter's River," at Portage des Sioux, 19 July 1815; "Treaty with the Wyandot, Etc. [Delaware, Seneca, Shawnee, Miami, Ojibwe, Odawa and Potawatomi]," at Spring Wells, Michigan Territory, 8 September 1815, in Charles J. Kappler, editor and compiler, *Indian Affairs, Laws and Treaties* (Washington, DC: Government Printing Office, 1904), 2:110-11, 111-12, 112-13, 113, 114, 117-19 (hereafter cited as Kappler).

6. *The Expeditions of Zebulon Montgomery Pike, to headwaters of the Mississippi River, Through Louisiana Territory, and in New Spain, During the Years 1805-6-7,* Elliott Coues, ed., 3 vols. (Minneapolis: Ross and Haines, Inc., 1965), 1:305; Hull quoted in R. David Edmunds, "'Unacquainted with the Laws of the Civilized World': American Attitudes toward the Métis Communities in the Old Northwest," in *The New Peoples: Being and Becoming Métis in North America,* ed. Jacqueline Peterson and Jennifer S. H. Brown (Winnipeg: University of Manitoba Press; Lincoln: University of Nebraska Press, 1985), 190; Long quoted in Jacqueline Louise Peterson, "The People in Between: Indian-White Marriage and the Genesis of a Métis Society and Culture in the Great Lakes Region, 1680-1830" (PhD diss., University of Illinois at Chicago, 1981), 133; Henry R. Schoolcraft, *Narrative Journal of Travels Through the Northwestern Regions of the United States Extending from Detroit through the Great Chain of American Lakes to the Source of the Mississippi River in the Year 1820,* ed. Mentor L. Williams, new forward by Philip P. Mason (1953; repr., East Lansing: Michigan State University Press, 1992), 221; William H. Keating, *Narrative of an Expedition to the Sources of St. Peter's River, Lake Winnepeek, Lake of the Woods, &c.* (Minneapolis, MN: Ross and Haines, 1959), 75.

7. Long quoted in Peterson, "The People in Between," 133; Keating, *Narrative of an Expedition,* 75, 76.

8. "Treaty with the Wyandots, Etc.," at Greenville, 3 August 1795, in Kappler, 2:41.

9. William Cronon, *Changes in the Land: Indians, Colonists, and the Ecology of New England* (New York: Hill and Wang; 1983) 54-81, 183n4 (Winthrop's theorizations of God-sanctioned land use). See also Francis Jennings, *The Invasion of America; Indians, Colonialism, and the Cant of Conquest* (New York: W. W. Norton, 1975), 128-45, esp. 134-36. Bernard W. Sheehan, *Seeds of Extinction; Jeffersonian Philanthropy and the American Indian* (Chapel Hill: University of North Carolina Press for the Omohundro Institute of Early American History and Culture, 1973), is the classic analysis of Anglo-American social evolutionist thought as it related to Native peoples; see also Robert A. Williams' discussion of the influence of the Scottish Common Sense school on

American thinking in *Linking Arms Together: American Indian Treaty Visions of Law and Peace, 1600–1800* (New York: Oxford University Press, 1997); Margaret T. Hodgen, *Early Anthropology in the Sixteenth and Seventeenth Centuries* (Philadelphia: University of Pennsylvania Press, 1964) examines social evolutionism as it was deployed in the first European efforts to theorize the existence of the so-called New World and reveals that its roots dated back to borrowings from classical Greek and Roman writings on distant peoples. A recent treatment that considers the Lockean roots is Patrick Wolfe, "Settler Colonialism and the Elimination of the Native," *Journal of Genocide Research* 8, no. 4 (2006): 387–409.

10. David D. Smits, "The 'Squaw Drudge': A Prime Index of Savagism," *Ethnohistory* 29 (Autumn, 1982): 281–306, provides a thorough assessment of European perceptions of Native gender roles, especially focusing on the European belief that Native gender roles violated the "natural" gender hierarchy of male dominance; see Susan Sleeper-Smith, "Women, Kin, and Catholicism: New Perspectives on the Fur Trade," *Ethnohistory* 47 (Spring 2000): 424–25 ("frontier Catholicism") and Peterson, "Prelude to Red River: A Social Portrait of the Great Lakes Métis," *Ethnohistory* 25 (Winter 1978): 52–53 (French gender roles in agriculture, French owning farms).

11. Keating, *Narrative of an Expedition*, 75; see Peterson, "Prelude to Red River," 52–53 (describing "ribbon" farms) and Peterson, "The People in Between: Indian-White Marriage and the Genesis of a Métis Society and Culture in the Great Lakes Region, 1680–1830," (PhD diss., University of Illinois at Chicago, 1981), 129 (general "backwardness" of the French).

12. Heng, "The Invention of Race in the European Middle Ages" I and II; for the traders' interconnected economic and political efforts, see Ronald N. Satz, "Chippewa Treaty Rights: The Reserved Rights of Wisconsin's Chippewa Indians in Historical Perspective," Transactions of the Wisconsin Academy of Sciences, Arts and Letters. 79 (1991; repr., Madison: 1994), 6–31; and Robert A. Trennert, *Indian Traders on the Middle Border: The House of Ewing, 1827–1854* (Lincoln: University of Nebraska Press, 1981), 23–118, for a thorough study of an individual mercantile firm that was deeply involved in treaty provisioning and politics. An important new study of the systematic exploitation of Native resources as part of the American state-building project is Michael John Witgen, *Seeing Red: Indigenous Land, American Expansion, and the Political Economy of Plunder in North America* (Chapel Hill: University of North Carolina Press for the Omohundro Institute of Early American History and Culture, 2022). See also Michael Witgen, "Seeing Red: Race, Citizenship, and Indigeneity in the Old Northwest," *Journal of the Early Republic* 38 (Winter 2018): 581–611.

13. "Treaty with the Wyandot, Etc.," ["Treaty of Maumee Rapids,"] 29 September 1817, Kappler, 2:145. For the currently preferred name, see "Treaty of the Maumee Rapids (1817)," *Ohio History Central*, July 1, 2005, http://www.ohiohistorycentral.org/entry.php?rec=1414. Accessed July 20, 2011.

14. Lewis Cass and Duncan McArthur to George Graham, 30 September 1817, American State Papers, Class 2, Indian Affairs, volume 2, selected and edited by Walter Lowrie and Walter S. Franklin (Washington, DC: Gales and Seaton, 1834), 139 (hereafter cited as ASP: IA).

15. George Graham to Lewis Cass and Duncan McArthur, 19 May 1817, ASP: IA, 2:137.

16. Of the tribes that did not retain fee simple lands, the Ojibwes and Potawatomis ceded all their lands in Ohio, while Odawas retained two tracts of land but did not hold them by individual patents, preferring communal landownership instead. See "Treaty with the Wyandot, Etc.," ["Treaty of Maumee Rapids,"] 29 September 1817, Kappler, 2:146 (fee simple provisions); 147 (terms of Odawa cession), 150–51 (terms of Ojibwe and Potawatomi cessions). For the names of tribal persons receiving allotted lands, see "Schedule," 152–55. For a further examination of Native land retention strategies in the Lower Great Lakes, see Rebecca Kugel, "Planning to Stay: Native Strategies to Remain in the Great Lakes Post-War of 1812," *Middle West Review* 2 (Spring 2016): 1–26.

17. Lewis Cass and Duncan McArthur to George Graham, 30 September 1817, ASP: IA, 2:139 ("mutual demands"), George Graham to Lewis Cass and Duncan McArthur, 19 May 1817, ASP: IA, 2:137 ("life estates"). "Treaty with the Wyandot, Etc.," ["Treaty of Maumee Rapids,"] 29 September 1817, Kappler, 2:47–48, Article 8, for a descriptive list of the twenty-three adoptive kinfolk. For Sawendebans, see 149; for Alexander and Richard G. Godfroy, see 148–49; for Shane, see 148 (and also John Sugden, *Tecumseh, A Life* (New York: Henry Holt, 1997), 379, 413n1); for widows, see 148 (Sarah Williams, Catharine Walker); for the multiracial "children of the late William M'Collock," and "the children of the late Shawnese chief captain Logan," see 148. In these last two instances, the number of children was left unspecified, making impossible an exact tally of the number of people who received land grants under the treaty. Thus, twenty-three represents the lowest number of persons by assuming a minimum of only two children in each of these cases. There could, in fact, have been several more.

18. "Treaty with the Wyandot, Etc.," ["Treaty of Maumee Rapids,"] 29 September 1817, Kappler, 2:148 ("taken prisoner," "ever since lived"). So-called white captives among Native peoples were a source of endless fascination for Anglo-Americans in the early republic; for representative analyses by historians, see Helen Hornbeck Tanner, "Coocoohchee: Mohawk Medicine Woman," *American Indian Culture and Research Journal* 3, no. 3 (1979): 23–41, Colin Calloway, "Simon Girty: Interpreter and Intermediary," in James A. Clifton, ed., *Being and Becoming Indian; Biographical Studies of North American Frontiers* (Chicago: Dorsey Press, 1989), 38–58, and two recent analyses of Frances Slocum, Susan Sleeper-Smith's assessment in *Indian Women and French Men: Rethinking Cultural Encounter in the Western Great Lakes* (Amherst: University of Massachusetts Press, 2001), 124–25, 136–39, and James Joseph Buss's longer treatment in *Winning the West With Words: Language and Conquest in the Lower Great Lakes* (Norman: University of Oklahoma Press, 2011), 134–62. John Demos, *The Unredeemed Captive: A Family Story from Early America* (New York: A. A. Knopf, 1994), discusses seventeenth-century New England and reveals the duration of the English/American anxiety over captives, while June Namias, *White Captives: Gender and Ethnicity on the American Frontier* (Chapel Hill: University of North Carolina Press, 1993), presents a feminist reading of captivity. See also Kathryn Zabelle Derounian-Stodola, *The Indian Captivity Narrative, 1550–1900* (New York: Maxwell Macmillan International, 1993); see also James Axtell, *The Invasion Within: The Contest of Cultures in Colonial North America* (New York: Oxford University Press, 1985).

19. Lewis Cass and Duncan McArthur to George Graham, 30 September 1817, ASP: IA, 2:139 ("Indians by blood"). For representative Congressional efforts to prevent "whites" from claiming lands at treaties or as private gifts or purchases from Native

individuals, see U. S. House Journal. 1st Congress, 2nd Session, 22 July 1790, 137–38, "An Act to regulate trade and intercourse with the Indian tribes"; U. S. House Journal. 2nd Congress, 2nd Session, 1 March 1793, 329–33, "An Act to regulate Trade and Intercourse with the Indian Tribes," U. S. House Journal. 4th Congress, 1st Session, 19 May 1796, 469–74, esp. Sections 5, 12, "An Act to regulate Trade and Intercourse with the Indian Tribes, and to preserve Peace on the Frontiers." Library of Congress, http://www.loc.gov. Accessed 6 February 2016. Buss, *Winning the West with Words*, 73–96, provides a perceptive treatment of Wyandot adaptations and the role of multiracial Wyandots and Anglophone adoptees; additionally, see Martin W. Walsh, "The 'Heathen Party': Methodist Observation of the Ohio Wyandots," *American Indian Quarterly* 16 (Spring 1992): 189–202. Additional discussions of the relationship between cultural orientation and racial identity in the Great Lakes region include Sleeper-Smith, *Indian Women and French Men*; and Lucy Eldersveld Murphy, *Great Lakes Creoles: A French-Indian Community on the Northern Borderlands, Prairie du Chien, 1750–1860* (New York: Cambridge University Press, 2014).

20. "Treaty with the Wyandot, Etc.," ["Treaty of Maumee Rapids,"] 29 September 1817, Kappler, 2:148 ("by blood or adoption").

21. "Treaty with the Wyandot, Etc.," ["Treaty of Maumee Rapids,"] 29 September 1817, Kappler, 2:149 ("Sawendebans, or Yellow Hair"), (the Godfroys as "adopted children") 148–49.

22. "Amendments Proposed to the Treaty with the Wyandots, Senecas, Delawares, Shawanees, Pattawatamies, Ottowas, and Chippewas," 29 December 1817, ASP: IA, 2:149 ("unprecedented," "at variance with"); "Treaty with the Wyandot, Etc.," ["Treaty of St. Mary's,"] 17 September 1818, Kappler, 2:162–63 ("Indian reservations"). For the land grants to individuals with their peculiar restrictions, see William E. Peters, *Ohio Lands and Their Subdivisions* (Athens, OH: W. E. Peters, 1918), 2nd ed., 216, 220–21, 223, 225, 226, 228–29, 231. See also Kugel, "Planning to Stay," for a more detailed discussion of the treaties' place in tribal plans to remain in northwestern Ohio.

23. "Treaty with the Wyandot, Etc.," ["Treaty of Maumee Rapids,"]" 29 September 1817, Kappler, 2:149 (Sawendebans described as Tondaganie's adopted son); for Sawendebans identified as the trader Peter Minor, see "Treaty with the Ottawa," 30 August 1831, at Maumee Rapids, Kappler, 2:338 (claim of Peter Minor), 336 (grant to Sawendebans or Peter Minor). The Godfroys are identified as adopted Potawatomi children in "Treaty with the Wyandot, Etc.," 148–49, and as the sons of the Indian agent, G[abriel] Godfroy, in James A. Clifton, *The Prairie People: Continuity and Change in Potawatomi Indian Culture, 1665–1965* (Lawrence: University of Kansas Press, 1977), 224.

24. Linda Gordon, *The Great Arizona Orphan Abduction* (Cambridge, MA: Harvard University Press, 1999) 6–15, 119–22. Although formal legal adoption was almost unheard of before the middle of the nineteenth century, orphaned, abandoned, or simply poor children were reabsorbed into families by being bound as indentured servants, a traditional early modern social mechanism for reincorporating unattached individuals into normative patriarchal family units. In theory, children would be fed, lodged, and taught a trade in exchange for their labor, though see Marilyn Irvin Holt, *The Orphan Trains: Placing Out in America* (Lincoln: University of Nebraska Press, 1992). By the 1850s, child welfare advocates had come to believe that poor, usually Catholic, urban children would flourish in wholesome rural environments, and children were sent on so-called

orphan trains to Midwestern and Western farming communities where, again, their labor was of paramount interest to the families who took them in. Protestant American missionaries brought these expectations with them to the Great Lakes country in the 1830s. For representative examples, see 6 April 1836, 19 February 1837, 10 March 1837, Ely Diaries, Ely Papers, box 1, Minnesota Historical Society (hereafter cited as MHS). For a tribal effort to hold onto its own orphaned children, see Julie L. Reed, *Serving the Nation: Cherokee Sovereignty and Social Welfare, 1800–1907* (Norman: University of Oklahoma Press, 2016). For treatments of the often more problematic forms of incorporation of Native youth into tribal societies in other regions of North America, see James F. Brooks, *Captives and Cousins: Slavery, Kinship, and Community in the Southwest Borderlands* (Chapel Hill: University of North Carolina Press for the Omohundro Institute of Early American History and Culture, 2002); Juliana Barr, *Peace Came in the Form of a Woman: Indians and Spaniards in the Texas Borderlands* (Chapel Hill: University of North Carolina Press, 2007); and Christina Snyder, *Slavery in Indian Country; The Changing Face of Captivity in Early America* (Cambridge, MA: Harvard University Press, 2010). For the observations of a present-day Miami educator on belonging to multiple tribal nations, see George Ironstrack, "*nahi meehtohseeniwinki: iilinweeyankwi neehi ssi meehtohseeniwiyankwi aatotamankwi*: To Live Well: Our Language and Our Lives," in James Joseph Buss and C. Joseph Genetin-Pilawa, eds., *Beyond Two Worlds: Critical Conversations on Language and Power in Native North America* (Albany: State University of New York Press, 2014), 181–208.

25. Zhingwaabe Aasin (as Shinguabe Wossin) in "Journal of the Commissioners, appointed to hold a treaty with the Chippeways, on Lake Superior in 1826," in "Documents Relating to the Negotiation of the Treaty of August 5, 1826, with the Chippewa Indians," 838, roll 1, NARA, RG 75, T494; unnamed "Menomonie chief" in "Journal of the Proceedings at treaty held by Gov. Cass and Col. McKenney with the Indians at the Buttes des Morts—near Green Bay," in "Documents Relating to . . . the Treaty of 11 August 1827, with the Menomonie Indians," 14, roll 2, NARA, RG 75, T494. The tribes involved in the original peace-making effort held at Prairie du Chien in 1825 included the Dakotas, Ojibwes, Sacs, Foxes, Menominis, Ioways, Ho-chunks, and the United Band of Ojibwes, Odawas and Potawatomis; see "Treaty with the Sioux, Etc.," 19 August 1825, at Prairie du Chien, Kappler, 2: 250. For "making of relatives," see Bethel Saler, *The Settlers' Empire: Colonialism and State Formation in America's Old Northwest* (Philadelphia: University of Pennsylvania Press, 2015). See Bohaker, *Doodem and Council Fire,* for an excellent new treatment of tribal understandings of adoption as an expansive, incorporative process among communities identifying as Anishinaabe; see, too, the insightful discussion of the multiple layers and networks of kin ties and obligations that informed Anishinaabe political processes and decision-making in Heidi Kiiwetinepinesiik Stark, "Marked by Fire: Anishinaabe Articulations of Nationhood in Treaty Making with the United States and Canada," *American Indian Quarterly* 36 (Spring 2012): 119–49.

26. Bruce White, "The Woman Who Married the Beaver: Trade Patterns and Gender Roles in the Ojibwa Fur Trade," *Ethnohistory* 46 (Winter 1999): 109–47; Bohaker, *Doodem and Council Fire*; see also Diamond Jenness, *The Ojibwa of Parry Island: Their Social and Religious Life*. National Museum of Canada, Bulletin 78, Anthropology Series. (Ottawa: Department of Mines, 1935), 22–23, for a discussion of Ojibwe

understandings that all living beings share identical forms of social personhood and live in identically constructed social worlds. The classic articulation of Ojibwe understanding of human and Other Than Human persons is A. Irving Hallowell, "Ojibwa Ontology, Behavior, and World View," in Dennis Tedlock and Barbara Tedlock, *Teachings from the American Earth: Indian Religion and Philosophy* (New York: Liveright Co., 1975), 141–78. For anthropological discussions of adoption in Ojibwe society, see Sister M. Inez Hilger, *Chippewa Child Life and Its Cultural Background*. Smithsonian Institution Bureau of American Ethnology, Bulletin 146 (Washington, DC: Government Printing Office, 1907) 33–35; Ruth Landes, *Ojibwa Sociology*. Columbia University Contributions to Anthropology 29 (New York: Columbia University Press, 1937), 16–17.

27. "Proceedings of a Council with the Chippewa Indians," *Iowa Journal of History and Politics* 5 (1911): 416. Two versions of the 1837 treaty proceedings exist. Better known and more widely accessible is the version that appeared without attribution in 1837 in the Dubuque *Iowa News* and was later reprinted in the *Iowa Journal of History and Politics*. A second version, written by the treaty commission's recording secretary, Verplanck Van Antwerp, is included in the microfilmed records of treaty negotiations in NARA, RG 75, T494. Titled "Proceedings of a Council held by Governor Henry Dodge with the Chiefs and principal men of the Chippewa Nation of Indians near Fort Snelling, at the confluence of the St. Peter and Mississippi Rivers, commencing on the 20th day of July 1837," 548–68, roll 3, NARA, RG 75, T494, this version includes (553) a parenthetical note from Van Antwerp stating "Sha-go-bai is a half breed."

28. White, "The Woman Who Married the Beaver"; Bohaker, *Doodem and Council Fire*, expands significantly on this point.

29. "Treaty with the Potawatomis," 2 October 1818, at St. Mary's, Kappler, 2:169; "Treaty with the Wea," 2 October 1818, at St. Mary's, 169; "Treaty with the Miami," 6 October 1818, at St. Mary's, 171–74.

30. "Treaty with the Potawatomis," 2 October 1818, at St. Mary's, Kappler, 2:169 ("sister of Topinibe"); "Treaty with the Wea," 2 October 1818, at St. Mary's, 169 ("sister of Jacco"). Sleeper-Smith's extended discussion of Kakima in *Indian Women and French Men*, 90–91, 93–95, also describes the widespread pattern of Native women incorporating foreign men into tribal societies by means of marriage; see also Bohaker, *Doodem and Council Fire*. For an early recognition of this practice, see Sylvia Van Kirk, "Toward a Feminist Perspective in Native History," in *Papers of the Eighteenth Algonquian Conference*, William Cowan, ed. (Ottawa: Carleton University Press, 1987), 386.

31. "Treaty with the Wea," 2 October 1818, at St. Mary's, Kappler, 2:169 ("within the limits"), 170 ("not to be conveyed"), 169. For lands granted to Kakima's children, see "Schedule," appended to "Treaty with the Potawatomis," 2 October 1818, 169. The fourth tribe to negotiate at St Mary's in October, 1818 was the Delawares who also preserved lands through holdings granted to individuals. The treaty does not provide any information about the six people, however, but it is nonetheless possible that the Delawares were also vesting land in the hands of the multiracial kin of tribal leaders. See "Treaty with the Delawares," 3 October 1818, at St. Mary's, Kappler, 2:170–71. A deeply informative analysis of how tribal kinship, especially the relationships between Native uncles and their multiracial nephews, operated in another region of North America is Theda Perdue, *"Mixed Blood" Indians: Racial Construction in the Early South* (Athens: University of Georgia Press, 2003).

32. "Treaty with the Miami," 6 October 1818, at St. Mary's, Kappler, 2:172; see also Article 3, 2:173–74, for the twenty-nine individuals granted lands. For biographical information on Richardville, see R. David Edmunds, "Richardville, Jean Baptiste (Peshewa)," in *The Encyclopedia of North American Indians,* ed. Frederick E. Hoxie (New York: Houghton Mifflin Company, 1996), 549–50. See also the longer treatment of Richardville's career by Bradley Birzer, "Jean Baptiste Richardville, Miami Métis," in *Enduring Nations: Native Americans in the Midwest,* ed. R. David Edmunds (Urbana: University of Illinois Press, 2008), 94–108.

33. R. David Edmunds, "Potawatomi," in *The Encyclopedia of North American Indians,* ed. Frederick E. Hoxie (New York: Houghton Mifflin, 1996), 506–8; see also Edmunds, *The Potawatomi.* For the Ohio Odawas' retention of land through grants of land, see "Treaty with the Ottawa," 18 February 1833, Kappler, 2:392–93 (Articles 2 and 3); for the Ho-chunk [Winnebagoes] see "Treaty with the Winnebago," 1 August 1829, Kappler, 2:301–2. For another study that explores the strategies of mixed-race tribal families, including the creation of reservations expressly for the multiracial tribal populations, see Jameson ("Jimmy") Sweet, *The 'Mixed-Blood' Moment: Race, Law, and Mixed-Ancestry Indians in the Nineteenth Century* (forthcoming). See also Nicole St-Onge, "Familial Foes? French-Sioux Families and Plains Métis Brigades in the Nineteenth Century," *American Indian Quarterly* 39 (Summer 2015): 302–37, for an exploration of comparable kinship strategies between multiracial French-Dakota families of the western Great Lakes and the Plains Métis of the Canadian Plains.

34. Stewart Rafert, "Godfroy, Francois (Palonswa)," in *The Encyclopedia of North American Indians,* ed. Frederick E. Hoxie (New York: Houghton Mifflin, 1996), 223–24; Birzer, in Edmunds, ed., *Enduring Nations,* 102 (on Lafontaine), 103–5 (Godfroy family); James M. McClurken, "Augustin Hamlin Jr.: Ottawa Identity and the Politics of Persistence," in *Being and Becoming Indian: Biographical Studies of North American Frontiers,* James A. Clifton, ed. (Chicago: Dorsey, 1989), 82–111; Edmunds, *The Potawatomis,* 222 (multiracial Potawatomi families). Other multiracial leaders rose to prominence who did not claim French ancestry, among them Billy Caldwell and Alexander Robinson of the United Band, but the French-descended population, numbering in the tens of thousands, formed an obvious majority in the region. It seems likely that, once this largest "white" population revealed itself to possess a different identity, it would remain the focus of American attention and perplexity. Indeed, Americans often collapsed all persons of multiracial ancestry into the category of French in recognition of this group's predominance.

35. 1 July 1843, Alexis Bailly to T. Hartley Crawford, 416, roll 388, National Archives and Records Administration, Record Group 75, Microcopy 234 (hereafter cited as NARA, RG 75, M234). For a sampling of treaties in which multiracial French kin identified their indigenous mothers, see "Treaty with the Ottawa, Etc.," 29 August 1821," at Chicago, Kappler, 2:199–200; "Treaty with the Potawatomi," 16 October 1826, at the Mississinewa River, Kappler, 2:276–77; "Treaty with the Chippewa, Etc.," 29 July 1829, at Prairie du Chien (with the Ojibwes, Odawas and Potawatomis), Kappler, 2:298; "Treaty with the Winnebago," 1 August 1829, at Prairie du Chien, Kappler, 2:301–2.

36. For a representative sampling of this and similar phrases, see Charles P. Babcock to William Medill, 26 May 1849, 160, roll 390, NARA, RG 75, M234 ("the red men of the forest"); Buss, *Winning the West with Words,* 119 ("daughter of the forest"). Variations

on the phrase describing Native peoples as "red men of the forest" were so well-known that William Apess, the Pequot author, lecturer, and reformer titled (perhaps ironically) his 1829 autobiography *A Son of the Forest.*

37. See Harriet Ritvo, *The Animal Estate: The English and Other Creatures in the Victorian Age* (Cambridge, MA: Harvard University Press, 1987) on constructs associated with animal breeding; Melissa L. Meyer, *Thicker Than Water: The Origins of Blood as Symbol and Ritual* (New York: Routledge, 2005) on the presumed properties of blood, and Stephen Jay Gould, *The Mismeasure of Man* (New York: W. W. Norton, 1981) on the pre-Darwinian science of "race."

38. George Boyd to Henry Dodge, 25 August 1839, 77, roll 318 ("notorious fact"), (*"all Indians"* [italics in original]), ("entire control"), ("Traders & half blood relatives"), ("designing & unprincipled"); George Boyd to Henry Dodge, 28 August 1839, 50, roll 318 ("influence," "their miserable halfbreed French Relations"), NARA, RG 75, M 234.

39. An important recent treatment of gifting among Great Lakes Native communities is Cary Miller, "Gifts as Treaties: The Political Use of Received Gifts in Anishinaabe Communities, 1820–1832," *American Indian Quarterly.* 26, no. 2 (Spring 2002): 221–45; see also the discussion in Bohaker, *Doodem and Council Fire.* The classic study of British understandings of gifting and their attempts to maneuver within what they understood as the Indigenous diplomatic system remains Wilbur R. Jacobs, *Wilderness Politics and Indian Gifts: The Northern Colonial Frontier, 1748–1763* (1950; repr., Lincoln: University of Nebraska Press, 1967); see also Edmunds' discussion of the Potawatomis' experiences with gifting as they negotiated multiple treaties with the Americans in the 1820s and early 1830s in *The Potawatomis.*

40. Dougherty quoted in James A. Clifton, *The Prairie People: Continuity and Change in Potawatomi Indian Culture, 1665–1965* (Lawrence: University of Kansas Press, 1977), 322; see also Birzer, "Jean Baptiste Richardville," in Edmunds, *Enduring Nations,* 94–108, for representative criticism of the ostentatious lifestyle of a tribal leader. For contemporaneous Anglo-American views of "half breeds" manipulating or colluding with tribal leaders, see Anselm J. Gerwing, "The Chicago Indian Treaty of 1833," *Journal of the Illinois State Historical Society,* 57 (Summer 1964): 117–42. In a thoughtful contrast, see Edmunds, *The Potawatomi,* 222–30, especially 228–30, 242, 248, which views the postwar efforts of multiracial leaders as good faith attempts to adapt to the growing Anglo-American presence and considers how they might have strategized to adopt specific Anglo-American occupations and land use patterns to the exclusion of others.

41. Birzer, "Jean Baptiste Richardville," in Edmunds, *Enduring Nations,* 94–108, 105; Edmunds, *The Potawatomis,* 242, 248.

42. "Speech of 'Sha-go-bai [Zhaagobe],'" in "Proceedings of a Council with the Chippewa Indians," 416; Chandonnais, spelled "Chandonai," quoted in "Journal of the pre-ceedings," "Treaty with the 'United Nation of Chippewa, Ottowa and Potawatamie,'" 26 September 1833, at Chicago, 0083, roll 3, NARA, RG 75, T494.

43. For the traders' combined economic and political efforts, see Satz, "Chippewa Treaty Rights," 6–31; and John P. Bowes, *Land Too Good for Indians; Northern Indian Removal* (Norman: University of Oklahoma Press, 2016). For a thorough study of a mercantile firm deeply involved in politics and treaty provisioning, see Trennert, *Indian Traders on the Middle Border,* 23–118. An excellent recent treatment of the Federal trading factory system and the political machinations of private traders to dismantle it,

is David Andrew Nichols, *Engines of Diplomacy: Indian Trading Factories and the Negotiation of American Empire* (Chapel Hill: University of North Carolina; 2016). See also, Michael John Witgen, *Seeing Red: Indigenous Land, American Expansion, and the Political Economy of Plunder in North America* (Chapel Hill: University of North Carolina Press for the Omohundro Institute of Early American History and Culture, 2022).

44. Satz, "Chippewa Treaty Rights." For an outstanding but often overlooked analysis of financial speculation in the western Great Lakes and how it was built on manipulating the Indian treaty and provisioning payments, see Kathleen Neils Conzen, "The Winnebago Urban System: Indian Policy and Townsite Promotion on the Upper Mississippi," in *Cities and Markets: Studies in the Organization of Human Space,* Rondo Cameron and Leo F. Schnore, eds. (Lanham, MD: University Press of America, 1997), 272–92, while Bruce M. White, "The Regional Context of the Removal Order of 1850," in *Fish in the Lakes, Wild Rice, and Game in Abundance: Testimony on Behalf of Mille Lacs Ojibwe Hunting and Fishing Rights,* James M. McClurken, compiler (East Lansing: Michigan State University, 2000), 141–328, provides a detailed examination of a particular series of political collusions in Minnesota and Wisconsin involving the annuity payments due the Ojibwe people. An additional treatment is James A. Clifton, "Wisconsin Death March: Explaining the Extremes in Old Northwest Indian Removal," *Transactions of the Wisconsin Academy of Sciences, Arts and Letters* 75 (1987), 1–39. Most recently, Larry Nesper, *"Our Relations . . . the Mixed Bloods:" Indigenous Transformation and Dispossession in the Western Great Lakes* (Albany: State University Press of New York; 2021) explores another effort by Anglo American land speculators to manipulate the multiracial identity of persons of French and Ojibwe ancestry to gain access to lands thought to contain valuable minerals.

45. Charles E. Cleland, *Rites of Conquest: The History and Culture of Michigan's Native Americans* (Ann Arbor: University of Michigan Press, 1992), 212–18, discusses the 1819 Treaty of Saginaw in some depth; see also 213 (quantities of alcohol); 215 (eleven multiracial children, Ojibwe leader kept drunk). Also see Kappler, "Treaty with the Chippewa, 1819," 24 September 1819, at Saginaw, 2:185–86 (full list of persons initially granted land under treaty).

46. Kappler, "Treaty with the Chippewa [*sic*, Ojibwe]," 5 August 1826, at Fond du Lac, 2:269 ("half breeds and Chippewas"), 272–73 (Schedule).

47. Conzen, "Winnebago Urban System," Satz, "Chippewa Treaty Rights," Cleland, *Rites of Conquest.* For representative treaties with separate payments for Native peoples and their "half-breed relations," see "Proceedings of a Council with the Chippewa Indians," 408–37; Kappler, "Treaty with the "Ottawa, Chippewa, and Pottawatamie, Nations of Indians," 29 August 1821, at Chicago, 2:198–201; "Treaty with the Chippewa [*sic*, Ojibwe]," 5 August 1826, at Fond du Lac, 2:268–73; "Treaty with the Potawatomi," 16 October 1826, at the Mississinewa River, 2:273–77; "Treaty with the Sacs and Foxes, Mdewakanton, Wahpekute, Wahpeton and Sisseton Dakotas, the Omahas, Ioways, Ottoes and Missourias," 15 July 1830, at Prairie du Chien, 2:305–10, and "Treaty with the Ottawa," 18 February 1833, at Maumee Rapids, Ohio, 2:392–94; "Treaty with the Chippewa, Etc. [Odawas and Potawatomis]," 26 September 1833, at Chicago, 2:402–15. All quotations are from "Treaty with the Sac and Foxes," 2:307.

48. "Report of Contested Election," 732 (descent from "pure European"); House Committee on Elections, Michigan Election, 19th Congress, 1st Session, Rep. No. 69,

13 February 1826, 7 ("so-called half breeds"); see also the longer report of the Congressional investigation, "A Report of the Proceedings in Relation to the Contested Election for Delegate to the Nineteenth Congress, from the Territory of Michigan...," in *The Territorial Papers of the United States*, vol. 11, The Territory of Michigan, 1820–1829, ed. Clarence E. Carter (Washington, DC: Government Printing Office, 1945), 730–75. For two outstanding recent assessments of the social and political repercussions of the American takeover of the Great Lakes region, see Michael Witgen, *An Infinity of Nations; How the Native New World Shaped Early North America* (Philadelphia: University of Pennsylvania Press, 2012), 340–46, and Lucy Eldersveld Murphy, *Great Lakes Creoles: A French-Indian Community on the Northern Borderlands, Prairie du Chien, 1750–1860* (New York: Cambridge University Press, 2014). For a general discussion of the so-called Yankee emigrants, see Russell E. Bidlack, *The Yankee Meets the Frenchman: River Raisin 1817–1830* (Ann Arbor: Historical Society of Michigan Press, 1965). For New England racial hierarchies and perceptions that persons of color, especially "Indians," had long vanished, see Jean M. O'Brien, *Firsting and Lasting: Writing Indians Out of Existence in New England* (Minneapolis: University of Minnesota Press, 2010) and Daniel Mandell, *Tribe, Race, History: Native Americans in Southern New England, 1780–1880* (Baltimore: Johns Hopkins University Press, 2008); for the erasure of race-based slavery and an African-American presence in the region, see Joanne Pope Melish, *Disowning Slavery: Gradual Emancipation and "Race" in New England, 1780–1860* (Ithaca, NY: Cornell University Press, 1998).

49. "Proceedings of a Council with the Chippewa Indians," 435 ("half-breed relations"); Kappler, "Treaty of Washington," 28 March 1836, with the Odawas and Ojibwes, 2:452 ("half-breeds"). The classic articulation of gendered public and private spheres in American life and culture is Nancy F. Cott, *The Bonds of Womanhood: "Woman's Sphere" in New England, 1780–1835* (New Haven, CT: Yale University Press, 1977). For a new examination of the complications generated by American efforts to impose their own conceptions and practices of marriage on Native peoples in the old *pays d'en haute*, see Catherine J. Denial, *Making Marriage: Husbands, Wives, and the American State in Dakota and Ojibwe Country* (St. Paul: Minnesota Historical Society Press, 2013).

50. "Speech of Carron," in "Journal of the proceedings at a Council held at Green Bay by Col. Stambaugh, US Agent, with the Menominie [sic] Indians," in "Documents Relating to the Negotiation of the Treaty of February 8, 1831, with the Menominee," 451 ("our children the half breeds"), roll 2, NARA, RG 75, T494; "Speech of La Grand," 5 January 1843, 406 ("our half breed children"), roll 388, NARA, RG 75, M234; "Speech of "Maw-Zaw-Zid" [Maangozid] in "Journal of the Commissioners, appointed to hold a treaty with the Chippeways, on Lake Superior in 1826," in "Documents Relating to the Negotiation of the Treaty of August 5, 1826, with the Chippewa Indians," 844 ("live in our hearts"), roll 1, NARA, RG 75, T494; Buffalo and Broken Nose quoted in Leonard Wheeler to David Greene, May 3, 1843, box 3, American Board of Commissioners for Foreign Missions Papers, MHS (originals at the Houghton Library, Harvard University; cited hereafter as ABCFM Papers).

51. Proceedings of a Council with the Chippewa Indians," *Iowa Journal of History and Politics* 5 (1911): 425 (Speech of "Ma-ghe-ga-bo [Mayaajigaabow]"); 416 (Speech of "Sha-go-bai [Zhaagobe]"). Also see the discussion of women's marriages as alliance-building practices in Bohaker, *Doodem and Council Fire*; see also the perceptive analysis

of Native understandings of marriage in Sylvia Van Kirk, "Toward a Feminist Perspective in Native History," in *Papers of the Eighteenth Algonquian Conference*, William Cowan, ed. (Ottawa, ON.: Carleton University Press, 1987), 377–89.

52. Grizzly Bear and Sku-a-ne-ne quoted in "Journal of George B. Porter, Governor of the Territory of Michigan and Superintendent of Indian Affairs, on his visit to Green Bay, in pursuance of the following Letter of Instructions from the Honorable Lewis Cass, Secretary of War," in "Documents Relating to the Negotiation of the Treaty of October 27, 1832, with the Menominee," 607, 616, roll 2, NARA, RG 75, T494; see also 606 for translation into English of Sku-a-ne-ne's name. "Speech of Pay-a-jig [Bayezhig]," "Proceedings of a Council with the Chippewa Indians," 415.

53. "Journal of Porter," in "Documents Relating to the Negotiation of the Treaty of October 27, 1832, with the Menominee," 607 ("live among"), roll 2, NARA, RG 75, T494; "Speech of Shinguaba Wossin [Zhingwaabe Aasin]," and "Speech of Snake River Ogima," in "Journal of the Commissioners, appointed to hold a treaty with the Chippeways, on Lake Superior in 1826," in "Documents Relating to the Negotiation of the Treaty of August 5, 1826, with the Chippewa Indians," 838, 844, roll 1, NARA, RG 75, T494. The Snake River *ogimaa's* name was not given. George Boyd to Henry Dodge, 28 August 1839, 77 ("designing traders and half breeds"), roll 318, NARA, RG 75, M234.

54. David Roediger, *The Wages of Whiteness: Race and the Making of the American Working Class* (London: Verso Press, 1991); Noel Ignatiev, *How the Irish Became White* (New York: Routledge, 1995); Matthew Frye Jacobson, *Whiteness of a Different Color: European Immigrants and the Alchemy of Race* (Cambridge, MA: Harvard University Press, 1998).

Chapter 3

1. "Testimony of Ay-ne-we-gah-bowh-e-quay," 29 July 1914, 1048, box 6, Ransom J. Powell Papers, Minnesota Historical Society (hereafter cited as Powell Papers, MHS).

2. Testimony of Day-dah-bah-saush," 31 October 1914, 10 ("pants and hats"). For pursuit of a hunting and trapping lifestyle, and avoidance of acquisitive behavior see "Testimony of Ay-ne-we-gah-bowh-e-quay," 29 July 1914, 1044 and "Testimony of Bay-bah-daung-ay-aush," 29 July 1914, 1025; for Indigenous dress and participation in Indigenous religious ceremonies, see "Testimony of Way-way-zo-e-quay," 29 July 1914, 1046–48, and "Testimony of Bah-ne-tah-nah-be-tung," 30 September 1914, 228. Also significant was membership in an Ojibwe clan other than the Eagle Clan, which was understood to be the "half breed clan"; see "Testimony of John ("Jack") Porter," 25 September 1914, 109–10, "Testimony of Bah-ne-tah-nah-be-tung," 30 September 1914, 228, and "Testimony of Nah-be-tah-nah-be-tung [possibly alternate rendering of Bah-ne-tah-nah-be-tung]," 30 September 1914, 237, all in box 6, Powell Papers, MHS.

3. "Testimony of Ain-dus-o-ge-shig," 24 September 1914, 85–86; see also 81–82 (Ain-dus-o-ge-shig identifies his grandparents by name), box 6, Powell Papers, MHS.

4. An early analysis of these remarkable court testimonies, with a focus on the ways that racialized identity was used to dispossess Ojibwes of their lands is David L. Beaulieu, "Curly Hair and Big Feet: Physical Anthropology and Implementation of Land Allotment on the White Earth Chippewa Reservation," *American Indian Quarterly* 8 (Fall 1984), 281–314; more recently, Jill Doerfler has explored past Ojibwe conceptions of

their identity as part of a White Earth Ojibwe initiative to reimagine a more Indigenous form of tribal inclusion in *Those Who Belong: Identity, Family, Blood, and Citizenship among the White Earth Anishinaabeg* (East Lansing: Michigan State University Press, 2015); for an incisive analysis of the conflation of old-fashioned racialism with "modern" genetics, see Kimberly Tallbear, *Native American DNA: Tribal Belonging and the False Promise of Genetic Science* (Minneapolis: University of Minnesota Press, 2013).

5. "Treaty with the Wyandot, Etc., [Treaty of Greenville]," 3 August 1795, at Greenville, Kappler, 2:41 (all quotes). The literature on North American multiracial peoples of Native and European heritage is extensive. For a representative sampling that includes both the Canadian and US literature, see Jennifer S. H. Brown, *Strangers in Blood: Fur Trade Company Families in Indian Country* (Vancouver: University of British Columbia Press, 1980), Sylvia Van Kirk, *Many Tender Ties: Women in Fur Trade Society, 1670–1870* (Norman: University of Oklahoma Press, 1980), Jacqueline Louise Peterson, "The People in Between: Indian-White Marriage and the Genesis of a Métis Society and Culture in the Great Lakes Region, 1680–1830," (PhD diss., University of Illinois at Chicago, 1981), Jennifer S. H. Brown and Jacqueline L. Peterson, eds., *The New Peoples: Being and Becoming Métis in North America* (Lincoln: University of Nebraska Press, 1985), Tanis Chapman Thorne, *The Many Hands of My Relations: French and Indians on the Lower Missouri* (Columbia: University of Missouri Press, 1996), Heather Devine, *The People Who Own Themselves: Aboriginal Ethnogenesis in a Canadian Family, 1660–1900* (Calgary, AB: University of Calgary Press, 2004), Lucy Eldersveld Murphy, *Great Lakes Creoles: A French-Indian Community on the Northern Borderlands, Prairie du Chien, 1750–1860* (New York: Cambridge University Press, 2014), Melinda Marie Jetté, *At the Hearth of the Crossed Races: A French-Indian Community in Nineteenth Century Oregon, 1812–1818* (Corvallis: Oregon State University Press, 2015).

6. Alfred Brunson, *A Western Pioneer; or, Incidents of the Life and Times of Rev. Alfred Brunson*, 2 vols. (Cincinnati, OH: Hitchcock and Walden, 1879), 2:83 (Francophones as formal interpreters, American disparagement of Francophone interpreters); Brunson to James D. Doty, 23 November 1843, 0678 (Francophones as after-hours interpreters), roll 388, National Archives and Records Administration Microfilm, Record Group 75, Microcopy 234 (hereafter cited as NARA, RG 75, M 234); John H. Eaton to John McNeil and Pierre Menard, 30 March 1829 in "Documents Relating to the Negotiation of the Treaty of July 29, 1829, with the United Chippewa, Ottawa, and Potawatomi Indians," 0150–53 (Francophones as messengers, as guides for commissioners' parties); Thomas L. McKenney to Pierre Menard, 6 April 1829; 0154 (instructed to make preliminary arrangements with tribes); John McNeil, Pierre Menard and Caleb Atwater to Pierre Menard Jr., 25 June 1829; 0156 (negotiate a change of council venue, persuade individual tribal leaders to attend treaties); John McNeil, Pierre Menard and Caleb Atwater to Jacques Metté, 25 June 1829; 156–57 (persuade individual tribal leaders to attend treaties, purchase supplies), roll 2, National Archives and Records Administration Microfilm, Record Group 75, Microcopy T494 (hereafter cited as NARA, RG 75, T494).

7. David Curtis Skaggs and Larry Lee Nelson, eds., *The Sixty Years War for the Great Lakes, 1754–1814* (East Lansing: Michigan State University Press, 2001); for an excellent study of the process of state formation in the northwestern territory, see Bethel Saler, *The Settlers' Empire: Colonialism and State Formation in America's Old Northwest* (Philadelphia: University of Pennsylvania Press, 2015).

8. Lewis Cass and Duncan McArthur to George Graham, 30 September 1817, *American State Papers: Indian Affairs*. 2 vols. Compiled by Walter Lowrie and Walter A. Franklin (Washington, DC: Gales and Seaton, 1834), II, 138 ("been compelled to admit") (hereafter cited as ASP: IA); Kappler, "Treaty with the Ottawa, Etc.," 28 March 1836, at Washington, DC, 2:452 ("half-breed relatives," "in their power to aid," "their capacity to use"); "Treaty with the Chippewa" [Treaty of St. Peters], 29 July 1837, at Fort Snelling, Kappler, 2:492 ("their half breed relations"). For an extended discussion of tribal treaty-making strategies in the period after the War of 1812 and its attendant complexities, see Rebecca Kugel, "Planning to Stay: Native Strategies to Remain in the Great Lakes Post-War of 1812" *Middle West Review* 2 (Spring 2016): 1–26.

9. Frederic Baraga, *Dictionary of the Ojibway Language* (1878; repr., St. Paul: Minnesota Historical Society Press, 1992), part 2 (Ojibwe-English), 421 ("half-dark, half-white") (hereafter cited as Baraga, *Dictionary*). An informative discussion of multiracial persons in the Great Lakes country is Jennifer S. H. Brown and Theresa Schenck, "Métis, Mestizo, and Mixed-Blood," in *A Companion to American Indian History*, ed. Philip J. Deloria and Neal Salisbury (Malden, MA: Blackwell, 2002, 2004); 321–38; particularly 326–27 for analysis of "half breed" and "Bois-brulé" as interchangeable glosses and as ethnic identifiers. For more on the French ethnic specificity of "Bois-brulé," see John Francis McDermott, *A Glossary of Mississippi Valley French, 1673–1850*. Washington University Studies in Language and Literature, New Series, No. 12 (St. Louis: Washington University Press, 1941), 26 ("Bois-brulé"). See also Nicole St-Onge, "Familial Foes? French-Sioux Families and Plains Métis Brigades in the Nineteenth Century," *American Indian Quarterly* 39 (Summer 2015): 302–37," for a perceptive study of another population of French-Indigenous persons whose self-conceptualizations differed in a number of ways from those of Ojibwe "half breeds," but also embraced a number of commonalities, including use of the ethnonym ("Bois-brulé").

10. Baraga, *Dictionary*, 421 ("Wissakodewinini"). The word remains in the modern Ojibwe language as "wiisaakodewikwe," "wiisaakodewinini," and has come to mean "a person of mixed ancestry." See John D. Nichols and Earl Nyholm, *A Concise Dictionary of Minnesota Ojibwe* (Minneapolis: University of Minnesota Press, 1995), part 1 (Ojibwe-English), 120 (hereafter cited as Nichols and Nyholm, *Concise Dictionary*). For an explication of the two language cognates by an early representative of the American state, see James D. Doty to Martin Van Buren, 21 January 1839, quoted in St-Onge, "Familial Foes?," 303, 329n6.

11. Baraga, *Dictionary*, 17 ("aiabitawisid," "half breed man"); Nichols and Nyholm, *Concise Dictionary*, 15 ("ayaa"), 16 ("aabita"); xii (discussion of properties of preverbs); "Testimony of May-zhuc-e-ge-shig," 24 April 1914, 761 ("long ago," "white man gave," "Ah-be-tah-wiz-ee"), "Testimony of I-ah-baince," 10 March 1914, 558 ("have half one kind," "half breed"), box 5, Powell Papers, MHS. For speculation about third- and fourth-gendered person's abilities to occupy an identity as being "half each," see Roger M. Carpenter, "Womanish Men and Manlike Women: The Native American Berdache as Warrior," in Fay Yarbrough and Sandra Slater, eds., *Gender and Sexuality in Indigenous North America, 1400–1850* (Columbia: University of South Carolina Press, 2011), 146–84.

12. "A Report of the Proceedings in Relation to the Contested Election for Delegate to the Nineteenth Congress, from the Territory of Michigan . . . ," in *The Territorial Papers*

of the United States, vol. 11, The Territory of Michigan, 1820–1829, ed. Clarence E. Carter (Washington, DC: Government Printing Office, 1945), 732 ("pure European"); "Report to the Commissioner of Indian Affairs," John W. Edmonds, 9 February 1837, NARA, Record Group 75, Microcopy 574, "Special Files of the Office of Indian Affairs," roll 23, 0584–729, 0593 ("one of whose parents," "strictly construed," "habits"); see also Saler, *Settlers' Empire* for American understandings of the future of the Old Northwest.

13. St-Onge, "Familial Foes?," also demonstrates that multiracial Dakota and Lakota tribal persons retained forms of belonging in their tribes of origin as well as claiming a distinctive French (or Canadian) identity.

14. An astute recent discussion of Navajo clans is Kristina Jacobsen and Shirley Ann Bowman, "'Don't Even Talk to Me if You're Kinya'áanii [Towering House]': Adopted Clans, Kinship, and 'Blood' in Navajo Country," *Journal of the Native American Studies Association* 6, no. 1 (2019): 43–76. My thanks to a former student, Joaquín Malta, for initially reminding me of Navajo practices of clan creation and to current graduate student Danny Archuleta who reminded me of the Tohono O'odham practice of creating clans for in-marrying groups. For scholarly works on the topic, see also Gladys A. Reichard, *Social Life of the Navajo Indians: With Some Attention to Minor Ceremonies* (New York: Columbia University Press, 1928) and Paul G. Zolbrod, *Diné Bahane': The Navajo Creation Story* (Albuquerque: University of New Mexico Press, 1984); Alice Joseph, Rosamond Spicer, and Jane Chesky, *The Desert People* (Chicago: University of Chicago Press, 1949); Ruth Murray Underhill, *The Singing for Power: The Song Magic of the Papago Indians of Southern Arizona* (1939; repr., Berkeley: University of California Press, 1976.)

15. Christina Snyder, *Slavery in Indian Country: The Changing Face of Captivity in Early America* (Cambridge, MA: Harvard University Press, 2010), 115 ("Sawanogalga"), 117 (Yuchis).

16. William Whipple Warren, *A History of the Ojibway People* (1885; repr., St. Paul: Minnesota Historical Society Press, 1984), 9–20 (brief biographical sketch), 55 ("received opinions"); 54–75 (Warren's overall intellectual orientation), 57–60 (Warren's assertion of the accuracy of biblical history).

17. Warren, *History,* 174 ("mixed bloods of either tribe"); 163 (Warren's dating of the peace council to "about the year 1695"). For an anthropological analysis of cultural practices of intermarriage, gift exchanges and food sharing as part of tribal peace negotiations dating at least to the seventeenth century, see Harold Hickerson, "The Feast of the Dead Among the Seventeenth Century Algonkians of the Upper Great Lakes," *American Anthropologist* 62 (February 1960): 81–107; also "The Sociohistorical Significance of Two Chippewa Ceremonials," *American Anthropologist* 65 (February 1963): 67–85.

18. Warren, *History,* 43 (Ojibwe-descended Dakotas), 174 ("relatives by blood"). For detailed analysis of Ojibwe kinship, see Ruth Landes, *Ojibwa Sociology.* Columbia University Contributions to Anthropology, vol. 29 (New York: Columbia University Press, 1937).

19. Warren, *History,* 165 (all quotes); see also 167–69 for a description of Ojibwe-Dakota peacemaking rituals. For Dakota historical perspectives that pay particular attention to the importance of bodies of water and water-dwelling spiritual beings, see Gwen Westerman and Bruce White, *Mni Sota Makoce: The Land of the Dakota* (St. Paul: Minnesota Historical Society Press, 2012), 18–22, 58–59, 73–74, 91–93.

20. Warren, *History*, 106–7 (uncle-nephew bond ruptured), 166 ("distinguished," "hated Ojibway blood"), 166–69 (shooting of multitribal Ojibwe), 171 ("sudden and secret flight"). For instances of Dakotas similarly fearful of attacks by Ojibwes contemporary with Warren's life, see Martha Coleman Bray, ed., *The Journals of Joseph N. Nicollet; A Scientist on the Mississippi Headwaters, with Notes on Indian Life, 1836–37* (St. Paul: Minnesota Historical Society Press, 1970), 31–32; also, ethnographer Ruth Landes reported that Dakota memories of Ojibwes as "centuries-long enemies," endured well into the twentieth century. See Landes, *The Mystic Lake Sioux* (Madison: University of Wisconsin Press), 9–10.

21. James F. Brooks, *Captives and Cousins: Slavery, Kinship, and Community in the Southwest Borderlands* (Chapel Hill: University of North Carolina Press for the Omohundro Institute of Early American History and Culture, 2002), 45–80; Snyder, *Slavery in Indian Country*, 152–56 (Joseph Brown's narrative).

22. Warren, *History*, 172 ("closely related"); 219 ("Ma-mong-e-se-da" and "camp was fired upon"); 220 ("in the Dakota tongue," "firing ceased immediately," "in the style of a chief"). On p. 219, Warren further identified Wabasha as the first of the three Dakota tribal leaders to bear this name.

23. Warren, *History*, 171 ("the ties of consanguinity," "harmed not," "war raged"); 165 (Wolf Clan Ojibwe leaders named and their villages identified as Rice Lake, Pokegama on Snake River, and Mille Lacs). See also Bray, *The Journals of Joseph N. Nicollet*, 45–46, for similar peaceful relations in another local region between the Ojibwe village of Sandy Lake and Dakota village at St. Anthony's Falls.

24. "Testimony of John ("Jack") Porter," 25 Sept 1914, 108–9, box 5, Powell Papers, MHS; "Kinojens," in Baraga's spelling, means "Little Pike," see Baraga, *Dictionary*, 190 ("Kinoje, pike"). See Nichols and Nyholm, *Concise Dictionary*, 227, for the present-day double vowel orthography of the name as Ginoozhe with ginoozhens as the diminutive. Ginoozhens was not the only multitribal Ojibwe-Dakota person recalled by Ojibwe witnesses in the early twentieth century. See also "Testimony of Shin-ow-aince," 30 January 1914," "Testimony of Way-dum-e-quay-on," 23 June 1914, 1002; boxes 5 and 6, Powell Papers, MHS.

25. "Testimony of John ("Jack") Porter," 25 Sept 1914, 108–9, boxes 5 and 6, Powell Papers, MHS.

26. Warren, *History*, 10 (elevated female character upon conversion); 11 (women's adoption of European-style housekeeping and cooking); 59 ("the sacred book of God"); 61 ("wild hunter state," "savage and unenlightened state," "bloody and exterminating warfare"); 265 ("drudges"); 370–71, 385–86 (women's dress and cleanliness).

27. Warren, *History*, 72 ("inveterate and hereditary enemies"); 263, 266–68 (instances of winter alliances and details of peacemaking rituals). A recent reexamination of Dakota-Ojibwe relationships argues persuasively for the importance of peaceful interactions between the two nations in contrast to the usual emphasis on warfare. See Gwen Westerman and Bruce White, *Mni Sota Makoce; The Land of the Dakota* (St. Paul: Minnesota Historical Society Press, 2012), 39, 81, 89, 91–93.

28. Warren, 270 (all quotes); for the larger discussion of the Ojibwe who learned his in-married wife's Dakota language, see 269–74.

29. Warren, *History*, 174 (all quotes). For a general discussion of Ojibwe-Dakota seasonal peacemaking practices and sharing of material resources, see Harold Hickerson, *The

Southwestern Chippewa, An Ethnohistorical Study. American Anthropological Association Memoir 92 (Menasha, WI: George B. Banta Co., Inc.; 1962), 12–29. For intertribal sharing of hunting resources, involving Dakotas and Ho-chunks, see Gary Anderson, *Kinsmen of Another Kind; Dakota-White Relations in the Upper Mississippi Valley, 1650–1862* (Lincoln: University of Nebraska Press, 1984), 126. Anderson's discussion of the Dakota-Ho-chunk peace initiative is notable for its suggestion that this seasonal practice extended beyond just Ojibwes and Dakotas.

30. Warren, *History,* 174 ("the mixed bloods of either tribe"), 165 ("blood relations"); Acts 17:26 ("of one blood"); Genesis 11: 1–9 (Tower of Babel), King James Version (hereafter cited as KJV).

31. Heidi Bohaker, *Doodem and Council Fire: Anishinaabe Governance through Alliance* (Toronto: The Osgoode Society for Canadian Legal History and University of Toronto Press, 2020), especially 135–69. It is also possible that all Ojibwe clans possessed mediating functions. Warren, *History,* 45–51, indicates that they were understood to have different socio-political responsibilities.

32. A caveat is in order here. Warren stated in his introduction to *History of the Ojibways,* 26–27, that he had plans to publish several additional studies of Ojibwe life and culture. He may have anticipated writing a description of current Ojibwe life and culture in one of these studies before his early death at age 28.

33. George Irving Quimby, *Indian Life in the Upper Great Lakes, 11,000 B.C. to A.D. 1800* (Chicago: University of Chicago Press, 1960), 154 ("British medals," "arms and seals."); for Ojibwe clans, see 125–26, 151, 153; for Potawatomis, see Quimby, "Some Notes on Kinship and Kinship Terminology among the Potawatomi of the Huron," *Papers of the Michigan Academy of Science, Arts, and Letters,* 25 (1940), 553–63; for Odawas, see Truman Michelson, "Note on the Gentes of the Ottawa," *American Anthropologist* 13 (April-June 1911): 338. For the presence of the Eagle Clan among Minnesota-dwelling Ojibwes, see "Testimony of Bah-ne-tah-nah-be-tung [also given as "Nah-be-tah-nah-be-tung"]," 30 September 1914, 223–24, 237–38; "Testimony of Jack Porter," 25 September 1914, 109–10; "Testimony of Ah-ke-waince," 28 September 1914, 196–97, box 6, Powell Papers, MHS. Another early reference to Minnesota Ojibwes claiming kinship ties with a multiracial individual based on a shared clan identity is found in William Johnston, "Letters on the Fur Trade," in *Historical Collections of the Michigan Pioneer and Historical Society,* ed. J. Sharpless Fox, vol. 37 (1909–1910), 132–207; 177. See also Larry Nesper, *"Our Relations . . . the Mixed Bloods,"* for an analysis of how similar categories of identity developed in Wisconsin Ojibwe communities and were manipulated by Anglo-American economic interests, once again playing upon supposed differences between mixed-blood and full-blood Ojibwes. It is unclear if Ojibwe and other Anishinaabe-identifying peoples in Canada also created these clans. The most recent treatment by Bohaker, *Doodem and Council Fire,* does not discuss their presence.

34. "Schoolcraft's Narrative of an Expedition Through the Upper Mississippi to Itasca Lake," in *Schoolcraft's Expedition to Lake Itasca; The Discovery of the Source of the Mississippi,* ed. Philip P. Mason (East Lansing: Michigan State University Press, 1993), 120 ("war-chief of Snake River," "principal chief"); 121 ("a flag, tobacco, wampum," "he would himself go," "protection").

35. Kappler, "Treaty with the Chippewa [Ojibwes]," 5 August 1826, at Fond du Lac, 2:270 ("Chaucopee") and ("Kaubemappa"); "Proceedings of a Council with the

Chippewa Indians," *Iowa Journal of History and Politics* 5 (1911): 408–37 (hereafter cited as "Proceedings of a Council I"), 410–14 (Ojibwe leaders remonstrate with Dodge); 421 (inadequacy of translation); see also Brunson, *A Western Pioneer*, 83 (inadequacy of interpreters); Henry Dodge to Caleb A. Harris, 7 August 1837, in "Documents Relating to the Negotiation of the Treaty of July 29, 1837, with the Chippewa Indians," 542 (unclear instructions), 543 (doubts about negotiating by himself), roll 3, NARA, RG 75, T494.

The St. Peters Treaty of 7 August 1837 is unique in that two different versions of the journal of proceedings survive, making comparisons possible between them. While substantially the same, there are nonetheless noticeable differences between the two versions, including additional material in the second (and longer) journal that the Commission's secretary, Verplanck Van Antwerp, sent to the Commissioner of Indian Affairs at the conclusion of his service. The first draft appeared in the Dubuque *Iowa News*, a regional newspaper, shortly after the treaty negotiations concluded in late July; it seems to have been a rough draft of the final version. This first draft also appears to have been written by Van Antwerp though this is not specified. For clarity in citations, the two journals are identified as "Proceedings" I and II.

36. "Proceedings of a Council I," 423 ("half breed relatives"); 416 (all other quotes).

37. "Proceedings of a Council II," 552 ("Shagobai is a half breed"); "Proceedings of a Council I," 416 ("the country that you want to buy from us").

38. "Proceedings of a Council I," 417 ("When I came here"), 418 (Hole-in-the-Day speaks in support), 426 ("our half breeds"), 430 ("our traders"). For an excellent discussion of the several official positions that individual Ojibwe political figures might occupy, with discussion of their corresponding duties, see Cary Miller, *Ogimaag, Anishinaabeg Leadership, 1760–1845* (Lincoln: University of Nebraska Press, 2010). As Miller notes, the same person might occupy more than one position at a time, perhaps a conceptual parallel to occupying more than one tribal or ethnic identity simultaneously.

39. The definitive scholarly study, upon which this discussion is based, is Thomas Vennum Jr., *The Ojibwa Dance Drum: Its History and Construction.* Smithsonian Folklife Series, no. 2 (Washington, DC: Smithsonian Institution Press, 1982); 45 ("copied and passed on"); see also 44–51 for his full discussion of Tail Feather Woman's initial vision and its central themes; also 64–65. The earliest anthropological treatment of the ceremony is Samuel A. Barrett, *The Dream Dance of the Chippewa and Menominee Indians of Northern Wisconsin.* Bulletin of the Public Museum of the City of Milwaukee, no. 1 (Milwaukee, 1911). A discerning recent treatment of the Drum Dance in the context of one specific Ojibwe Reservation is Erik M. Redix, *The Murder of Joe White: Ojibwe Leadership and Colonialism in Wisconsin* (East Lansing: Michigan State University Press, 2014), 192–204. For an informative discussion of Tail Feather Woman's ongoing importance to both Dakotas and Ojibwes in the present day, see Bruce M. White, "Honoring Wiyaka Sinte Win/Tail Feather Woman and her Vision," http://www.minnesotahistory.net/wptest/?page_id=882. Accessed 2/17/2017.

40. All quotes from Fred K. Blessing field notes, cited in Bruce White, "Honoring Wiyaka Sinte Win/Tail Feather Woman and her Vision," http://www.minnesotahistory.net/wptest/?page_id=882. Accessed 2/17/2017.

41. White, "Honoring Wiyaka Sinte Win/Tail Feather Woman and her Vision."

Chapter 4

1. Edmund Franklin Ely Diaries, 16 February 1837 ("called me a Frenchman," Maangozid tells Ely the incident occurred on this date); 17 August 1836 (Maangosid's conversion); box 1, Edmund Franklin Ely and Family Papers, Minnesota Historical Society (hereafter Ely Diaries, Ely Papers, MHS). For further discussion of Maangosid's encounter with Christianity, see Rebecca Kugel, "Religion Mixed with Politics: The 1836 Conversion of Mang'osid of Fond du Lac," *Ethnohistory* 37 (Spring 1900): 126–57. The spelling of Maangosid's name has been changed to reflect current orthographic practice.

2. For Ojibwe social formation and early experiences with the French, see "Memoir on the Manners, Customs, and Religion of the Savages of North America; by Nicholas Perrot" in *The Indian Tribes of the Upper Mississippi Valley and Region of the Great Lakes,* ed. and trans. Emma Helen Blair (Cleveland, OH: Arthur H. Clark Company, 1911), 1:25–272, 109–10; "History of the Savage Peoples Who Are Allies of New France," by Claude Charles Le Roy, Sieur de Bacqueville de la Potherie, in Blair, *The Indian Tribes,* 1:277; Harold Hickerson, *The Southwestern Chippewa: An Ethnohistorical Study,* American Anthropological Association Memoir 92 (Menasha, WI: George B. Banta, 1962), 65–71; Harold Hickerson, *The Chippewa and Their Neighbors: A Study in Ethnohistory* (New York: Holt, Rinehart and Winston, 1970), 42–49; and Heidi Bohaker, "'Nindoodemag:' The Significance of Algonquian Kinship Networks in the Eastern Great Lakes Region, 1600–1701," *William and Mary Quarterly,* 3rd ser., 63 (January 2006): 23–29. For an extended Native-centered interpretation of French and British efforts at colonization, see Heidi Bohaker, *Doodem and Council Fire: Anishinaabe Governance through Alliance* (Toronto: University of Toronto Press published for The Osgoode Society for Canadian Legal History, 2020); for Ojibwe movements westward, see Laura Peers, *The Ojibwa of Western Canada, 1780–1879* (Winnipeg: University of Manitoba Press, 1994).

3. Lahontan's work was translated into English as *New Voyages to North-America by the Baron de Lahontan* within a year of its original publication. The English translation was used in this work. See *New Voyages to North-America by the Baron de Lahontan,* 2 vols. (1703; repr., Chicago: A. C. McClurg, 1905) 2:738 ("the French," "the Country"). Though Lahontan's work was not published until the early eighteenth century, he left New France in the 1690s never to return. His familiarity with the Algonkian-language word for the French thus dates from the earlier century, indicating its existence by that time.

4. Frederick Webb Hodge, *Handbook of American Indians North of Mexico* (Washington, DC: Government Printing Office, 1907), 351 (all quotes); Frederic Baraga, *Dictionary of the Ojibway Language* (1878; repr., St. Paul: Minnesota Historical Society Press, 1992), 2:254, "Mitig." See also 1:291–92 ("Wood," "wooden box," "wooden canoe," "wooden house," etc.).

5. Testimony of James H. Van Nett, 25 September 1914, p. 131 ("the first Frenchman," "was building," "out of oak logs," "the way the Frenchman"), box 6, Powell Papers, MHS; Alexander F. Chamberlain, *The Language of the Mississagas of Skugog* (Philadelphia: MacCalla and Company, 1892), 34 ("thought it meant," "he carries a trunk"), 65, 9 (Naawagiizhigokwe identified by name, knowledge attested to). In the late nineteenth century at the time Chamberlain was working, the Mississauga language was still considered separate from Anishinaabemowin, the Ojibwe language. More recently, linguists

have classified them as varying forms of one widespread language. See discussions of Anishinaabemowin in Bohaker, *Doodem and Council Fire.*

6. Warren, *History of the Ojibway People,* 47; Bohaker, "'Nindoodemag,'" 35.

7. Martha Coleman Bray, ed., *The Journals of Joseph N. Nicollet, A Scientist on the Mississippi Headwaters, with Notes on Indian Life, 1836–37* (St. Paul: Minnesota Historical Society Press, 1970), 113 ("traders that wear a hat"); Christina Snyder, *Slavery in Indian Country: The Changing Face of Captivity in Early America* (Cambridge, MA: Harvard University Press, 2010), 124 ("their arms upon," "was never done," "observed the French"), 280n85.

8. Bohaker, "'Nindoodemag,'" 23 ("spectacular council"); Gilles Havard, *The Great Peace of Montreal of 1701: French-Native Diplomacy in the Seventeenth Century,* trans. Phyllis Aronoff and Howard Scott (Montreal: McGill-Queen's University Press, 2001).

9. The literature on eighteenth century Native encounters with and resistance to colonizing European powers in eastern North America is extensive. For a representative selection of important treatments, see Fred Anderson, *Crucible of War: The Seven Years' War and the Fate of Empire in British North America, 1754–1766* (New York: Alfred A. Knopf, 2000); Colin G. Calloway, *Crown and Calumet: British-Indian Relations, 1783–1815* (Norman: University of Oklahoma Press, 1987); Calloway, *The Scratch of a Pen: 1763 and the Transformation of North America* (New York: Oxford University Press, 2006); Gregory Evans Dowd, *A Spirited Resistance: The North American Indian Struggle for Unity, 1745–1815* (Baltimore: Johns Hopkins University Press, 1992); and Dowd, *War Under Heaven: Pontiac, the Indian Nations, and the British Empire* (Baltimore: Johns Hopkins University Press, 2002); R. David Edmunds, *The Shawnee Prophet* (Lincoln: University of Nebraska Press, 1983); Eric Hinderaker, *Elusive Empires: Constructing Colonialism in the Ohio Valley, 1673–1800* (Cambridge: Cambridge University Press, 1997), R. Douglas Hurt, *The Ohio Frontier: Crucible of the Old Northwest, 1720–1830* (Bloomington: Indiana University Press, 1996); Michael N. McConnell, *A Country Between: The Upper Ohio Valley and Its Peoples, 1724–1774* (Lincoln: University of Nebraska Press, 1992); David C. Skaggs and Larry Nelson, eds., *The Sixty Years' War for the Great Lakes, 1754–1816* (East Lansing: Michigan State University Press, 2001); John Sugden, *Blue Jacket: Warrior of the Shawnees* (Lincoln: University of Nebraska Press, 2000); Richard White, *The Middle Ground: Indians, Empires, and Republics in the Great Lakes Region, 1650–1815* (Cambridge: Cambridge University Press, 1991); Keith R. Widder, *Beyond Pontiac's Shadow: Michilimackinac and the Anglo-Indian War of 1763* (East Lansing: Michigan State University Press, 2013); Timothy D. Willig, *Restoring the Chain of Friendship: British Policy and the Indians of the Great Lakes, 1783–1815* (Lincoln: University of Nebraska Press, 2008). For rituals of repossession at war's end, see Helen Hornbeck Tanner, ed., *Atlas of Great Lakes History* (Norman: University of Oklahoma Press, 1987), 47–53.

10. For political fallout of the French evacuation, see citations in note 7 above, especially Dowd, Edmunds, McConnell, and Sugden. For the Great Lakes fur trade itself, see Arthur J. Ray, *Indians in the Fur Trade: Their Role as Trappers, Hunters, and Middlemen in the Lands Southwest of Hudson Bay, 1660–1870* (Toronto: University of Toronto Press, 1974); E. E. Rich, *The Fur Trade and the Northwest to 1857* (Toronto: McClelland and Stewart, 1967); William J. Eccles, "The Fur Trade and Eighteenth-Century Imperialism," *William and Mary Quarterly,* 3rd series, 40 (July 1983), 341–62; also see Eccles, *The*

Canadian Frontier 1534–1760 (New York: Holt Rinehart and Winston, 1969), 132–39, 161–85. The classic study of the Canadian fur trade, which recognized the importance of the culturally resonant trading practices developed by French and Native peoples, is the economic historian Harold A. Innis, *The Fur Trade in Canada* (New Haven, CT: Yale University Press, 1930). An excellent study of the lives and work of the voyageurs, with a focus on British North America, is Carolyn Podruchny, *Making the Voyageur World: Travelers and Traders in the North American Fur Trade* (Lincoln: University of Nebraska Press, 2006), while Jacqueline Peterson, "The People in Between: Indian-White Marriage and the Genesis of a Métis Society in the Great Lakes Region, 1680–1830 (PhD diss., University of Illinois at Chicago Circle, 1981), 104–53, discusses the development of the Great Lakes fur trade towns. Lucy Eldersveld Murphy, *Great Lakes Creoles: A French-Indian Community on the Northern Borderlands, Prairie du Chien, 1750–1860* (New York: Cambridge University Press, 2014), provides an engrossing in-depth study of one such community and its transformation into a "white" American town. See also Elizabeth T. Baird, "O-De-Jit-Wa-Win-Wing; Contes du Temps Passé," box 4, Henry S. and Elizabeth T. Baird Papers, Wisconsin State Historical Society. Of Odawa, French, and Scottish ancestry, Elizabeth Thérèse Fisher Baird's memoirs reveal her self-identification as French.

11. Podruchny, *Making the Voyageur World*, 9, 22–31; Allan Greer, *Peasant, Lord, and Merchant: Rural Society in Three Quebec Parishes, 1740–1840* (Toronto: University of Toronto Press, 1985); Edith J. Burley, *Servants of the Honourable Company: Work, Discipline, and Conflict in the Hudson's Bay Company, 1770–1879* (Toronto: Oxford University Press, 1997); see also Allan Kulikoff, *From British Peasants to Colonial American Farmers* (Chapel Hill: University of North Carolina Press, 2000); and for a comparison with an emerging free labor work environment in another rigidly hierarchical occupation, see Marcus Rediker, *Between the Devil and the Deep Blue Sea: Merchant Seamen, Pirates, and the Anglo-American Maritime World, 1700–1750* (Cambridge: Cambridge University Press, 1987).

12. Podruchny, *Making the Voyageur World*, 9, 22–31; Rich, *The Fur Trade and the Northwest to 1857*, 189–90; see also Laura Peers, *The Ojibwa of Western Canada*. The classic study of the American Fur Company is David Lavender, *A Fist in the Wilderness* (New York: Doubleday, 1964); see also Arthur Ray, *Indians in the Fur Trade: Their Roles as Trappers, Hunters, and Middlemen in the Lands Southwest of Hudson Bay, 1660–1870* (Toronto: University of Toronto Press, 1974).

13. For detailed discussion of fur trade class relations between elites and voyageurs, see Podruchny, *Making the Voyageur World*, esp. chap. 5; an excellent published primary source that treats class relations at length is *"The Orders of the Dreamed": George Nelson on Cree and Northern Ojibwa Religions and Myth* (St. Paul: Minnesota Historical Society Press, 1988), edited with commentary by Jennifer S. H. Brown and Robert Brightman. For examples of labor status distinctions in the western Great Lakes Ojibwe villages, see 10 September 1833 (voyageurs transport missionaries' baggage); 23 September 1833 (elite does not labor with hands); 14 and 26 September 1833 (elite help unload foundered canoe, elite forced to paddle when voyageurs disabled), "Diary Kept by the Reverend William Thurston Boutwell, Missionary to the Ojibwa Indians, 1832–1837," Boutwell Journal, William Thurston Boutwell and Family Papers, MHS (hereafter cited as Boutwell Journal, Boutwell Papers).

14. Boutwell Journal, 29 June 1833 ("cook" for trader and other elite travelers); 27 June 1832 ("in their handkerchief"); see also 12 November 1833 (Boutwell hires a "man" to fish for him); 28 and 33 September 1833 (voyageurs sleep under canoe, elite sleep in tents); 30 September 1833 (Boutwell sleeps in trader's tent); Boutwell Papers, MHS; Ely Diaries, 22 May 1834 (trader and voyageurs split two fish), box 1, Ely Papers, MHS. For traders' efforts at establishing their authority, see Podruchny, *Making the Voyageur World*, 134–64, especially 146–51; and Brown and Brightman, *"The Orders of the Dreamed."*

15. Despite the overall cultural association of hunting with men, young Ojibwe girls were also given celebrations after their first kill, suggesting Ojibwes regarded the self-sufficiency demonstrated by successful hunting as an adult life skill worthy of recognition for all people who acquired it regardless of gender. See Chantal Norrgard, *Seasons of Change: Labor, Treaty Rights, and Ojibwe Nationhood* (Chapel Hill: University of North Carolina Press, 2014), 47–48.

16. Bohaker, "Kinship Networks," 39 ("acceptable masculinity"), 40–41 (enduring social significance of hunting); Cary Miller, *Ogimaag; Anishinaabeg Leadership, 1760–1845* (Lincoln: University of Nebraska Press, 2010), especially 21–63 for Ojibwe beliefs about spiritual power and hunting practices; Norrgard, *Seasons of Change*, 31, 43–50, esp. 47–48 (respectful hunting, hunting rituals, feasts for both young girls and boys); Larry Nesper, *The Walleye War: The Struggle for Ojibwe Spearfishing and Treaty Rights* (Lincoln: University of Nebraska Press, 2002), 38–41 (solidarity of kinship, historic significance of hunting for Ojibwe men's identities). See also Robert Brightman, *Grateful Prey: Rock Cree Human-Animal Relationships* (Berkeley: University of California Press, 1993).

17. Henry R. Schoolcraft, *Narrative Journal of Travels through the Northwestern Regions of the United States extending from Detroit through the Great Chain of American Lakes to the Sources of the Mississippi River in the year 1820* (1821; repr., East Lansing: Michigan State University Press, 1992, Mentor L. Williams, ed., 59 (all quotes); see also 502. The "Indians" are identified by name and tribal heritage on p. 366. (Hereafter cited as *Narrative Journal.*) Podruchny, *Making the Voyageur World*, discusses voyageur work culture in detail; see especially chps. 3–6. For anti-authoritarian play and spontaneity, see Mikhail Bakhtin. *Rabelais and his World*. (1965 [Russian]; repr., Bloomington: Indiana University Press, 1984.

18. Ely Diaries, 30 May 1835 (all quotes), Ely Papers, MHS. The Ojibwe-language word for lacrosse is baaga'adowewin. "The Ojibwe Peoples' Dictionary," https://ojibwe .lib.umn.edu/, accessed 7 July 2020.

19. Boutwell Journal, 10 July 1832 ("Our voyageurs," "after the dance," "presented their tobacco"), 16 May 1833 ("invite[d] the Frenchmen"), see also 3 May 1833 (another example of the French being invited to partake of maple sugar), Boutwell Journal, Boutwell Papers, MHS. For first fruits ceremonies, see Sister M. Inez Hilger, *Chippewa Child Life and Its Cultural Background*. Smithsonian Institution Bureau of American Ethnology Bulletin 146 (Washington, DC: Government Printing Office, 1951), 111–12.

20. *The Journals of Joseph N. Nicollet, A Scientist on the Mississippi Headwaters, with Notes on Indian Life, 1836–37*, Martha Coleman Bray., ed. (St. Paul: Minnesota Historical Society, 1970), 81 ("French from France"), 115 ("beyond the sea"), 82–83, 112–18 (actions and speeches of tribal leaders); Joseph N. Nicollet, *Report Intended to*

Illustrate a Map of the Hydrographical Basin on the Upper Mississippi River. Senate Document No. 237. 26th Congress, 2nd Session, 1840–41 (Washington, DC: Blair and Rives; 1843), 55 (*"Frenchman of the olden time"*).

Nicollet was very much aware and more than a little uncomfortable that Ojibwes regarded his presence as an opportunity to renew ties with the French. The full context of his remarks, taken from both his journals and his official Report are worth a more detailed examination. In his journal he noted that the Ojibwes distinguished him from the North American French population, referring to him as a *"Kayaté-wernit-tig-oj* (which means "a Frenchman of the olden time")." [Present-day spelling of this phrase would be Geté wemitigoozhe.] "The Ojibwe Peoples' Dictionary," https://ojibwe.lib.umn .edu/, accessed 23 July 2020. In a footnote in his official *Report Intended to Illustrate a Map,* Nicollet included a second phrase in "the Chippeway tongue" which located the French homeland while further distinguishing between the two populations of Frenchmen. Nicollet's transcription of the Ojibwe-language phrase seems garbled, but the content is nevertheless significant. Ojibwes, he wrote, distinguished him from North American French, describing him as *"Awas komigo wer-nittig-oj,* viz: a Frenchman from beyond the waters; which expression is translated by the Canadians, *un Francais de France."* Nicollet, *Report,* 55 (all quotes, italics in original).

21. Boutwell Journal, 9 February 1833 (all quotes; request that Indian agent be notified); see also 18 February 1833 (Bizhiki's son's death and funeral), 4 March and 3 May 1833 (references to Bizhiki as elderly), box 1, Boutwell Papers, MHS. When he asked for the flag for his son's grave, Bizhiki also told Boutwell that he had expected, upon his own death, that his deceased son would be recognized as chief. Given Bizhiki's advanced age, it is probable his son had already assumed a number of leadership duties before his untimely demise.

22. Boutwell Journal, 8 March 1836, box 1, Boutwell Papers, MHS. See Boutwell Journal for Big Cloud's political activities.

23. Nicollet, *Report,* 115 ("being the first," "showing us how"), Sherman Hall to David Greene, 24 October 1838, box 2, ABCFM Papers, MHS (all remaining quotes).

24. William H. Keating, *Narrative of an Expedition to the Source of St. Peter's River* (1823; repr., Minneapolis: Ross and Haines, 1959), 2:164 (all quotes). For the present-day spelling of the phrase "Wemetegogin gegakepatese," as *Wemigitoozhe gagibaadizi,* see John D. Nichols and Earl Nyholm, *A Concise Dictionary of Minnesota Ojibwe* (Minneapolis: University of Minnesota Press, 1995), 2:182 ("foolish"), 183 ("Frenchman"). See also "The Ojibwe Peoples' Dictionary," https://ojibwe.lib.umn.edu/, accessed 23 July 2020. Keating's translation of *Wemitigoozhe* contained layers of complexity. Though he did not seem to recognize that the word translated as "Frenchman," he did observe in a footnote that "Wemetegogin does not properly mean a white man, but one who elevates logs into the air, probably from the beams or eaves used in the construction of white men's cabins." Keating, *Narrative of an Expedition,* 2:164. At the same time, some of his confusion may have been due to the efforts of his interpreter, Charles Bruce, to characterize the several ethno-national populations of the western Great Lakes in terms Americans would understand. In the first decades of sustained contact with Americans, a number of bilingual men who served as interpreters struggled to make regional understandings of whiteness and race comprehensible to Anglo-Americans. For more on Bruce, see Keating, *Narrative of an Expedition,* 2:148; Theresa M. Schenck, *All Our Relations;*

Chippewa Mixed-Bloods and the Treaty of 1837 (Winnipeg, ON: Centre for Rupert's Land Studies; Madison, WI: Amik Press, 2010), 31–32.

25. Keating, *Narrative of an Expedition*, 2:164. An excellent recent analysis of Ojibwe women's gendered work and overall societal importance is Brenda J. Child, *Holding Our World Together: Ojibwe Women and the Survival of Community* (New York: Viking Press, Penguin Library of American Indian History, 2012). Classic anthropological studies of Ojibwe labor that recognized their gendered nature include Frances Densmore, *Chippewa Customs* (1929; repr. St. Paul: Minnesota Historical Society Press, 1979) and Sister M. Inez Hilger, *Chippewa Child Life and Its Cultural Background*, Smithsonian Institution Bureau of American Ethnology Bulletin 146 (Washington, DC: United States Government Printing Office, 1951). The close correlation between men and hunting was further sanctioned in oral narratives of Nanabo'zho, the Ojibwe culture hero, who was also the first hunter. See William Jones, *Ojibwa Texts*, Truman Michelson, ed. Publications of the American Ethnological Society, vol 7, parts 1 and 2 (New York: G. E. Stechert, 1917, 1919); 235–79, esp. 251–71.

26. Thomas Vennum Jr., *Wild Rice and the Ojibway People* (St. Paul: Minnesota Historical Society Press, 1988), 81–150, esp. 99–100. For *bawa' iganaakoon*, see p. 99. The gendered labor of ricing changed markedly in the twentieth century, with both women and men participating in all aspects of the harvesting process. In addition to Vennum, *Wild Rice and the Ojibway People*, see Child, *Holding Our World Together*, 24–27, 97–120; see also Norrgard, *Seasons of Change*, 4–5, 22–23.

27. Norrgard, *Seasons of Change*, 31, quotes Mille Lacs elder Maud Kegg describing the "way the Indians [Ojibwes] made their living long ago." For a similar articulation of the gendered concept of "making a living" from the perspective of another Native nation, see Colleen O'Neill, *Working the Navajo Way: Labor and Culture in the Twentieth Century* (Lawrence: University of Kansas Press, 2005), 55–80, esp. 65–66.

28. There are tantalizing references in much earlier records that describe the concern of Great Lakes Native peoples that tribal individuals were becoming too much like the French. As early as the Jesuit Relation of 1632, a young man of the Algonquin tribal nation stated "[s]ome of my own people cast upon me the reproach that I am becoming a Frenchman." The issue for these seventeenth century Algonquins was not with French labor practices, but the fear that conversion to Christianity would cause the young man to "leav[e] my own nation." Jesuit Relation of 1632 quoted in Jacqueline Louise Peterson, "The People In Between: Indian-White Marriage and the Genesis of a Métis Society and Culture in the Great Lakes Region, 1680–1830 (PhD diss., University of Illinois at Chicago Circle, 1981), 41.

29. Ely Diaries, 28 February 1839 ("dwelling House"); 27 April 1839 (all other quotes) [emphasis added], box 1, Ely Papers, MHS. "Bwaanens" was the diminutive form of Bwaan, or Dakota. In the nineteenth century, Bwaanens was usually translated as "Little Sioux." "The Ojibwe Peoples' Dictionary." https://ojibwe.lib.umn.edu/. Accessed 17 March 2021.

30. M. M. Hoffmann, *Church Founders of the Old Northwest: Loras and Cretin and Other Captains of Christ* (Milwaukee: Bruce Publishing Company, 1937), 167–68 (all quotes); see also Robert Galler, "Making Common Cause: Yanktonais and Catholic Missionaries on the Northern Plains," *Ethnohistory* 55 (Summer 2008): 446–47.

31. Ely Diaries, 28 June 1834 (guides); 18 October 1834, 18 and 19 October 1846 (mail carriers); 1 September 1834 (packers at portages); 2 September 1834 (short terms jobs

paid on completion), 7 September 1837 (Ely attempts to pay in kind); 2 October 1837 (Ojibwe men employed by American Fur Company), box 1, Ely Papers, MHS; Boutwell Journal 27 June 1832 (insisting on cash in hand), Boutwell Papers, MHS. For perceptions of the inabilities of Europeans and their descendants to perform Ojibwe men's tasks, see 23 October 1833, 28 June 1834, box 1, Ely Diaries, Ely Papers, MHS; Boutwell Journal, 12 July 1832, Boutwell Papers, MHS; also, Keating, *Narrative of an Expedition,* 1:230–32, 2:163–64.

32. Ely Diaries, 28 and 29 June 1834 (separate food), box 1, Ely Papers, MHS; Schoolcraft, *Narrative Journal of Travels,* 128 (expedition camps across river from Ojibwe village). Interestingly, when the Ojibwes of Fond du Lac negotiated with Ely about the location of his mission, they insisted he build the mission on the opposite side of the river from the Ojibwe community. Ely Diaries, 15 and 21 May 1837.

33. Ely Diaries, 18 October 1834 (Ojibwe traveler carrying mail), 28 June 1834 (Ojibwe men hiring as guides for missionaries), box 1, Ely Papers, MHS.

34. Ely Diaries, 28 June 1834 (all quotes), box 1, Ely Papers, MHS. Italics in original.

35. Ely Diaries, 20 May 1836 ("forerunner of Americans"), box 1, Ely Papers, MHS.

36. Ely Diaries, 21 May 1836 ("Agents of Americans"); box 1, Ely Papers, MHS; see also Boutwell to Greene, 3 December 1838 (missionaries attend treaty, consult with Americans), box 2, ABCFM Papers, MHS. For the treaty itself, see Charles J. Kappler, *Indian Affairs, Laws and Treaties,* "Treaty with the Chippewas," at St. Peters, 29 July 1837 (Washington, DC: Government Printing Office, 1904), 2:491–93.

37. ABCFM missionaries adopted the practice of giving Ojibwe converts "civilized" Anglo-American names, yet another indication of the changed status such persons were expected to represent. Ely gave Madweweyaash the name "William Talcott," after a personal friend and financial supporter of the ABCFM. In his diaries, Ely usually refers to Madweweyaash as "William." Cf Ely Diaries, 11 March 1836, 13 March 1836, 11 April 1836, 16 April 1836, box 1, Ely Papers, MHS. For Ely's years at Fond du Lac and his prominence in the conversions of Ojibwe individuals, see Rebecca Kugel, "Religion Mixed with Politics."

38. Ely Diaries, 6 June 1838 ("found the Saviour," residing near Ely's house), 13 August 1836 (wearing American-style clothing), box 1, Ely Papers, MHS; Ayer to Greene, 4 October 1837 ("live like civilized people"), box 2, ABCFM Papers, MHS.

39. Ely Diaries, 13 August 1836 ("laugh[ed] at him," "tak[ing] Indian dress," participation in wild rice harvesting); 7 November 1836 (Madweweyaash's continued reliance on hunting); 7 June 1838 ("principal men"), box 1, Ely Papers, MHS; see also Ely to Greene, 7 November 1836, box 2, ABCFM Papers, MHS (Madweweyaash continues hunting). For Madweweyaash's waged work for Ely, see Ely Diaries, 29 August and 7 September 1837, 7 June 1838, box 1, Ely Papers, MHS.

40. Ely Papers, 7 June 1838 ("assembled at lodge," "Indians do not like," "i.e. hired"; Ely hires Madweweyaash for wages), box 1, Ely Papers, MHS; "*nind anoki,*" "I work," "*nind anokia,*" "I make him work," "*nind anokitas,*" "I work for myself," "*nind anokitawa,*" "I work for him," "*Anôkitagan,*" "hireling," "servant," Baraga, *Dictionary,* 2:41. Another verb, "*nind anona*" meant "I hire him"; Baraga, *Dictionary,* 2:41; "*nind anonigo,*" meant "I am hired," Baraga, *Dictionary,* 1:134. For additional words formed from the stems *anoki-* and *anona-,* see Baraga, *Dictionary,* 2:41–42. In the present-day Ojibwe language, all verbs with the root anooki- indicate hired labor. See "anooki, s/he hires, orders, commissions

(someone)," "The Ojibwe Peoples' Dictionary," https://ojibwe.lib.umn.edu/. Accessed 3 November 2020.

41. Ely Diaries, 20 May 1836 ("get possession of," "to do with them"); 7 June 1838 ("I told them," "You can kill animals," "[W]e had rather"), box 1, Ely Papers, MHS. For instances of Madweweyaash's problematic labor for Ely, see Ely Diaries, 16 February and 29 August 1837 (William fishes for Ely); 7 September 1837 (Ely pays William in food and clothing); 11 September 1837 (Ely gives William "an old Blanket coat" in lieu of cash for catching and salting fish), box 1, Ely Papers, MHS.

42. Child, *Holding Our World Together*, 24–27, 97–111; Susan Sleeper-Smith, *Indigenous Prosperity and American Conquest: Indian Women of the Ohio River Valley, 1690–1792* (Chapel Hill: University of North Carolina Press for the Omohundro Institute of Early American History and Culture, 2018).

Chapter 5

1. James D. Doty to Martin Van Buren, 21 January 1839, quoted in Nicole St-Onge, "Familial Foes? French-Sioux Families and Plains Métis Brigades in the Nineteenth Century." *American Indian Quarterly* 39 (Summer 2015), 302–37 ("Bois Brulés," regional usage of both the French and English ethnonyms); Theresa M. Schenck, *William W. Warren; The Life, Letters, and Times of an Ojibwe Leader* (Lincoln: University of Nebraska Press, 2007), 61 ("Half Breeds"). For the broader context of multiracial persons in North America, see Jennifer S. H. Brown and Theresa Schenck, eds., "Métis, Mestizo, and Mixed-Blood," in *A Companion to American Indian History*, ed. Philip J. Deloria and Neal Salisbury (Malden, MA: Blackwell Publishing, 2002, 2004), 321–38. William Whipple Warren, *History of the Ojibway People* (1885; repr., St. Paul: Minnesota Historical Society Press, 1984), 80, 95–105, 108–12, for LaPointe's place in Ojibwe oral history; Louise Phelps Kellogg, *The French Régime in Wisconsin and the Northwest* (New York: Cooper Square Publishers, 1968), 104–12, and Helen Hornbeck Tanner, ed., *Atlas of Great Lakes Indian History* (Norman: University of Oklahoma Press for the Newberry Library, 1987), 29–39, for the seventeenth and eighteenth century European colonial history of the LaPointe region; Philip M. Mason, ed., *Schoolcraft's Expedition to Lake Itasca: The Discovery of the Source of the Mississippi* (1834; repr., East Lansing: Michigan State University Press, 1993), 118 (for the establishment of the Subagency at LaPointe). David Greene to Jeremiah Evarts, 27 July 1829 (support for mission among fur traders), David Greene to Sherman Hall and William T. Boutwell, 10 June 1832 [*sic*, 1831] (establishment of LaPointe mission), box 1, American Board of Commissioners for Foreign Missions Papers, Minnesota Historical Society (hereafter cited as ABCFM Papers, MHS).

2. "Affidavit of Henry Blatchford," 28 June 1847, 445 ("under the influence of Liquor," "in several places," "remonstrating," "shameful conduct," "as a gentleman," "pen and ink"); "Affidavit of Michel Dufault," 28 June 1847, 442 ("chasing," "tearing," "child at her Breast," "embrac[ed]," "resisting his attempts"), roll 389, National Archives and Records Administration, Record Group 75, Microcopy 234 (hereafter cited as NARA, RG 75, M234). See Schenck, *William W. Warren*, 29 (name of daughter); 33 (DuFault identified as William Warren's cousin); 50 (in 1848, one year after the assault, Charlotte and Sophia named as still living with Matilda and William); Julia Warren Spears, "Interesting Reminiscences of Early Frontier Days," 2–3, in Julia A. Warren Spears

Papers, Minnesota Historical Society (hereafter cited as Spears Papers) (Julia describes living with William's family in 1847 and moving to live with an aunt in 1848); Henry M. Rice to William Medill, 30 June 1847, 350 (describes duration of Hays' alcoholic binge), roll 389, NARA, RG 75, M234.

3. Warren, *History of the Ojibway People*, 384–86.

4. Schenck, *William Warren*, 36; Robert Stuart to T. Hartley Crawford, 11 February 1844, 53 (William Aitken's residence), roll 389, NARA, RG 75, M234.

5. William Warren to Henry Dodge, 28 June 1847, 440–41 (Warren states Hays' behavior had lost him the respect of the Ojibwes; and while he made no direct mention of Hays' assaults on the Warren women, it seems reasonable to infer that this was one aspect of Hays' behavior that had lost him Ojibwe respect); Henry Dodge to Medill, 22 July 1847, 438–39 (prior complaints against Hays, William Warren's support among some government officials), roll 389, NARA, RG 75, M234; Dodge to Medill, 7 August 1847, 446–47 (Warren's support among LaPointe inhabitants); Dodge to Medill, 30 May 1847, 430–32 (Dodge's gubernatorial duties), roll 389, NARA, RG 75, M234. For sexual assaults on Ojibwe women, see John S. Livermore to Orlando Brown, 11 September 1849, 272 (an Ojibwe woman defends herself against a trader's clerk), 273 (an intoxicated "Frenchman" "attempted force upon" an Ojibwe woman), roll 390, NARA, RG 75, M 234; John S. Livermore to Orlando Brown, 1 January 1850, 345 (subagency interpreter convicted of attempted rape of an Ojibwe "young woman"), roll 390, NARA, RG 75, M 234. The classic articulation of the nineteenth century ideology of separately gendered "spheres" for women and men is Barbara Welter, "The Cult of True Womanhood, 1820–1860" *American Quarterly* 18, no. 2, pt. 1 (Summer 1966), 151–74.

6. William W. Warren to Henry Dodge, 28 June 1847, 441 (all quotes); "Affidavit of Henry Blatchford," 28 June 1847, 445 (indicates that beyond the physical assault on her person, Matilda was "otherwise injured"). All additional references: roll 389, NARA, RG 75, M234.

7. Henry M. Rice to William Medill, 30 June 1847, 350 (all quotes; Medill to Rice, 17 June 1847, 342 (Rice negotiates with Ho-chunks); 343 (Rice indicates Medill has asked him to go to LaPointe); Isaac A. Verplanck to Medill, 12 June 1847, 409 (commissioners delayed; Dodge to Medill, 7 August 1847, 446–47 (letters lost in mail). All additional references: roll 389, NARA, RG 75, M234.

8. Henry R. Schoolcraft, *Narrative Journal of Travels Through the Northwestern Regions of the United States . . . in the Year 1820* (East Lansing: Michigan State University Press, 1953), calculated several of the distances from LaPointe to Little Falls. Schoolcraft gave the distance from LaPointe to Fond du Lac as 114 miles (140); and from Fond du Lac to Sandy Lake as 126 miles (160). On the journey from Sandy Lake to Little Falls, he did not make precise mileage calculations, noting daily travel times instead. The expedition took four days to make that part of the trip, starting in the afternoon of 25 July and reaching Little Falls about noon on 28 July, pausing for a day and a half to hunt for buffalo once they reached the prairie lands south of Crow Wing River. Their four-day journey was thus longer than the trip would have been for a party that traveled straight through without stopping. The most accurate account of the Sandy Lake to Crow Wing leg of the journey was by C. C. Trowbridge, who provided daily estimations of mileage as 28 miles for July 25, 100 miles for July 26, and "about 90 miles" for 27 July (p. 490). Trowbridge also noted that the expedition passed Crow Wing River "about noon" on that day

(p. 489). Since they had embarked that morning at 5 A.M. and camped for the night at 5 P.M., the mouth of the Crow Wing River was about at the day's halfway point, or forty-five miles. See "The Journal and Letters of Charles Christopher Trowbridge, Expedition of 1820," in Schoolcraft, *Narrative Journal*, 461–500. For the distance from Crow Wing to Little Falls, see F. Paul Prucha, "Fort Ripley: The Post and the Military Reservation," *Minnesota History* 28 (September 1947), 211, which gives distances from Crow Wing to Fort Ripley (7 miles) and Fort Ripley to Little Falls (15 miles); and Augustus Aspinwall Reminiscence (p. 13), which gives the distance from Little Falls to Swan River as 3 miles. Augustus Aspinwall Reminiscence, February 10, 1902. Copies at the Minnesota Historical Society. Originals owned by Mrs. Leonard W. Nelson, Spokane, Washington. No present-day town remains at Swan River. I estimate the total number of miles traveled by Matilda's party was 438 on a voyage of between six and eight days.

9. 31 March and 6 April 1836 (As a young teen Matilda participates in women's subsistence activities at her mother's sugar bush); 3 September and 28 October 1837 (Matilda travels by canoe with her mother and siblings from Fond du Lac to Sandy Lake); 15 September 1834 (Matilda's mother personally transports her children in her own canoe). Edmund Franklin Ely Diaries, box 1, Edmund Franklin Ely and Family Papers, Minnesota Historical Society [hereafter Ely Diaries, Ely Papers, MHS]. Frances Densmore, *Chippewa Customs* (1929, repr., St. Paul: Minnesota Historical Society Press, 1979), 119–23, provides a unique first-hand oral account by an Ojibwe woman of women's labor over the course of a typical nineteenth century year, while the overall book features a number of women as consultants. Their comments on their labor reveal how integral women's work was to overall tribal cultural practices. Similarly, Sister M. Inez Hilger, *Chippewa Child Life and Its Cultural Background*. Smithsonian Institution, Bureau of American Ethnology Bulletin 146 (Washington, DC: US Government Printing Office, 1951), contains numerous descriptions of women's work as it involved childrearing and motherhood. An excellent recent discussion that centers on Native women's agricultural labor is Susan Sleeper-Smith, *Indigenous Prosperity and American Conquest: Indian Women of the Ohio River Valley, 1690–1792*. (Chapel Hill: University of North Carolina Press for the Omohundro Institute of Early American History and Culture, 2018). For a historical discussion of Ojibwe women that centers their productive and provisioning work, see Brenda J. Child, *Holding Our World Together: Ojibwe Women and the Survival of Community* (New York: Viking, 2012), especially 1–62; see also Erik M. Redix, *The Murder of Joe White: Ojibwe Leadership and Colonialism in Wisconsin* (East Lansing: Michigan State University Press, 2014), 101–14.

10. Henry M. Rice to William Medill, 30 June 1847, 350 ("been beastly intoxicated"); Gen. Isaac A. Verplanck to Medill, 10 July 1847, 417 ("canoes, tents," Henry Rice to escort Wisconsin *ogimak* to treaty site); William W. Warren to Medill, 1 September 1847, 449 ("Interpreter for the U. States"). See also Verplanck to William Marcy, 5 June 47, 407–8 and Verplanck to Medill, 12 June 1847, 409 (inquiries to Indian Office go unanswered); Verplanck to Marcy, 2 July 1847, 410–11 (Mix's illness); Verplanck to Medill, 5 July 1847, 412–14 (arrives at LaPointe, Hays missing, decides to hold treaty at Fond du Lac at Henry Rice's urging); Rice to Medill, 17 June 1847, 342–43 (Rice gives reasons not to hold treaty at LaPointe); all additional references: roll 389, NARA, RG 75, M234. See Schoolcraft, *Narrative*, 477–79, on travel times from LaPointe to Fond du Lac.

11. Dodge to Medill, 22 July 1847, 438 (all quotes), date of receipt of Warren's letter recorded on back of page; Hays to Medill, 11 August 1847, 0333 ("representations unfavorable"); Richmond to Hays, 20 August 1847, 380 ("make enquiries," "all the facts, "the opportunity"), all additional references: roll 389, NARA, RG 75, M234.

12. Hays to Hall et al., 15 September 1847, 0371 ("abusing the wife"), roll 389, RG 75 M234; Francis Paul Prucha, *The Great Father: The United States Government and the American Indians* (Lincoln: University of Nebraska Press, 1986) 31–34, 40–42 (trade and intercourse acts, their specific mandate to keeping alcohol from Indian country). For the efforts of Hays' family to get him a job with the Indian Office, see Alexander Hays to "Colonel Dodge," 21 June 1847, 0443; General Samuel Hays to Medill, 3 January 1848, 0033 and 17 January 1848, 0034, all: roll 389, NARA, RG 75, M234. For the Hays family, see John W. Jordan, *Genealogical and Personal History of Western Pennsylvania*, 2 vols. (New York: Lewis Historical Publishing Company, 1915), 2:851–56. For an in-depth analysis of the importance of gentlemanly status and comportment for elite Anglo-American men (and a suggestion why William Warren would both challenge and assert their own claim to such status) see Timothy J. Williams, *Intellectual Manhood: University, Self, and Society in the Antebellum South* (Chapel Hill: University of North Carolina Press, 2015).

13. Hays to Richmond, 2 September 1847, 367 ("[t]he charge of abusing"), roll 389, NARA, RG 75 M234. In the 1840s, the word "abuse" was generally understood to describe individual bad actions, along the lines of the verbs "to use ill" or "to mistreat." It also frequently described verbal behavior, as in the phrase "to use abusive language." Its twenty-first century meaning as the systematic use of violence and/or cruelty to control another person was not included in these earliest editions. Quotations ("to use ill," "to mistreat") from entry for "abuse" in the definitive early Webster's *American Dictionary of the English Language,* 1828, http://www.webstersdictionary1828. Accessed 12 September 2021.

14. Hays to Richmond, 2 September 1847, 367 (all quotes), roll 389, NARA, RG 75, M234.

15. Hays to Richmond, 2 September 1847, 367 ("my character," "seen proper," "shall endeavor"); Edmund F. Ely to Hays, 16 September 1847, 375 ("gentlemanly"); Sherman Hall to Hays, 16 September 1847, 373 ("opinion"), all references: roll 389, NARA, RG 75, M234. For use of honorific "Esquire," see Jeremiah Russell to Hays, 16 September 1847, 379, roll 389, NARA, RG 75, M234, and the letters of Ely and Hall cited above. Also see "Journal of Rev. S. Hall," 5 August—26 September 1831, box 1, ABCFM Papers, MHS, for reference to "H. R. Schoolcraft, Esq." Ironically, Hall had performed William and Matilda's marriage ceremony at the LaPointe mission four years earlier. See "Church Records, LaPointe," 10 August 1843, LaPointe Church Records, 1833–1867, ABCFM Papers, Minnesota Historical Society (originals in "Records of the Protestant Mission Church, Madeline Island," Chicago Historical Society, Chicago, Illinois).

16. Hays to Richmond, 2 September 1847, 370 ("If you have taken the trouble"), 368 ("If anyone states"), roll 389, NARA, RG 75, M234.

17. Verplanck to Medill, 29 August 1848, quoted in Schenck, *William Warren,* 43–44 ("the best Interpreter in the country"); Hays to Richmond, 2 September 1847, 368–69 (Hays and Warren's conversations while visiting Ojibwes, Hays' claims of Warren's disloyalty), roll 389, NARA, RG 75, M234.

18. Verplanck to Medill, 1 November 1847, 423 ("without fraud," "without presents," "without providing for debts"); 420 ("Lepointe gentlemen," "seven Indians"), roll 389, NARA, RG 75, M234; William Warren to George Warren, 18 December 1849, quoted in Schenck, *William Warren*, 58 ("hard times," "dire necessity"), 4 (William Warren born at LaPointe). For letters and petitions alleging fraud and coercion, see Nodin of Snake River to "the President of the United States," 3 September 1847, 396 (claims treaty was misinterpreted, blames Warren); "Statement of Charles H. Oakes," 11 September 1847, 397–98 (alleges threats made concerning annuities); "Statement of Bazile H. Beaulieu, James Ermatinger, et al.," 28 August 1847, 399 (Warren's interpretations inaccurate, allege irregularities in obtaining signatures); "Statement of Clement H. Beaulieu," 30 August 1847, 400 (Warren's interpretation faulty, Warren gives incorrect information); Richmond to Medill, 14 October 1847, 390–91 (Warren's interpretation faulty); "Affidavit of Isaac A. Verplanck," 2 November 1847, 428 (swears to accuracy of interpretation and legitimacy of negotiations); see also Verplanck to Medill, 1 November 1847, above, for Verplanck's detailed defense of the treaty and descriptions of AFC actions to derail it; Rice to Medill, 6 November 1847, 403–4 (describes actions of American Fur Company personnel to sink the treaty), all above: roll 389, NARA, RG 75, M234.

19. William Warren to George Warren, 13 April 1849, quoted in Schenck, *William Warren*, 50 ("accommodating all," "come every day"); Blatchford to Edward Warren, 29 December 1848, quoted in Schenck, *William Warren*, 47–48 ("whenever he writes"); see also Schenck, *William Warren*, 47, 187n4 (birth and baptism of Warrens' third child). For the Ojibwe land cession at the 1837 Treaty of Fort Snelling, see Charles C. Royce, comp., "Indian Land Cessions in the United States," in *Eighteenth Annual Report of the Bureau of American Ethnology to the Secretary of the Smithsonian Institution, 1896–97*, by J. W. Powell, vol. 18, pt. 2 (1896–97), Plate 140 (Map 33). For fur traders intermittently occupying the Crow Wing site, see Rhoda R. Gilman, Carolyn Gilman, and Deborah M. Stultz, *The Red River Trails: Oxcart Routes between St. Paul and the Selkirk Settlement, 1820–1879* (St. Paul: Minnesota Historical Society Press, 1979), 7–10; for the construction of the American fort, see F. Paul Prucha, "Fort Ripley: The Post and the Military Reservation," *Minnesota History* 28 (September 1947): 205–24.

20. William Warren to George Warren, 1 March 1849, quoted in Schenck, *William Warren*, 48 ("My wife and children"); William Warren to George Warren, 13 April 1849, quoted in Schenck, *William Warren*, 50 ("I have got to keeping"), 47 (birth of Warrens' third child).

21. Schenck, *William Warren*, 50 (all quotes; reference to fifteen people for Sunday dinner); 187n7 (presence of Charlotte and Sophia in household). For the experiences of young multiracial women at the Mackinaw Mission School, and the skills they particularly sought to learn, see Rebecca Kugel, "Reworking Ethnicity: Gender, Work Roles, and Contending Redefinitions of the Great Lakes Métis, 1820–42," in R. David Edmunds, ed., *Enduring Nations: Native American in the Midwest* (Urbana: University of Illinois Press, 2008), especially 162–64. See also Densmore, *Chippewa Customs* and Hilger, *Chippewa Child Life*, both cited in note 7 above. Contrast the meals the Warrens offered with the typical starch-heavy fare served in American institutions like the Mackinac boarding school, in Keith R. Widder, *Battle for the Soul: Métis Children Encounter Evangelical Protestants at Mackinaw Mission, 1823–1837* (East Lansing: Michigan State

University Press, 1999), 110. A rare reference to the skills of multiracial women cooking "before an open fire" is described in Elizabeth T. Baird's "O-De-Jit-We-Wi-Wing; Contes du Temps Passé," p. 24, box 4, Henry S. and Elizabeth T. Baird Papers, Wisconsin State Historical Society.

22. Schenck, *William Warren*; 54–60; see also appendix B, 179, for Warren's complete published writings. That the Indian Office questionnaire was sent to Rice was not unusual; as a matter of course Indian Office personnel contacted Anglo-American settlers to provide information about tribal peoples; they infrequently asked Native people for information. William was employed as Rice's clerk when the questionnaire was sent out and Rice asked him to supply the answers to its many questions.

23. "Memoir of William W. Warren," J. Fletcher Williams in *History of the Ojibway People* (1885; repr., St. Paul: Minnesota Historical Society Press, 1984), 14–16; Schenck, *William Warren*, 98–122, for discussions of Warren's legislative career, his involvement in newspaper debates, and other public intellectual work.

24. "Treaty with the Chippewa [Ojibwe]," at Fort Snelling near St. Peter's, 29 July 1837, in Charles J. Kappler, ed. and comp., *Indian Affairs, Laws and Treaties* (Washington, DC: Government Printing Office, 1904), 2:492 ("half-breed relations") [Hereafter Kappler]. W. Warren to G. Warren, 4 February 1851 ("Half Breeds"), quoted in Schenck, *William Warren*, 119; Warren to Editor of the *Minnesota Democrat*, 28 January 1851 ("strongest ties"), quoted in Schenck, *William Warren*, 107.

25. W. Warren to G. Warren, n.d. [c. December 1850] ("our common interest"), quoted in Schenck, *William Warren*, 65; W. Warren to G. Warren, first letter of 15 January 1851 ("in a manner"), quoted in Schenck, *William Warren*, 110; Christina Snyder, "The Rise and Fall and Rise of Civilizations: Indian Intellectual Culture during the Removal Era," *Journal of American History* (September 2017), 391 (number of students), 390–91 (years of operation); see also Snyder's recent monograph, *Great Crossings; Indians, Settlers, and Slaves in the Age of Jackson* (New York: Oxford University Press, 2017).

26. W. Warren to Henry Schoolcraft, 22 September 1849 ("fast degenerating"), quoted in Schenck, *William Warren*, 55; W. Warren to Alexander Ramsey, 21 January 1851 ("guaranteed," "their eventual civilization"), Schenck, *William Warren*, 117; W. Warren to G. Warren, 31 March 1850 ("perpetual annuity"), Schenck, *William Warren*, 63.

27. W. Warren to Alexander Ramsey, 21 January 1851 ("living by agriculture"), quoted in Schenck, *William Warren*, 114; W. Warren to Henry Schoolcraft, 22 September 1849 ("fast degenerating"), Schenck, *William Warren*, 55; W. Warren to G. Warren, n.d. [c. 31 March 1850] ("come to this country"), Schenck, *William Warren*, 64.

28. W. Warren to the Editor of the *Minnesota Democrat*, 31 December 1851 ("teachings of civilization"), quoted in Schenck, *William Warren*, 145; W. Warren "To the Half Breeds of Red River," 15 March 1850 (all remaining quotes); Gertrude Ann Rhodes Fonds, additional manuscript 345, British Columbia Provincial Archives, Victoria, British Columbia, Canada. I am indebted to Dr. Cary Miller, Associate Vice President, Indigenous Curriculum, Academics, and Research at the University of Manitoba, for bringing this document to my attention.

29. William Watts Folwell, *A History of Minnesota*, 2nd. ed. 4 vols. (St. Paul: Minnesota Historical Society Press, 1922) 1:360–64 (for economic boom and attendant problems); Bruce M. White, "The Regional Context of the Removal Order of 1850," in *Fish in the Lakes, Wild Rice, and Game in Abundance: Testimony on Behalf of Mille Lacs Ojibwe*

Hunting and Fishing Rights, comp. James M. McClurken (East Lansing: Michigan State University Press, 2000), 154–55 (population boom).

30. There is an extensive literature on Native and Native-descended women in fur trade society. For important representative works, see Jacqueline L. Peterson, "Prelude to Red River: A Social Portrait of the Great Lakes Métis," *Ethnohistory* 25 (Winter 1978): 41–67, Jennifer S. H. Brown, *Strangers in Blood: Fur Trade Company Families in Indian Country* (Vancouver: University of British Columbia, 1980), and Susan Sleeper-Smith, *Indian Women and French Men: Rethinking Cultural Encounter in the Western Great Lakes* (Amherst: University of Massachusetts Press, 2001). Theresa M. Schenck, comp. and ed., *All Our Relations; Chippewa Mixed-Bloods and the Treaty of 1837.* Centre for Rupert's Land Studies, University of Winnipeg (Madison, WI: Amik Press, 2010), 15–16; provides a description of the Aitken family, with dates of parents' marriages and children's baptisms. See also Keith R. Widder, *Battle for the Soul: Métis Children Encounter Evangelical Protestants at Mackinaw Mission, 1823–1837* (East Lansing: Michigan State University Press, 1999) for an in-depth study of the mission school that Matilda attended.

31. Schenck, *William Warren,* 173, 196n1; n.d., newspaper clipping, Sauk Rapids *Frontiersman,* MHS. It is unclear from extant records if Sam Abbe acknowledged his paternity of Matilda Warren's child.

32. For Matilda and her family, see "Inhabitants of Chippewa Agency and Gull Lake, Cass County, Minnesota Territory, 2 December 1857," household 7; for her brother-in-law, Truman Warren, see household 6; for Aitken family members, see household 11; for total population of 196 persons, see second to last unnumbered page. Census of Inhabitants of the Territory of Minnesota, 1857, www.ancestry.com. Accessed 25 July 2019.

33. Julia A. Spears, "History of White Earth," in *A Pioneer History of Becker County, Minnesota,* ed. Alvin H. Wilcox (St. Paul: Pioneer Press Company, 1907), 250 (Matilda, identified by her third husband's name as Mrs. Fountain, is listed along with her four oldest children as part of the departing party. Curiously, the youngest, allegedly fathered by Sam Abbe, is not listed). Julia A. A. Wood Memoir quoted in Schenck, *William Warren,* 164 (original in William H. Wood and Family Papers, MHS) indicated that Matilda spoke little English. See "Free Inhabitants of Chippewa Agency in Cass County, Minnesota, 16 June 1860," household 174 (household with boarder), 1860 United States Federal Census, www.ancestry.com. Accessed 26 July 2019; "Inhabitants of Chippewa Agency, Cass County, Minnesota, 20 August 1870," household 30 (Matilda lists occupation as seamstress, household contains boarder), 1870 United States Federal Census www.ancestry.com. Accessed 26 July 2019. Contrast Matilda's wage work with the experiences of her sister-in-law, Julia Warren Spears, who was hired as a teacher and later boarding school matron in Julia Warren Spears, "Interesting Reminiscences of Early Frontier Days," 5, in Spears Papers, MHS. For the history of White Earth, see Melissa L. Meyer's pathbreaking study, *The White Earth Tragedy: Ethnicity and Dispossession at a Minnesota Anishinaabe Reservation, 1889–1920* (Lincoln: University of Nebraska Press, 1994).

34. Jean M. O'Brien, "Memory and Mobility: Grandma's Mahnomen, White Earth," *Ethnohistory* 64 (July 2017), 345–77. See also "Free Inhabitants of Chippewa Agency in Cass County, Minnesota, 16 June 1860," household 174 (household with child and boarder), 1860 United States Federal Census, www.ancestry.com. Accessed 26 July 2019.

"Inhabitants of Chippewa Agency, Cass County, Minnesota, 20 August 1870," household 30 (household with grandchildren), 1870 United States Federal Census, www.ancestry.com. Accessed 26 July 2019. "Inhabitants in White Earth Agency, Becker County, Minnesota, 2 June 1880," household 8-1 (Matilda's household with daughter, grandchildren); nearby households of kinfolk are household 13-1 (Charlotte Warren Price's household), household 18-2 (Sophia Warren's household), 1880 United States Federal Census, www.ancestry.com. Accessed August 8, 2019. This pattern persisted and is also revealed in Reservation censuses of the late nineteenth and early twentieth centuries, though these censuses must be used with care as they do not clearly indicate household groups and neglect to include non-Native spouses and other non-Native kin. Nonetheless, Matilda Warren Fountain, her children Madeline Warren Uran, William V. Warren, and Lillie Warren McLean, their spouses (if tribal members) and children, plus a cousin, Emma Lynde Morgan, are listed together on every annual census. For examples, see "Census of the White Earth Mississippi Chippewa Indians of White Earth Agency, 1896," unnumbered pages, individuals 94–116; "Census of the White Earth Mississippi Chippewa Indians of the White Earth Agency, Minnesota," June 30, 1897, pp. 5–6, individuals 100–120; and "Census of the Chippewa (White Earth Mississippi Band) Indians of White Earth Agency, Minnesota," 1898, unnumbered pages, individuals 107–29. Meyer, *The White Earth Tragedy*, describes Federal Indian policy as it particularly affected Minnesota Ojibwes.

35. O'Brien, "Memory and Mobility"; see also Brenda J. Child, "Wilma's Jingle Dress; Ojibwe Women and Healing in the Early Twentieth Century," in *Reflections on American Indian History: Honoring the Past*, ed. Albert L. Hurtado (Norman: University of Oklahoma Press, 2006), 113–36.

Conclusion

1. Carron quoted in "Journal of the proceedings at a Council held at Green Bay by Col. Stambaugh, US Agent, with the Menominie Indians," Treaty of 8 February 1831 at Green Bay, 0451 ("our children the half breeds"), roll 2, NARA, RG 75, T494; Marten to Lyman Warren, n.d., 404 ("our half breed relations"), roll 388, NARA, RG 75, M234.

2. Jill Doerfler, *Those Who Belong: Identity, Family, Blood, and Citizenship among the White Earth Anishinaabeg* (East Lansing: Michigan State University Press, 2015).

Bibliography

Manuscript Sources

British Columbia Provincial Archives, Victoria, British Columbia, Canada

Gertrude Ann Rhodes Fonds Papers, Additional Manuscript 345, "W. Warren 'To the Half Breeds of Red River,' 15 March 1850."

Minnesota Historical Society Manuscripts

American Board of Commissioners for Foreign Missions (ABCFM) Papers. Copies at the Minnesota Historical Society. Originals at the Houghton Library, Harvard University, Cambridge, Massachusetts.

William Thurston Boutwell Papers.

Edmund Franklin Ely and Family Papers. Copies at the Minnesota Historical Society. Originals at the St. Louis County Historical Society, Duluth, Minnesota.

Charles Eugene Flandrau and Family Papers.

LaPointe Church Records, 1833–1867. Copies at the Minnesota Historical Society. Originals in "Records of the Protestant Mission Church, Madeline Island," Chicago Historical Society, Chicago, Illinois.

Ransom Judd Powell Papers.

Julia A. Warren Spears and Family Papers.

James F. Sutherland Papers.

National Archives and Records Administration

Documents Relating to the Negotiation of Ratified and Unratified Treaties with Various Indian Tribes, 1801–1869. National Archives Microfilm Publications, Record Group 75, Microcopy T494, Rolls 1–6.

Letters Received by the Office of Indian Affairs, 1824–1881. National Archives Microfilm Publications, Record Group 75, Microcopy 234, Rolls 318, 388–390.

Special Files of the Office of Indian Affairs, 1807–1904. National Archives Microfilm Publications, Record Group 75, Microcopy 574, Rolls 18, 29, 31, 34.

Wisconsin State Historical Society Manuscripts

Elizabeth T. Baird, "O-De-Jit-Wa-Wi-Wing; Contes du Temps Passé." Box 4. Henry S. and Elizabeth T. Baird Papers.

Published Primary Sources

American State Papers: Indian Affairs. 2 vols. Volume 1, compiled by Walter Lowrie and Matthew St. Clair Clarke; volume 2, compiled by Walter Lowrie and Walter S. Franklin. Washington, DC: Gales and Seaton, 1832, 1834.

Bacqueville de la Potherie, Claude Charles LeRoy. "History of the Savage Peoples Who Are Allies of New France." In The Indian Tribes of the Upper Mississippi Valley and the Great Lakes Region, edited and translated by Emma Helen Blair. 2 vols. Cleveland, OH: Arthur H. Clark Company, 1911.

Baraga, Frederic. Dictionary of the Ojibway Language. St. Paul: Minnesota Historical Society Press, 1992. First published 1878 by Beauchemin and Valois (Montreal) as A Dictionary of the Otchipwe Language.

Bray, Martha Coleman, ed. The Journals of Joseph N. Nicollet: A Scientist on the Mississippi Headwaters, with Notes on Indian Life, 1836–37. Translated by André Fertey. St. Paul: Minnesota Historical Society Press, 1970.

Carter, Clarence E., ed. The Territory of Michigan, 1820–1829. Vol. 11 of The Territorial Papers of the United States. Washington, DC: Government Printing Office, 1945.

Coues, Elliott, ed. The Expeditions of Zebulon Montgomery Pike, to Headwaters of the Mississippi River, Through Louisiana Territory, and in New Spain, During the Years 1805-6-7. 3 vols. Minneapolis: Ross and Haines, 1965. First published 1810 by C. and A. Conrad (Philadelphia).

Johnston, William. "Letters on the Fur Trade." In Historical Collections of the Michigan Pioneer and Historical Society, edited by J. Sharpless Fox. Vol. 37. 1909–1910.

Keating, William H. Narrative of an Expedition to the Source of St. Peter's River. Minneapolis, MN: Ross and Haines, 1959. First published 1824 by H. C. Carey and I. Lea (Philadelphia).

Lom d'Arce de Lahontan, Louis-Armand de, Baron de Lahontan. New Voyages to North America by the Baron de Lahontan. 2 vols. Chicago: A. C. McClurg, 1905. First published 1703 by La Haye (no place identified).

Mason, Philip M., ed. Schoolcraft's Expedition to Lake Itasca: The Discovery of the Source of the Mississippi. East Lansing: Michigan State University Press, 1993. First published 1834 by Harper and Brothers (New York).

Nelson, George. "The Orders of the Dreamed": George Nelson on Cree and Northern Ojibwa Religions and Myth, edited with commentary by Jennifer S. H. Brown and Robert Brightman. St. Paul: Minnesota Historical Society Press, 1988.

Nicollet, Joseph N. Report Intended to Illustrate a Map of the Hydrographical Basin on the Upper Mississippi River. Senate Document No. 237. 26th Congress, 2nd Session, 1840–41. Washington, DC: Blair and Rives, 1843.

Perrot, Nicholas. "Memoir on the Manners, Customs, and Religions of the Savages of North America" in Emma Helen Blair, editor and translator, The Indian Tribes of the Upper Mississippi Valley and Region of the Great Lakes. Cleveland, OH: Arthur H. Clark Company, 1911. 2 vols.

"Proceedings of a Council with the Chippewa Indians," Iowa Journal of History and Politics 5 (1911): 408–37.

Schoolcraft, Henry Rowe. Narrative Journal of Travels Through the Northwestern Regions of the United States Extending from Detroit through the Great Chain of American

Lakes to the Source of the Mississippi River in the Year 1820. Edited by Mentor L. Williams, new foreword by Philip P. Mason. East Lansing: Michigan State University Press, 1992. First published 1953; citations to 1992 edition.

Spears, Julia A. "History of White Earth." In *A Pioneer History of Becker County, Minnesota* edited by Alvin H. Wilcox, 246–53. St. Paul, MN: Pioneer Press Company, 1907.

Warren, William Whipple. *History of the Ojibway People.* St. Paul: Minnesota Historical Society Press, 1984. First published 1885; citations to 1984 edition.

Published Secondary Sources

Andersen, Chris. *"Métis": Race, Recognition, and the Struggle for Indigenous Peoplehood.* Vancouver: University of British Columbia Press, 2014.

Anderson, Fred. *Crucible of War: The Seven Years' War and the Fate of Empire in British North America, 1754-1766.* New York: Alfred A. Knopf, 2000.

Anderson, Gary Clayton. *Kinsmen of Another Kind: Dakota-White Relations in the Upper Mississippi Valley, 1650-1862.* Lincoln: University of Nebraska Press, 1984.

Aron, Stephen. *How the West Was Lost: The Transformation of Kentucky from Daniel Boone to Henry Clay.* Baltimore: Johns Hopkins University Press, 1996.

Axtell, James. *The Invasion Within: The Contest of Cultures in Colonial North America.* New York: Oxford University Press, 1985.

Bakhtin, Mikhail. *Rabelais and His World.* Bloomington: Indiana University Press, 1984. First published 1965 in Russian.

Baraga, Frederick. *Chippewa Indians, as Recorded by Rev. Frederick Baraga in 1847. Studia Slovenica,* vol. 10, 7–79. New York: Studia Slovenica, League of Slovenian Americans, 1976. First published 1847.

Barr, Juliana. *Peace Came in the Form of a Woman: Indians and Spaniards in the Texas Borderlands.* Chapel Hill: University of North Carolina Press, 2007.

Barrett, Samuel A. "The Dream Dance of the Chippewa and Menominee Indians of Northern Wisconsin." *Bulletin of the Public Museum of the City of Milwaukee* 1. Milwaukee, WI: 1911.

Beckert, Sven. *Empire of Cotton: A Global History.* New York: Alfred A. Knopf, 2014.

Berlin, Ira. *Many Thousands Gone: The First Two Centuries of Slavery in North America.* Cambridge, MA: Harvard University Press, 1998.

Bidlack, Russell E. *The Yankee Meets the Frenchman: River Raisin 1817-1830.* Ann Arbor: Historical Society of Michigan Press, 1965.

Bieder, Robert E. *Science Encounters the Indian, 1820-1880: The Early Years of American Ethnology.* Norman: University of Oklahoma Press, 1986.

Birzer, Bradley J. "Jean Baptiste Richardville, Miami Métis." In *Enduring Nations: Native Americans in the Midwest,* edited by R. David Edmunds, 94–108. Urbana: University of Illinois Press, 2008.

Bohaker, Heidi. *Doodem and Council Fire: Anishinaabe Governance through Alliance.* Toronto: University of Toronto Press for The Osgoode Society for Canadian Legal History, 2020.

———. "'Nindoodemag:' The Significance of Algonquian Kinship Networks in the Eastern Great Lakes Region, 1600-1701." *William and Mary Quarterly* 3rd ser., 63, no. 1 (January 2006): 23–52.

Bowes, John P. *Land Too Good for Indians: Northern Indian Removal*. Norman: University of Oklahoma Press, 2016.

Boydston, Jeanne. *Home and Work: Housework, Wages, and the Ideology of Labor in the Early Republic*. New York: Oxford University Press, 1990.

Bridenthal, Renate, Claudia Koontz, and Susan Stuard, eds. *Becoming Visible: Women in European History*. 2nd ed. Boston: Houghton Mifflin, 1987.

Brightman, Robert. *Grateful Prey: Rock Cree Human-Animal Relationships*. Berkeley: University of California Press, 1993.

Brooks, James F. *Captives and Cousins: Slavery, Kinship, and Community in the Southwest Borderlands*. Chapel Hill: University of North Carolina Press for the Omohundro Institute of Early American History and Culture, 2002.

Brown, Jennifer S. H. *Strangers in Blood: Fur Trade Company Families in Indian Country*. Vancouver: University of British Columbia Press, 1980.

———, and Theresa Schenck. "Métis, Mestizo, and Mixed-Blood." In *A Companion to American Indian History*, edited by Philip J. Deloria and Neal Salisbury, 321–38. Malden, MA: Blackwell, 2002.

———, and Jacqueline L. Peterson, eds. *The New Peoples: Being and Becoming Métis in North America*. Lincoln: University of Nebraska Press, 1985.

Brunson, Alfred. *A Western Pioneer; or, Incidents of the Life and Times of Rev. Alfred Brunson*. 2 vols. Cincinnati, OH: Hitchcock and Walden, 1879.

Burley, Edith J. *Servants of the Honourable Company: Work, Discipline, and Conflict in the Hudson's Bay Company, 1770–1879*. Toronto: Oxford University Press, 1997.

Buss, James Joseph. *Winning the West with Words: Language and Conquest in the Lower Great Lakes*. Norman: University of Oklahoma Press, 2011.

Caffrey, Margaret M. "Complementary Power: Men and Women of the Lenni Lenape." *American Indian Quarterly* 24 (Winter 2000): 44–63.

Calloway, Colin G. *Crown and Calumet: British-Indian Relations, 1783–1815*. Norman: University of Oklahoma Press, 1987.

———. *The Scratch of a Pen: 1763 and the Transformation of North America*. New York: Oxford University Press, 2006.

———. "Simon Girty: Interpreter and Intermediary." In *Being and Becoming Indian: Biographical Studies of North American Frontiers*, edited by James A. Clifton, 38–58. Chicago: Dorsey Press, 1989.

Carpenter, Roger M. "Womanish Men and Manlike Women: The Native American Berdache as Warrior." In *Gender and Sexuality in Indigenous North America, 1400–1850*, edited by Sandra Slater and Fay A. Yarbrough, 146–64. Columbia: University of South Carolina Press, 2011. Reflecting current views that the term "berdache" is inaccurate and offensive to many persons on the LGBTQI+ spectrum, the title of this chapter has been revised to "Womanish Men and Manlike Women: The Native American Two-spirit as Warrior."

Chamberlain, Alexander F. *The Language of the Mississaga of Skugog*. Philadelphia: MacCall and Company, 1892.

Child, Brenda J. *Holding Our World Together: Ojibwe Women and the Survival of Community*. New York: Viking, 2012.

Chute, Janet. *The Legacy of Shingwaukonse: A Century of Native Leadership.* Toronto: University of Toronto Press, 1998.

Cleland, Charles E. *Rites of Conquest: The History and Culture of Michigan's Native Americans.* Ann Arbor: University of Michigan Press, 1992.

Clifton, James A. "Wisconsin Death March: Explaining the Extremes in Old Northwest Indian Removal." *Transactions of the Wisconsin Academy of Sciences, Arts and Letters* 75 (1987): 1–39.

———. *The Prairie People: Continuity and Change in Potawatomi Indian Culture, 1665–1965.* Lawrence: University of Kansas Press, 1977.

Collier, Jane Fishburne. *Marriage and Inequality in Classless Societies.* Stanford, CA: Stanford University Press, 1988.

Conzen, Kathleen Neils. "The Winnebago Urban System: Indian Policy and Townsite Promotion on the Upper Mississippi." In *Cities and Markets: Studies in the Organization of Human Space,* edited by Rondo Cameron and Leo F. Schnore, 269–310. Lanham, MD: University Press of America, 1997.

Cott, Nancy F. *The Bonds of Womanhood: "Woman's Sphere" in New England, 1780–1835.* New Haven, CT: Yale University Press, 1977.

Cronon, William. *Changes in the Land: Indians, Colonists, and the Ecology of New England.* New York: Hill and Wang, 1983.

DeMallie, Raymond J. "Touching the Pen: Plains Indian Treaty Councils in Ethnohistorical Perspective." In *Ethnicity on the Great Plains,* edited by Frederick C. Luebke, 38–53. Lincoln: University of Nebraska Press, 1980.

Demos, John. *The Unredeemed Captive: A Family Story from Early America.* New York: A. A. Knopf, 1994.

Denial, Catherine J. *Making Marriage: Husbands, Wives, and the American State in Dakota and Ojibwe Country.* St. Paul: Minnesota Historical Society Press, 2013.

Densmore, Frances. *Chippewa Customs.* St. Paul: Minnesota Historical Society Press, 1979. First published as the Smithsonian Institution, Bureau of American Ethnology. Bulletin 86. Washington, DC: Government Printing Office, 1929.

Derounian-Stodola, Kathryn Zabelle. *The Indian Captivity Narrative, 1550–1900.* New York: Maxwell Macmillan International, 1993.

Devine, Heather. *The People Who Own Themselves: Aboriginal Ethnogenesis in a Canadian Family, 1660–1900.* Calgary, AB: University of Calgary Press, 2004.

Dowd, Gregory Evans. *A Spirited Resistance: The North American Indian Struggle for Unity, 1745–1815.* Baltimore: Johns Hopkins University Press, 1992.

———. *War Under Heaven: Pontiac, the Indian Nations, and the British Empire.* Baltimore: Johns Hopkins University Press 2002.

Eccles, William J. *The Canadian Frontier, 1534–1760.* New York: Holt Rinehart and Winston, 1969.

———. "The Fur Trade and Eighteenth-Century Imperialism." *William and Mary Quarterly,* 3rd ser., 40 (July 1983): 341–62.

Edmunds, R. David. "Potawatomi." In *The Encyclopedia of North American Indians,* edited by Frederick E. Hoxie, 506–508. New York: Houghton Mifflin, 1996.

———. *The Potawatomis: Keepers of the Fire.* Norman: University of Oklahoma Press, 1978.

———. "Richardville, Jean Baptiste (Peshewa)." In *The Encyclopedia of North American Indians,* edited by Frederick E. Hoxie, 549–50. New York: Houghton Mifflin, 1996.

———. *The Shawnee Prophet.* Lincoln: University of Nebraska Press, 1983.

———. "'Unacquainted with the Laws of the Civilized World': American Attitudes toward the Métis Communities in the Old Northwest." In *The New Peoples: Being and Becoming Métis in North America,* edited by Jacqueline Peterson and Jennifer S. H. Brown, 185–91. Winnipeg: University of Manitoba Press; Lincoln: University of Nebraska Press, 1985.

Ethridge, Robbie, and Sheri M. Shuck-Hall, eds. *Mapping the Mississippian Shatter Zone: The Colonial Indian Slave Trade and Regional Instability in the American South.* Lincoln: University of Nebraska Press, 2009.

Etienne, Mona, and Eleanor Burke Leacock, eds. *Women and Colonization: Anthropological Perspectives.* New York: Praeger, 1980.

Faragher, John Mack. *Daniel Boone: The Life and Legend of an American Pioneer.* New York: Henry Holt, 1992.

Folwell, William Watts. *A History of Minnesota.* 2nd. ed. 4 vols. St. Paul: Minnesota Historical Society Press, 1922.

Frederickson, George M. *The Black Image in the White Mind: The Debate on Afro-American Character and Destiny, 1817–1914.* New York: Harper and Row, 1971.

Fur, Gunlög. *A Nation of Women: Gender and Colonial Encounters Among the Delaware Indians.* Philadelphia: University of Pennsylvania Press, 2009.

———. "'Some Women Are Wiser Than Some Men': Gender and Native American History." In *Clearing a Path: Theorizing the Past in Native American Studies,* edited by Nancy Shoemaker, 75–103. New York: Routledge, 2002.

Gallay, Allan. *The Indian Slave Trade: The Rise of the English Empire in the American South, 1670–1717.* New Haven, CT: Yale University Press, 2002.

Galler, Robert. "Making Common Cause: Yanktonais and Catholic Missionaries on the Northern Plains." *Ethnohistory* 55 (Summer, 2008): 439–64.

Gerwing, Anselm J. "The Chicago Indian Treaty of 1833." *Journal of the Illinois State Historical Society,* 57 (Summer, 1964): 117–42.

Gilman, Rhoda R., Carolyn Gilman, and Deborah M. Stultz. *The Red River Trails: Oxcart Routes between St. Paul and the Selkirk Settlement, 1820–1879.* St. Paul: Minnesota Historical Society Press, 1979.

Gordon, Linda. *The Great Arizona Orphan Abduction.* Cambridge, MA: Harvard University Press, 1999.

Gould, Stephen Jay. *The Mismeasure of Man.* Rev. ed. New York: W. W. Norton, 1995.

Greer, Allan. *Peasant, Lord, and Merchant: Rural Society in Three Quebec Parishes, 1740–1840.* Toronto: University of Toronto Press, 1985.

Gross, Ariela J. *What Blood Won't Tell: A History of Race on Trial in America.* Cambridge, MA: Harvard University Press, 2008.

Hallowell, A. Irving. "Ojibwa Ontology, Behavior, and World View." In *Teachings from the American Earth: Indian Religion and Philosophy,* edited by Dennis Tedlock and Barbara Tedlock, 141–78. New York: Liveright, 1975.

Hannaford, Ivan. *Race: The History of an Idea in the West.* Baltimore: Johns Hopkins University Press, 1996.

Hartman, Mary S. *The Household and the Making of History: A Subversive View of the Western Past.* Cambridge: Cambridge University Press, 2004.

Havard, Gilles. *The Great Peace of Montreal of 1701: French-Native Diplomacy in the Seventeenth Century.* Translated by Phyllis Aronoff and Howard Scott. Montreal: McGill-Queen's University Press, 2001.

Heng, Geraldine. "The Invention of Race in the European Middle Ages I: Race Studies, Modernity, and the Middle Ages." *Literature Compass* 8, no. 5 (2011): 315–31.

———. "The Invention of Race in the European Middle Ages II: Locations of Medieval Race." *Literature Compass* 8, no. 5 (2011): 332–50.

Hickerson, Harold. *The Chippewa and Their Neighbors: A Study in Ethnohistory.* New York: Holt Rinehart and Winston, 1970.

———. "The Feast of the Dead Among the Seventeenth Century Algonkians of the Upper Great Lakes." *American Anthropologist* 62 (February 1960): 81–107.

———. "The Sociohistorical Significance of Two Chippewa Ceremonials." *American Anthropologist* 65 (February 1963): 67–85.

———. *The Southwestern Chippewa: An Ethnohistorical Study.* American Anthropological Association Memoir 92. Menasha, WI: George B. Banta Co., 1962.

Hilger, Sister M. Inez. *Chippewa Child Life and Its Cultural Background.* Smithsonian Institution. Bureau of American Ethnology. Bulletin 146. Washington, DC: Government Printing Office, 1951.

Hill, Sarah H. *Weaving New Worlds: Southeastern Cherokee Women and Their Basketry.* Chapel Hill: University of North Carolina Press, 1997.

Hinderaker, Eric. *Elusive Empires: Constructing Colonialism in the Ohio Valley, 1673–1800.* Cambridge: Cambridge University Press, 1997.

Hodge, Frederick Webb, ed. *Handbook of American Indians North of Mexico.* Smithsonian Institution, Bureau of American Ethnology. Bulletin 30, Part 2. Washington, DC: Government Printing Office, 1907, 1910.

Hodgen, Margaret T. *Early Anthropology in the Sixteenth and Seventeenth Centuries.* Philadelphia: University of Pennsylvania Press, 1964.

Hoffmann, M. M. *Church Founders of the Old Northwest: Loras and Cretin and Other Captains of Christ.* Milwaukee: Bruce Publishing Company, 1937.

Holt, Marilyn Irvin. *The Orphan Trains: Placing Out in America.* Lincoln: University of Nebraska Press, 1992.

Horsman, Reginald. *Race and Manifest Destiny: The Origins of American Racial Anglo-Saxonism.* Cambridge, MA: Harvard University Press, 1981.

Hudson, Nicholas. "From 'Nation' to 'Race': The Origin of Racial Classification in Eighteenth-Century Thought." *Eighteenth-Century Studies* 29 (Spring, 1996): 247–64.

Hurt, R. Douglas. *The Ohio Frontier: Crucible of the Old Northwest, 1720–1830.* Bloomington: Indiana University Press, 1996.

Ignatiev, Noel. *How the Irish Became White.* New York: Routledge, 1995.

Innis, Harold A. *The Fur Trade in Canada.* New Haven, CT: Yale University Press, 1930.

Jacobs, Wilbur R. *Wilderness Politics and Indian Gifts: The Northern Colonial Frontier, 1748–1763.* Lincoln: University of Nebraska Press, 1967. First published 1950; citations to 1967 edition.

Jacobsen, Kristina, and Shirley Ann Bowman. "'Don't Even Talk to Me if You're Kin-ya'áanii [Towering House]": Adopted Clans, Kinship, and 'Blood' in Navajo Country." *Journal of the Native American Studies Association* 6, no. 1 (2019): 43–76.

Jacobson, Matthew Frye. *Whiteness of a Different Color: European Immigrants and the Alchemy of Race.* Cambridge, MA: Harvard University Press, 1998.

Jenness, Diamond. *The Ojibwa of Parry Island: Their Social and Religious Life.* National Museum of Canada, Bulletin 78, Anthropology Series. Ottawa: Department of Mines, 1935.

Jennings, Francis. *The Ambiguous Iroquois Empire: The Covenant Chain Confederation of Indian Tribes with English Colonies from its Beginnings to the Lancaster Treaty of 1744.* New York: W. W. Norton, 1984.

———. *Empire of Fortune: Crowns, Colonies and Tribes in the Seven Years War in America.* New York: W. W. Norton, 1988.

———. *The Invasion of America: Indians, Colonialism, and the Cant of Conquest.* New York: W. W. Norton, 1975.

———. ed. *History and Culture of Iroquois Diplomacy: An Interdisciplinary Guide to the Treaties of the Six Nations and Their League.* With joint editor William N. Fenton, associate editor Mary A. Druke, and research editor David R. Miller. Syracuse, NY: Syracuse University Press, 1985.

Jetté, Melinda Marie. *At the Hearth of the Crossed Races: A French-Indian Community in Nineteenth-Century Oregon, 1812–1818.* Corvallis: Oregon State University Press, 2015.

Johnston, Basil. *The Manitous: The Spiritual World of the Ojibway.* New York: Harper Collins, 1995.

———. *Ojibway Ceremonies.* Toronto: McClelland and Stewart, 1982.

———. *Ojibway Heritage.* New York: Columbia University Press, 1976.

Jones, William, comp. *Ojibwa Texts.* Publications of the American Ethnological Society, edited by Truman Michelson. Vol 7. Parts 1 and 2. New York: G. E. Stechert and Co., 1917, 1919.

Jordan, John W. *Genealogical and Personal History of Western Pennsylvania.* 2 vols. New York: Lewis Historical Publishing Company, 1915.

Joseph, Alice, Rosamond Spicer, and Jane Chesky. *The Desert People.* Chicago: University of Chicago Press, 1949.

Kappler, Charles J., ed, and comp. *Indian Affairs: Laws and Treaties.* 2 vols. Washington, DC: Government Printing Office, 1904.

Kellogg, Louise Phelps. *The French Régime in Wisconsin and the Northwest.* New York: Cooper Square Publishers, 1968.

Klein, Laura F., and Lillian A. Ackerman, eds. *Women and Power in Native North America.* Norman: University of Oklahoma Press, 1995.

Kohl, Johann Georg. *Kitchi-Gami: Life Among the Lake Superior Ojibway.* St. Paul: Minnesota Historical Society, 1985. Originally published 1860 by Chapman and Hall (London).

Kugel, Rebecca. "Planning to Stay: Native Strategies to Remain in the Great Lakes Post-War of 1812." *Middle West Review* 2 (Spring 2016): 1–26.

———. "Religion Mixed with Politics: The 1836 Conversion of Mang'osid of Fond du Lac." *Ethnohistory* 37 (Spring 1990): 126–57.

———. "Reworking Ethnicity: Gender, Work Roles, and Contending Redefinitions of the Great Lakes Métis, 1820–42." In *Enduring Nations: Native American in the Midwest,* edited by R. David Edmunds, 160–81. Urbana: University of Illinois Press, 2008.

———. *To Be the Main Leaders of Our People: A History of Minnesota Ojibwe Politics, 1825–1898.* East Lansing: Michigan State University Press, 1998.

Kulikoff, Allan. *From British Peasants to Colonial American Farmers.* Chapel Hill: University of North Carolina Press, 2000.

Landes, Ruth. *The Mystic Lake Sioux.* Madison: University of Wisconsin Press. 1968.

———. *Ojibwa Sociology.* Columbia University Contributions to Anthropology, vol. 29. New York: Columbia University Press, 1937.

Lavender, David. *A Fist in the Wilderness.* New York: Doubleday, 1964.

Leacock, Eleanor Burke. "Matrilocality in a Simple Hunting Economy (Montagnais-Naskapi)." *Southwestern Journal of Anthropology* 11 (Spring 1955): 31–47.

———. "The Montagnais-Naskapi 'Hunting Territory' and the Fur Trade." American Anthropological Association Memoir 78. Menasha, WI: George B. Banta Co., 1954.

———. "Women's Status in Egalitarian Society: Implications for Social Evolution." *Current Anthropology* 19 (June 1978): 247–75.

Lewis, James Otto. *The Aboriginal Portfolio, or, a Collection of Portraits of the Most Celebrated Chiefs of the North American Indians.* Philadelphia: Lelhman and Duval, 1836.

Mandell, Daniel. *Tribe, Race, History: Native Americans in Southern New England, 1780–1880.* Baltimore: Johns Hopkins University Press, 2008.

McClurken, James M. "Augustin Hamlin Jr.: Ottawa Identity and the Politics of Persistence." In *Being and Becoming Indian: Biographical Studies of North American Frontiers,* edited by James A. Clifton, 82–111. Chicago: Dorsey, 1989.

McConnell, Michael N. *A Country Between: The Upper Ohio Valley and Its Peoples, 1724–1774.* Lincoln: University of Nebraska Press, 1992.

McDermott, John Francis. *A Glossary of Mississippi Valley French, 1673–1850.* Washington University Studies in Language and Literature, n.s., 12. St. Louis: Washington University Press, 1941.

McDonnell, Michael A. *Masters of Empire: Great Lakes Indians and the Making of America.* New York: Hill and Wang, 2015.

McNally, Michael D. *Honoring Elders: Aging, Authority, and Ojibwe Religion.* New York: Columbia University Press, 2009.

Melish, Joanne Pope. *Disowning Slavery: Gradual Emancipation and "Race" in New England, 1780–1860.* Ithaca, NY: Cornell University Press, 1998.

Merritt, Jane T. *At the Crossroads: Indians and Empires on a Mid-Atlantic Frontier, 1700–1763.* Chapel Hill: University of North Carolina Press, 2003.

Meyer, Melissa L. *Thicker Than Water: The Origins of Blood as Symbol and Ritual.* New York: Routledge, 2005.

———. *The White Earth Tragedy: Ethnicity and Dispossession at a Minnesota Anishinaabe Reservation, 1889–1920.* Lincoln: University of Nebraska Press, 1994.

Michelson, Truman. "Note on the Gentes of the Ottawa." *American Anthropologist* 13 (April–June 1911): 338.

Miles, Tiya. *The Dawn of Detroit: A Chronicle of Slavery and Freedom in the City of the Straits.* New York: New Press, 2017.

Miller, Cary. "Gifts as Treaties: The Political Use of Received Gifts in Anishinaabe Communities, 1820–1832." *American Indian Quarterly* 26 (Spring 2002): 221–45.

———. *Ogimaag: Anishinaabeg Leadership, 1760–1845*. Lincoln: University of Nebraska Press, 2010.

Murphy, Lucy Eldersveld. *A Gathering of Rivers: Indians, Métis, and Mining in the Western Great Lakes, 1737–1832*. Lincoln: University of Nebraska Press, 2004.

———. *Great Lakes Creoles: A French-Indian Community on the Northern Borderlands, Prairie du Chien, 1750–1860*. New York: Cambridge University Press, 2014.

Namias, June. *White Captives: Gender and Ethnicity on the American Frontier*. Chapel Hill: University of North Carolina Press, 1993.

Nesper, Larry. *The Walleye War: The Struggle for Ojibwe Spearfishing and Treaty Rights*. Lincoln: University of Nebraska Press, 2002.

Nichols, David Andrew. *Engines of Diplomacy: Indian Trading Factories and the Negotiation of American Empire*. Chapel Hill: University of North Carolina Press, 2016.

Nichols, John D., ed. "'Statement Made by the Indians': A Bilingual Petition of the Chippewas of Lake Superior, 1864." Centre for Research and Teaching of Canadian Native Languages. London, ON: University of Western Ontario, 1988.

Nichols, John D., and Earl Nyholm. *A Concise Dictionary of Minnesota Ojibwe*. Minneapolis: University of Minnesota Press, 1995.

Norrgard, Chantal. *Seasons of Change: Labor, Treaty Rights, and Ojibwe Nationhood*. Chapel Hill: University of North Carolina Press, 2014.

O'Brien, Jean M. *Firsting and Lasting: Writing Indians Out of Existence in New England*. Minneapolis: University of Minnesota Press, 2010.

———. "Memory and Mobility: Grandma's Mahnomen, White Earth." *Ethnohistory* 64 (July 2017): 345–77.

O'Neill, Colleen. *Working the Navajo Way: Labor and Culture in the Twentieth Century*. Lawrence: University of Kansas Press, 2005.

Peers, Laura. *The Ojibwa of Western Canada, 1780–1879*. Winnipeg: University of Manitoba Press, 1994.

Perdue, Theda. *Cherokee Women: Gender and Culture Change, 1700–1835*. Lincoln: University of Nebraska Press, 1998.

———. *"Mixed Blood" Indians: Racial Construction in the Early South*. Athens: University of Georgia Press, 2003.

Peters, William E. *Ohio Lands and Their Subdivisions*. 2nd ed. Athens, OH: W. E. Peters, 1918.

Peterson, Jacqueline L. "The People in Between: Indian-White Marriage and the Genesis of a Métis Society in the Great Lakes Region, 1680–1830. PhD diss., University of Illinois at Chicago Circle, 1981.

———. "Prelude to Red River: A Social Portrait of the Great Lakes Métis." *Ethnohistory* 25 (Winter 1978): 41–67.

Podruchny, Carolyn. *Making the Voyageur World: Travelers and Traders in the North American Fur Trade*. Lincoln: University of Nebraska Press, 2006.

Prucha, Francis Paul. "Fort Ripley: The Post and the Military Reservation." *Minnesota History,* 28 (September 1947): 205–24.

———. *The Great Father: The United States Government and the American Indians*. Lincoln: University of Nebraska Press, 1986.

Quimby, George Irving. *Indian Life in the Upper Great Lakes, 11,000 B.C. to A.D. 1800.* Chicago: University of Chicago Press, 1960.

——. "Some Notes on Kinship and Kinship Terminology among the Potawatomi of the Huron." *Papers of the Michigan Academy of Science, Arts, and Letters* 25 (1940): 553–63.

Rafert, Stewart. "Godfroy, Francois (Palonswa)." In *The Encyclopedia of North American Indians,* edited by Frederick E. Hoxie, 223–24. New York: Houghton Mifflin, 1996.

Ramirez-Shkwegnaabi, Benjamin. "The Dynamics of American Indian Diplomacy in the Great Lakes Region." *American Indian Culture and Research Journal* 27 (December 2003): 53–77.

Ray, Arthur J. *Indians in the Fur Trade: Their Role as Trappers, Hunters, and Middlemen in the Lands Southwest of Hudson Bay, 1660–1870.* Toronto: University of Toronto Press, 1974.

Rediker, Marcus. *Between the Devil and the Deep Blue Sea: Merchant Seamen, Pirates, and the Anglo-American Maritime World, 1700–1750.* Cambridge: Cambridge University Press, 1987.

Redix, Erik. *The Murder of Joe White: Ojibwe Leadership and Colonialism in Wisconsin.* East Lansing: Michigan State University Press, 2014.

Reed, Julie L. *Serving the Nation: Cherokee Sovereignty and Social Welfare, 1800–1907.* Norman: University of Oklahoma Press, 2016.

Reichard, Gladys A. *Social Life of the Navajo Indians: With Some Attention to Minor Ceremonies.* New York: Columbia University Press, 1928.

Rich, E. E. *The Fur Trade and the Northwest to 1857.* Toronto: McClelland and Stewart, 1967.

Richter, Daniel K. *The Ordeal of the Longhouse: The Peoples of the Iroquois League in the Era of European Colonization.* Chapel Hill: University of North Carolina Press for the Omohundro Institute of Early American History and Culture, 1992.

Ritvo, Harriet. *The Animal Estate: The English and Other Creatures in the Victorian Age.* Cambridge, MA: Harvard University Press, 1987.

Roediger, David. *The Wages of Whiteness: Race and the Making of the American Working Class.* London: Verso, 1991.

Rogin, Michael Paul. *Fathers and Children: Andrew Jackson and the Subjugation of the American Indian.* New York: Knopf, 1975.

Royce, Charles C., comp. "Indian Land Cessions in the United States." In *Eighteenth Annual Report of the Bureau of American Ethnology to the Secretary of the Smithsonian Institution, 1896–97,* by J. W. Powell, vol. 18, pt. 2 (1896–97).

Rushforth, Brett. *Bonds of Alliance: Indigenous and Atlantic Slaveries in New France.* Chapel Hill: University of North Carolina Press for the Omohundro Institute of Early American History and Culture, 2012.

Saler, Bethel. *The Settlers' Empire: Colonialism and State Formation in America's Old Northwest.* Philadelphia: University of Pennsylvania Press, 2015.

Satz, Ronald N. "Chippewa Treaty Rights: The Reserved Rights of Wisconsin's Chippewa Indians in Historical Perspective." *Transactions of the Wisconsin Academy of Sciences, Arts and Letters,* 79, no. 1 (1991): 1–251.

Schenck, Theresa M. *William W. Warren: The Life, Letters, and Times of an Ojibwe Leader.* Lincoln: University of Nebraska Press, 2007.

———, comp. and ed. *All Our Relations: Chippewa Mixed-Bloods and the Treaty of 1837*. Winnipeg, MB: Centre for Rupert's Land Studies, University of Winnipeg. Madison, WI: Amik Press, 2010.

Sheehan, Bernard W. *Seeds of Extinction: Jeffersonian Philanthropy and the American Indian*. Chapel Hill: University of North Carolina Press for the Omohundro Institute of Early American History and Culture, 1973.

Shoemaker, Nancy. "An Alliance Between Men: Gender Metaphors in Eighteenth-Century American Indian Diplomacy East of the Mississippi." *Ethnohistory* 46, no. 2 (1999): 239–63.

———. "How Indians Got to Be Red." *American Historical Review* 102 (June 1997): 625–44.

———. *A Strange Likeness: Becoming Red and White in Eighteenth-Century North America*. New York: Oxford University Press, 2004.

Skaggs, David C., and Larry Nelson, eds. *The Sixty Years' War for the Great Lakes, 1754–1816*. East Lansing: Michigan State University Press, 2001.

Sleeper-Smith, Susan. *Indian Women and French Men: Rethinking Cultural Encounter in the Western Great Lakes*. Amherst: University of Massachusetts Press, 2001.

———. *Indigenous Prosperity and American Conquest: Indian Women of the Ohio River Valley, 1690–1792*. Chapel Hill: University of North Carolina Press for the Omohundro Institute of Early American History and Culture, 2018.

———. "Women, Kin, and Catholicism: New Perspectives on the Fur Trade." *Ethnohistory* 47 (Spring 2000): 423–52.

Smedley, Audrey. *Race in North America: Origins and Evolution of a Worldview*. 3rd ed. Boulder, CO: Westview Press, 2007.

Smith, James G. E. "Leadership Among the Southwestern Ojibwa." National Museums of Canada, Publications in Ethnology, no 7. Ottawa: National Museums of Canada, 1973.

Smith, Katy Simpson. "'I Look on You . . . As My Children': Persistence and Change in Cherokee Motherhood, 1750–1835." *North Carolina Historical Review* 87 (October 2010): 403–30.

Smits, David D. "The 'Squaw Drudge': A Prime Index of Savagism," *Ethnohistory* 29 (Autumn 1982): 281–306.

Snyder, Christina. *Great Crossings: Indians, Settlers, and Slaves in the Age of Jackson*. New York: Oxford University Press, 2017.

———. "The Rise and Fall and Rise of Civilizations: Indian Intellectual Culture during the Removal Era." *Journal of American History* (September 2017): 386–409.

———. *Slavery in Indian Country: The Changing Face of Captivity in Early America*. Cambridge, MA: Harvard University Press, 2010.

Stanton, William. *The Leopard's Spots: Scientific Attitudes toward Race in America, 1815–1859*. Chicago: University of Chicago Press, 1960.

St-Onge, Nicole. "Familial Foes? French-Sioux Families and Plains Métis Brigades in the Nineteenth Century." *American Indian Quarterly* 39 (Summer 2015): 302–37.

Sugden, John. *Blue Jacket: Warrior of the Shawnees*. Lincoln: University of Nebraska Press, 2000.

———. *Tecumseh: A Life*. New York: Henry Holt, 1998.

Tanner, Helen Hornbeck, ed. *Atlas of Great Lakes Indian History*. Published for the Newberry Library. Norman: University of Oklahoma Press, 1987.
———. "Coocoohchee: Mohawk Medicine Woman." *American Indian Culture and Research Journal* 3, no. 3 (1979): 23–41.
Tanner, John. *The Falcon: A Narrative of the Captivity and Adventures of John Tanner*. New York: Penguin Books, 1994. First published 1830 by Baldwin and Cradock (London).
Taylor, Allan. "Captain Hendrick Aupaumut: The Dilemmas of an Intercultural Broker." *Ethnohistory* 43 (Summer 1996): 431–47.
———. *The Divided Ground: Indians, Settlers, and the Northern Borderland of the American Revolution*. New York: Alfred A. Knopf, 2006.
Thorne, Tanis Chapman. *The Many Hands of My Relations: French and Indians on the Lower Missouri*. Columbia: University of Missouri Press, 1996.
Trennert, Robert A. *Indian Traders on the Middle Border: The House of Ewing, 1827–1854*. Lincoln: University of Nebraska Press, 1981.
Underhill, Ruth Murray. *The Singing for Power: The Song Magic of the Papago Indians of Southern Arizona*. Berkeley: University of California Press, 1976. First published 1939; citations to the 1976 edition.
Usner Jr., Daniel H. *Indians, Settler, and Slaves in a Frontier Exchange Economy: The Lower Mississippi Valley before 1783*. Chapel Hill: University of North Carolina Press for the Omohundro Institute of Early American History and Culture, 1992.
Van Kirk, Sylvia. *Many Tender Ties: Women in Fur Trade Society, 1670–1870*. Norman: University of Oklahoma Press, 1980.
———. "Toward a Feminist Perspective in Native History." In *Papers of the Eighteenth Algonquian Conference*, edited by William Cowan. Ottawa, ON: Carleton University Press, 1987.
Vaughan, Alden T. "From White Man to Redskin: Changing Anglo-American Perceptions of the American Indian." *American Historical Review* 87 (October 1982): 917–53.
Vennum Jr., Thomas. *The Ojibwa Dance Drum: Its History and Construction*. Smithsonian Folklife Series No. 2. Washington, DC: Smithsonian Institution Press, 1982.
———. *Wild Rice and the Ojibway People*. St. Paul: Minnesota Historical Society Press, 1988.
Walsh, Martin W. "The 'Heathen Party': Methodist Observation of the Ohio Wyandots." *American Indian Quarterly* 16 (Spring 1992): 189–202.
Welter, Barbara. "The Cult of True Womanhood, 1820–1860." *American Quarterly* 18, no. 2, pt. 1 (Summer 1966): 151–74.
Westerman, Gwen, and Bruce M. White. *Mni Sota Makoce: The Land of the Dakota*. St. Paul: Minnesota Historical Society Press, 2012.
White, Bruce M. "The Regional Context of the Removal Order of 1850." In *Fish in the Lakes, Wild Rice, and Game in Abundance: Testimony on Behalf of Mille Lacs Ojibwe Hunting and Fishing Rights*, compiled by James M. McClurken. East Lansing: Michigan State University Press, 2000.
———. "The Woman Who Married the Beaver: Trade Patterns and Gender Roles in the Ojibwa Fur Trade," *Ethnohistory* 46 (Winter 1999): 109–47.

White, Richard. *The Middle Ground: Indians, Empires, and Republics in the Great Lakes Region, 1650–1815*. Cambridge: Cambridge University Press, 1991.

Widder, Keith R. *Battle for the Soul: Métis Children Encounter Evangelical Protestants at Mackinaw Mission, 1823–1837*. East Lansing: Michigan State University Press, 1999.

———. *Beyond Pontiac's Shadow: Michilimackinac and the Anglo-Indian War of 1763*. East Lansing: Michigan State University Press, 2013.

Wiesner, Merry E. *Women and Gender in Early Modern Europe*. Cambridge: Cambridge University Press, 1993.

Williams., J. Fletcher. "Memoir of William W. Warren." In *History of the Ojibway People*. St. Paul: Minnesota Historical Society Press, 1984. First published 1885; citations to the 1984 edition.

Williams, Robert A. *Linking Arms Together: American Indian Treaty Visions of Law and Peace, 1600–1800*. New York: Oxford University Press, 1997.

Williams, Timothy J. *Intellectual Manhood: University, Self, and Society in the Antebellum South*. Chapel Hill: University of North Carolina Press, 2015.

Willig, Timothy D. *Restoring the Chain of Friendship: British Policy and the Indians of the Great Lakes, 1783–1815*. Lincoln: University of Nebraska Press, 2008.

Witgen, Michael John. *An Infinity of Nations: How the Native New World Shaped Early North America*. Philadelphia: University of Pennsylvania Press, 2012.

———. *Seeing Red: Indigenous Land, American Expansion, and the Political Economy of Plunder in North America*. Chapel Hill: University of North Carolina Press for the Omohundro Institute of Early American History and Culture, 2022.

———. "Seeing Red: Race, Citizenship, and Indigeneity in the Old Northwest." *Journal of the Early Republic* 38 (Winter 2018): 581–611.

Wolfe, Patrick. "Settler Colonialism and the Elimination of the Native." *Journal of Genocide Research* 8, no. 4 (2006): 387–409.

———. *Settler Colonialism and the Transformation of Anthropology: The Politics and Poetics of an Ethnographic Event*. London: Cassell, 1999.

Zolbrod, Paul G. *Diné Bahane': The Navajo Creation Story*. Albuquerque: University of New Mexico Press, 1984.

Websites

https://www.aihc.amdigital.co.uk/
https://www.ancestry.com/
https://www.kingjamesbibleonline.org
https://www.loc.gov/
https://www.minnesotahistory.net/
https://www.archives.gov
https://ohiohistorycentral.org/
https://ojibwe.lib.umn.edu
https://webstersdictionary1828.com/

Index

References in italic type indicate images or image captions.

Abbe, Sam, 163–64, 165, 166, 222n33
ABCFM. *See* American Board of
  Commissioners for Foreign Missions
adoption, adoptees, 98, 195–96n24; and
  Maumee Rapids treaty, 54, 55–56, 68;
  mistreatment of, 93–94; Native and
  Anglo-American views, 57–58
AFC. *See* American Fur Company
Africans: enslavement of, 24
Agabe-gijik, 32
age: and status, 34, 35; and wisdom,
  32–33
agriculture, 46, 51, 121
Ah-be-tah-wiz-ee, 86. *See also*
  Ayaa'aabiitawisid
Ah be te ke zhick [Ap-te-ke-zhick], 29, 30
Ain-dus-o-ge-shig, 79, 108
Aitken, William A., 147
alcohol: introduction of, 152, 219n12
alcoholism: of James P. Hays, 151–52
Algonkian-speakers, 13, 32; ethnonym
  for French, 121–23
Algonquins, 121
alliances, 28, 31, 48, 58; with European
  powers, 22–23; French-Ojibwe,
  129–30; kin-based, 121, 173
American Board of Commissioners for
  Foreign Missions (ABCFM), 119, 137,
  144, 215n37
American Eagle, 101
American Fur Company (AFC), 69; and
  Treaty of Fond du Lac, 155–56

Anglo-Americans/Americans, 30, 39,
  50, 75, 89, 101, 120, 125, 131, 163,
  194n18; and Customs of All the
  Nations, 170–71; as elites, 154–55;
  gender expectations, 51, 141–42;
  as Gichimookomaanag, 27–28,
  186n17; on kinship, 70–71; at
  LaPointe, 144–45; mixed-bloods,
  99–100; on multiracial persons,
  42–43, 172–73; and Ojibwes, 160–61;
  patriarchy of, 148–49; on race, 76,
  143; race-based differences, 24–25;
  use of ethnonyms, 28–29; women's
  positions as, 146–47, 165–66
Anglophones: adopted by tribes, 54, 55,
  60, 68–69
animals: clans named for, 101. *See also*
  Other Than Human persons
Anishinaabe (Anichinabe),
  Anishinaabeg, 28–29. *See also*
  Ojibwes (Anishinaabeg)
Apaches: and Navajo clans, 88
Ap-te-ke-zhick [Ah be te ke zhick], 29, 30
assimilation, 175, 176; of Ojibwes,
  160–61; White Earth Reservation
  and, 166–67
Aupaumut, Hendrick, 13
autonomy, 12; personal, 127
Awaasi (Fish) Clan, 91
Aw ban aw bee, 6, 37
Ayaa'aabitawasid [Aiábitawisid], 86, 96,
  100

239

race, racial identity, 7, 24, 45; American construction of, 3–4, 15, 25–26, 39, 40, 69, 71, 76, 143, 171, 173, 175; French and, 50, 51, 52–53; of multiracial people, 66–67, 78–79; Native constructs of, 26–27; and social identity, 78–79, 80–81; treaty negotiation and, 53–54, 59
Radisson, Pierre-Esprit, 144
reciprocity, 20, 35, 127
Red men: Native use of, 25
Red Power era, 176
Red River region: Métis from, 161–62
refugees: cultural absorption of, 88
removal, 66, 149, 172
reservations, 54, 222–23n34; assimilation on, 166–67, 176
resistance, 48, 76
Rice, Henry, 149, 150, 151, 156, 158, 221n22
rice harvesting, 132, 138, 158, 214n26
Rice Lake, Wisc., 91, 94, 95
Richardville, Jean Baptiste (Peshewa), 61–62, 64, 116
Richmond, William: investigation of James Hays, 152–54
rituals: death, 129; diplomatic, 13, 57–58
Robinson, D. A., 158
Rock River ferry, 25

Sac, 25, 37
Saginaw, Mich., treaty of, 68–69
Sandy Lake Village, Minn., 27, 33, 125, 217–18n8
Sauks, 43, 121
Sault Ste. Marie (Baaweting), 40, 121, 130, 144
savage, savagery, 52, 63, 129
Sawanogalga (Shawnee people) moiety, 88
Sawendebans (Yellow Hair; Peter Minor), 55, 56, 57
Schoolcraft, Henry, 49, 50, 69, 83, 102, 128, 154
Scott, James C., 5
self-identity, self-identification, 40–41; of multiracial persons, 66–67

self-reliance, 12, 127, 131; Ojibwe, 136, 212n15
Senecas, 53, 54, 56
settler colonialism, 12, 163; and gendered labor roles, 140–41; land cessions, 46, 172; and subordination of tribes, 174–75
Seven Years' War, 21, 24, 27–28, 133; French defeat, 120, 124, 140
sexual assault, 21: on Indigenous women, 147–48, 217n5; on Matilda Warren, 145–46
sexuality, 21, 166
Shawnees, 1, 48, 59, 88; kinship terms, 18, 29–30; and Maumee Rapids Treaty, 53, 54, 55
Shinguabe Wossin. See Zhingwaabe Aasin
shooting stars: at Sandy Lake village, 33
Siouan-speakers, 13
Six Nations Iroquois Confederacy, 2, 18, 31, 123; political dominance, 20–21
skin color: and racial identity, 24, 25–26, 171
Sku-a-ne-ne (Little Brave), 73
slavery, 4, 24, 76
Slavery in Indian Country: The Changing Face of Captivity in Early America (Snyder), 93
Sleeper-Smith, Susan: Indigenous Prosperity and American Conquest, 140–41
Smith, William R., 103
Snake River, Wisc., 72, 102
Snyder, Christina: Slavery in Indian Country, 93
social evolution, 51, 64
social groups/collectivities, 1, 10, 20, 88; formation of, 121; power of, 52
social identities, 7; and forms of labor, 119–20; gender and, 120–21; of multitribal peoples, 95–97, 101; Ojibwes and, 78–79; race and, 67, 80–81
social landscape: Lower Great Lakes, 83–84, 88

somatic features: American racial
  definitions, 78–79
sovereignty: Indigenous, 162
speech, speakers, 13, 15; age and status,
  34; transcribed Native, 9–10
spirit beings, 33, 127, 179n2; Dakotas
  and, 91–92
spirituality, 32–33; of multitribal persons,
  105–6
Spotted Arm, 25
Spruce, 34
status: age and, 34
St. Croix River: Ojibwe kin groups on,
  91, 95
St. Louis, Mo., 48
St. Mary's, Ohio: treaty of, 56, 60,
  197–98nn30–32
St. Peters, Minn.: treaty of, 103, 107, 137,
  207–8n35
subordination/subjugation, 14, 39, 120,
  167; of multiracial people, 143–44; of
  tribes, 174–75; of voyageurs, 126–27,
  128, 133; of women, 19, 20–22; of
  youth, 32–33, 36–37
subsistence: and landholdings, 159–60
Swan River, Minn.: Matilda Warren at,
  149, 150–51

Tail Feather Woman (Wiyaka Sinte
  Win), 105–6, 107
Talcott, William. See Madweweyaash
Ta-Ma-Kake-Toke (The Woman That
  Spoke First), 112
Tanner, John, 32
Tarhe, 18, 30
Taucumwah, 62
Tecumseh, 48, 54
Tenskwatawa, 48
termination: as 1950s–60s Federal Indian
  policy, 176
Thames, Battle of the, 54
Those Who Belong: Identity, Family,
  Blood, and Citizenship among
  the White Earth Anishinaabeg
  (Doerfler), 176
Three Council Fires; Three Fires: and
  Greenville treaty negotiations, 7–8

Tohono O'odham: clan formation, 88
Tondaganie, 54, 57
Topinibe, 60
Trade and Intercourse Acts, 152, 219n12
traders, trade, 132, 145; French, 122–23,
  144; land-cession negotiations and,
  67–68; and multiracial identities,
  69–70
trading posts, 47, 122, 125–26; at Crow
  Wing, 156–57
translation: intercultural, 104
treaties, 1, 18, 67, 149; community
  involvement, 6–7; gift exchange,
  65–66; interpreters, 150, 151, 186n19;
  land-cession, 53, 172–73; multiracial/
  multitribal negotiators, 59–60,
  64–66; negotiations, 4–6, 53–54, 103,
  150–51, 173–74; tribal relationships
  and, 2–3; US negotiation of, 47–48.
  See also by location/name
Treaty of 1855, 34
Treaty of October 2, 1818, 61
Treaty of 16 October 1826, 30, 189n34
Treaty of 27 October 1832, 42
tribes/nations: American views of,
  42–43; belonging and inclusion in,
  43–44
Tuckabatchee, 88

United Band of Ojibwes, Odawas, and
  Potawatomis, 26, 66. See also Odawas;
  Ojibwes (Anishinaabeg); Potawatomis
United States, 15, 76, 172; coercive
  policies, 174–75; colonial political
  discourse, 3–4; use of Customs of
  All Nations, 23–24; and French
  population, 50–51; Greenville treaty
  negotiation, 7–8; and multiracial
  leaders, 64–67; and Northwest
  Territory expansion, 46–47, 86–87;
  racialized identities, 3–4, 7, 11–12,
  24–26, 45; treaty negotiations,
  47–48
Utes: in Navajo clans, 88

Van Antwerp, Verplanck, 104, 197n27,
  207–8n35

Printed in the USA
CPSIA information can be obtained
at www.ICGtesting.com
LVHW091609110923
757842LV00004B/69